To Mum

Love

The
GOOD GARDENER'S
GUIDE
to indoor and outdoor plants and flowers

The GOOD GARDENER'S GUIDE

to indoor and outdoor plants and flowers

EDITED BY FRANCES PERRY

MACDONALD AND JANE'S
LONDON

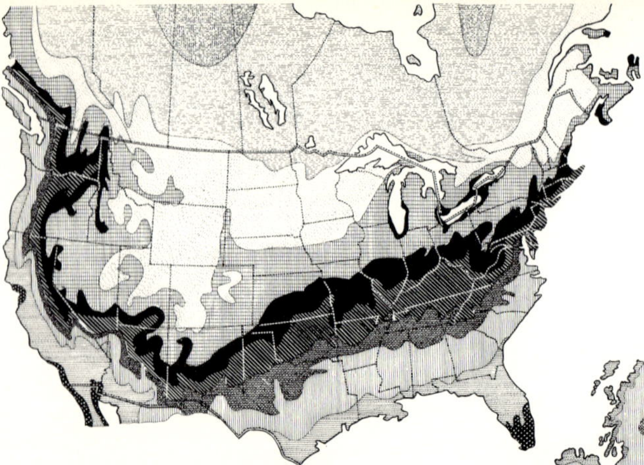

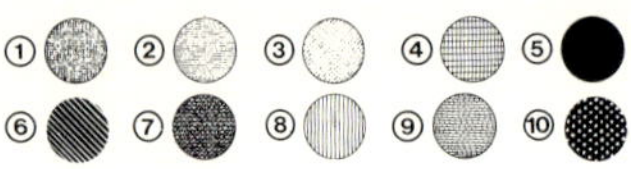

ZONES OF HARDINESS

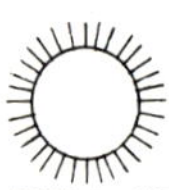

FULL SUN

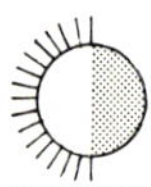

SEMISHADE

SHADE

SPARINGLY

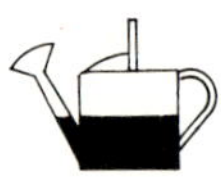

SUFFICIENTLY

GENEROUSLY

FLOWERING PERIOD
(FROM EARLIEST TO LATEST)

SHELTER FROM COLD

First published 1976 by Macdonald & Jane's
Macdonald and Jane's Publishers Ltd;
8, Shepherdess Walk, London N1 7LW
ISBN 0356 08296 9

Photoset by Tradespools Ltd, Frome, Somerset
Printed and bound by Officine Grafiche di Arnoldo Mondadori Editore, Verona

CONTENTS

INDOOR PLANTS

1 **MAIDENHAIR FERN**
Adianthum capillus-veneris:

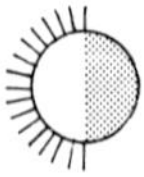

8

Family: Adiantaceae. Name from Greek *adiantos*, dry; the fronds repel water, a property first recorded by Theophrastus.
Place of origin: cosmopolitan; rare in Britain.
Description: a lovely and delicate deciduous fern with many basal fronds; numerous pinnules (small leaves) which are dark green, kidney-shaped, crenulate or lobate on the upper edge. Many distinct varieties once grown but now largely disappeared.
Use: as an indoor plant, or to decorate walls and recesses and damp, shady rockeries.
Planting: spring. Keep rhizomes near soil surface. For pot use, supply good drainage and a little lime.
Propagation: by division and by spores sown on damp peat and sand, covered with glass to maintain humidity.
Environment and light: adequate but not direct light, with fairly high humidity level. Avoid hot places, move as little as possible. Slight frost injures fronds; severe frost kills.
Type of soil: ordinary garden soil with peat.
Soil moisture: water plentifully during growing season; in winter keep soil moist only.

---

2 **ARALIA misnamed CASTOR-OIL PLANT**
Aralia sieboldii (more correctly *Fatsia japonica*)*:*

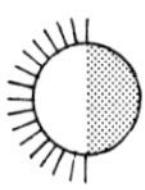

8

Family: Araliaceae. Name adapted from the Japanese name for this plant *Fat Si.*
Place of origin: Japan; introduced into Europe in 1838.
Description: a slow growing evergreen plant with large, bright green, smooth, shiny leaves with 7 or 9 (rarely 11) pointed, oblong lobes. Flowers on branching panicles in round, milky-white heads, succeeded by round, black, ivy-like berries.
Flowering time: autumn to winter.
Use: where hardy (temperate climates) makes a useful winter flowering shrub. The cream-splashed leaves of the variety *variegata* make this a good house plant for cool rooms.
Propagation: by cuttings from sucker shoots in spring, or by division.
Environment and light: adequate light indoors but never in direct sun. Half-shade outdoors.
Type of soil: any good garden soil outdoors; loam, peat or leaf mould and sand (equal parts) for pot work.
Soil moisture: water only when required.
Remarks: shorten straggly growths in spring.

3 ASPARAGUS FERN

Asparagus sprengeri (now more correctly A. densiflorus "Sprengeri"):

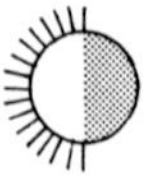

Family: Liliaceae. Name given by Theophrastus.
Place of origin: Southern Africa; introduced into Europe in 1890.
Description: a woody stemmed plant with long trailing (or widely climbing) branches 2–6 ft. (1–2 m) long, armed with small hooked prickles and small, flat, evergreen phylloclades, mostly in threes and 1–1½ in. (2·5–4 cm) long. Flowers tiny, white or pinkish, fragrant, in racemes. Fruit: bright red ½ in. (1 cm) berries.

Flowering time: early summer.
Use: as an indoor plant, especially suitable for hanging baskets.
Propagation: by division in spring or seed.
Environment and light: ample ventilation, plenty of light, but not direct sun.

Type of soil: dry, permeable and rich. If the soil is not sufficiently rich, the branches of the plant will droop. Feed in summer.
Soil moisture: water regularly, more frequently in the summer months.
Remarks: dwarfs and variegated forms occur.

---

4 ASPIDISTRA

Aspidistra elatior (A. lurida):

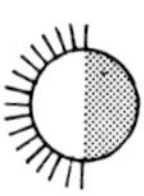

Family: Liliaceae. Name from Greek *aspidion*, a small round shield, referring to shape of stigma.
Place of origin: Central-eastern Asia; introduced 1822.
Description: perennial plants with underground rhizomatic stems, long and large radical leaves, upright and well stemmed, with complete, leathery, shiny green lamina, narrowing to a channelled stalk one-third the length of the blade. Purple, insignificant flowers close to ground. Also a variegated green and white leafed variety.

Flowering time: seldom; summer.
Use: withstands poor soil and light and considerable neglect, but needs good light for robust health.

Propagation: by division towards the end of autumn.
Environment and light: needs good light, but not sun; without adequate light the leaves become less shiny. Outdoors it grows well in warm, shady places.
Type of soil: ordinary soil with sand and peat, always with a little organic matter.

(7)

Soil moisture: water regularly two or three times weekly, and more often in summer.

5 AUCUBA; often known as LAUREL

Aucuba japonica:

7

Family: Cornaceae. Latinized from the Japanese name.
Place of origin: Himalayas to Japan; introduced in 1783.
Description: an evergreen shrub up to 12 ft. (3·6 m) with leathery, oblong, shiny leaves which are slightly dentate on smooth, stiff branches. Flowers 4-petalled in terminal male and female on separate plants. Later produce quantities of glossy green berries which turn red and persist all winter. Clones with variegated foliage and white or yellow berries occur.
Use: grown for its variety of foliage in shrubberies or for hedging. Makes a useful winter pot-plant if kept well away from sources of heat. In summer plunge the pots in soil outdoors in the shade and hand pollinate female plants to obtain fruits.
Propagation: roots easily from cuttings in spring or late summer.
Environment and light: outdoors in shade or half-shade.
Type of soil: loose, rich but not too calcareous.
Soil moisture: only water when soil is dry, and slightly more often in summer.
Remarks: since Aucubas are unisexual, male plants must be grown as well as female to obtain berries.

---

6 CALATHEA; MAKOY CALATHEA

Calathea makoyana:

10

Family: Marantaceae. Name from Greek *kalathos*, basket; the tough leaves of *c. discolor* are made into waterproof baskets in South America.
Place of origin: Tropical America (Brazil and Peru).
Description: herbaceous, rhizomatic plant about 18 in. (50 cm) high, with oval, rounded leaves on long stems, with dark green markings on a paler background; lower blade of the leaf is blotched in red.
Use: in temperate climates it is solely an indoor or greenhouse plant, much appreciated for its elegant foliage; in its places of origin it can be grown outdoors.
Propagation: by division of crowns in spring.
Environment and light: moist close atmosphere with night temperatures around 55°–60°F (12°–15°C). Shade from direct sun. Where possible keep the plant in the same place.
Type of soil: good drainage, loam mixed with sand and leaf-mould or peat.
Soil moisture: water regularly so that the soil is always moist, but do not soak.
Remarks: renew frequently; the rich leaf colourings fade with age.

7 CAMEDOREA; FEATHERS PALM

Chamaedorea elegans (Collinia elegans; Neanthe bella):

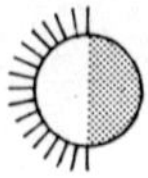

9

Family: Palmae. Name from Greek *chamai*, on the ground, *dorea*, gift, referring to the ease with which the fruit is gathered.
Place of origin: Mexico and Central America.
Description: a small palm, growing to a maximum height of 3–6 ft. (1–2 m) with pinnate leaves spaced along the stipe, with narrow, sharp segments, bright green in colour. The stipe (trunk) of the plant is ringed, and not unlike bamboo in appearance. Flowers dioecious, females followed by shining scarlet fruits.
Use: as an indoor, porch or greenhouse plant.
Propagation: by careful division in spring.
Environment and light: mild and fairly humid conditions. These palms grow in shade of tall trees in nature and dislike direct sunlight.
Type of soil: woodland type (two parts spongy peat to one each of loam and sand).
Soil moisture: water frequently, but not too copiously.
Remarks: the fruits are eaten by Mexicans and the young shoots like asparagus.

---

8 COCOS WEDDELIANA; WEDDEL PALM

Cocos weddeliana:

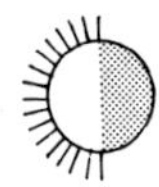

Family: Palmae. Now more correctly Microcoelum weddeliana (*Syagrus weddeliana*). Name from Greek *mikros*, small, *koilus*, hollow; there is a small hollow in the embryo of the fruits.
Place of origin: Brazil.
Description: a tree-like palm with black, fibre-netted trunk and arching sprays of fern-like leaves which bend over and almost reach the ground. Leaves with slender pinnules, glossy green, paler underneath.
Use: mostly used in the juvenile state, when it makes an elegant pot plant.
Propagation: by seeds sown early spring (75°–81°F) (25°–27°C).
Environment and light: likes light, but do not expose to direct sun.
Type of soil: well-rotted humus type, leaf-mould with added sand and rotted manure.
Soil moisture: water as required, sparingly in winter.
Remarks: a dry atmosphere causes the tips of the leaves to wither; too humid an atmosphere causes yellowing followed by death. Discard overlarge and leggy plants.

9 CROTON

Codiaeum variegatum:

(10)

Family: Euphorbiaceae. Latinized version of vernacular name *kodiho*.
Place of origin: Malayan archipelago and Pacific Islands; introduced in late nineteenth century.
Description: an evergreen shrub, represented in cultivation by *Codiaeum variegatum pictum* and its varieties. These vary greatly in leaf-shape and colouring from long and narrow to ovate, variously lobed and come in red, green and yellow, orange or near black or combinations of same, often speckled with other colours. Height 12–18 in. (30–45 cm) in pots but 6–10 ft. (2–3 cm) in tropical gardens.
Use: splendid pot plant on account of rich leaf colouring. In warm areas, such as the West Indies, often used for hedging or as specimen shrubs.
Propagation: by young soft cuttings in spring rooted with bottom heat (75°F (25°C)). Shoots drip latex when cut so dip in charcoal before insertion.
Environment and light: good light essential or colours dull. Avoid draughts or sudden temperature changes (which cause leaf drop), also direct sun through glass.
Type of soil: any good potting compost.
Soil moisture: water frequently and spray leaves daily in hot weather.

---

10 COLEUS

Coleus blumei: hybr.

(9)

Family: Labiatae. Name from Greek *koleos*, a sheath, from the way the stamens are enclosed.
Place of origin: India, Java, tropical Asia.
Description: an evergreen, sub-shrubby perennial with ornamental foliage of various colours and patternings —green, yellow, crimson, mauve and pink. Leaves nettle-shaped and sized, velvety to the touch with dentate margins. Spikes of weedy flowers which should be regularly removed.
Use: as a summer bedding plant, put outside when all risk of frost is over or, more generally, as a pot plant indoors.
Propagation: by soft cuttings in spring or late summer in the greenhouse, for plants with similarly coloured foliage; by seed for hybrids with variously coloured foliage.
Environment and light: outdoors in shade or half-shade; indoors well-lit. Ideal temperature 55°F (12°C).
Type of soil: light soil achieved by a mixture of garden soil, leaf-mould and sand.
Soil moisture: water as required.
Remarks: susceptible to mealy bugs and greenhouse white fly; old plants are usually discarded.

11 AUSTRALIAN DRACAENA; ERECT PALM LILY

Cordyline stricta:

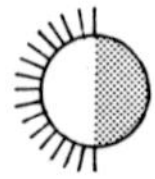

9

Family: Liliaceae.
Place of origin: Australia.
Description: an elegant palm-like plant of 3–8 ft. (1–2·5 m) with closely set, narrow 1–2 ft. (30–60 cm) leaves from upright, rigid stems. Sessile pale blue or lilac flowers in pyramidal panicles. The variety *grandis* has more highly coloured leaves.
Use: an excellent pot plant because of its beautiful leaves, or in shady borders in warm, frost-free gardens.
Propagation: by stem cuttings or air layers.
Environment and light: likes a lot of light, but not direct sun, and adequate warmth and humidity; keep away from draughts and sharp changes of temperature.
Type of soil: sandy loam with peat or leaf-mould and shredded sphagnum moss.
Soil moisture: water and spray frequently in summer and less in winter.

---

12 CABBAGE PALM; CORDYLINE

Cordyline terminalis:

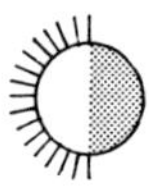

Family: Cordyline terminalis (often listed as *Dracaena terminalis*). Name from Greek *kordyle*, club or cudgel, referring to the shape of the roots.
Place of origin: S.E. Asia, Pacific Islands, Australia; introduced early nineteenth century.
Description: evergreen trees or shrubs with leathery or stiff lanceolate leaves. The species has produced many clones with foliage in various shades of green, flashed, striped or margined with red, purple or cream. This springs from a central growing point, which elongates to a short trunk with age. The white, cream or reddish flowers come in 1 ft. (30 cm) panicles.
Use: indoor plants remarkable for beautiful foliage.
Propagation: commercially by stem cuttings; the central stem, cut into 2–4 in. (5–10 cm) segments, placed in a propagating bench kept at (70–75°F, 21–24°C) will root from each leaf joint. Also by suckers or air layers.
Environment and light: likes light, but not direct sun, adequate humidity and warmth (50°–55°F (10°–12°C) winter temperature); no draughts or sharp changes of temperature.
Type of soil: peaty compost, or sandy loam with peat.
Soil moisture: frequently water and spray in summer; water much less in the winter months.

13 CYCAS; sometimes called SAGO PALM

Cycas revoluta:

Family: Cycadaceae. Name from Greek *kykas* used by Theophrastus to mean a palm. Despite their appearance the Cycadaceae are not related to the Palmae.
Place of origin: China and Japan.
Description: has a cylindrical trunk growing to 7 ft. (2·1 m) covered by the remains of leaf bases. Leaves consist of flat, slightly sickle-shaped pinnules, rolled at edges with sharp tips, dark green in colour, and lighter on the underside. Flowers dioecious and undistinguished; females produce red fruits.
Use: outdoor plant for parks and gardens in climatically favourable places; but also grown in pots indoors; during the winter, in the latter case, it must be kept in an airy place with very little humidity.
Propagation: by stem cuttings, 2–3 in. (5–8 cm) thick, rooted with bottom heat (65°–70°F (18°–20°C)). These should be dried for a few days before insertion. Also by seeds or suckers.
Environment and light: if grown outdoors, it prefers sheltered, half-shaded places; if indoors, try to avoid direct sun, but put in a well-lit place.
Type of soil: peaty compost.
Soil moisture: water copiously except in winter.

---

14 DIEFFENBACHIA; DUMB CANE; TUFTROOT

Dieffenbachia amoena:

Family: Araceae. The name derives from that of the German botanist J. F. Dieffenbach (1790–1863).
Place of origin: Tropical America; introduced in 1880.
Description: a polymorphous species with many named varieties. The original species has dark green, lanceolate leaves, 9 in. by 3 in. (22 cm by 7 cm) wide, with irregular cream marks between the veins.
Use: as an indoor plant.
Propagation: by air layering, basal suckers or stem cuttings rooted in heat (80°F (26·7°C)).
Environment and light: needs warm, moist conditions (aim at 65° (17°C)) and unlikely to thrive if temperature drops below 45°F (7°C). Avoid draughts and fumes. Good light away from direct sun.
Type of soil: Peat mixes or compost of loam, peat, leaf-mould and sand.
Soil moisture: water in summer; otherwise when soil is dry. Spray leaves frequently.
Remarks: the stems are extremely poisonous and to bite invites throat swellings and loss of speech—hence the name Dumb cane—or sometimes Mother-in-law plant.

15 SPOTTED DIEFFENBACHIA

Diffenbachia picta:

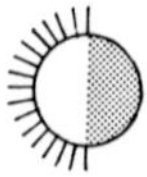

Family: Araceae.
Place of origin: Colombia, Venezuela, Ecuador; introduced in 1820.
Description: a plant with an upright, cylindrical stem of a certain firmness, quick-growing, with oval-oblong, green leaves with sharp points, heavily marked on both sides with ivory marbling and blotches. Usually about $1\frac{1}{2}$ ft. (50 cm) tall when used as pot plants; taller specimens can be cut up for propagation purposes.
Flowering time: summer, but seldom flowers.
Use: because of its foliage this is a striking indoor plant; its decorative quality lies above all in the variegation of the leaves.
Propagation: by layers and stem cuttings (see No. 14).
Environment and light: Dieffenbachias thrive in moist heat and shed their leaves if too cold. This species is more tolerant than most but nevertheless aim at minimum winter temperatures around 55°F (12°C).
Type of soil: rich, preferably made up of a mixture of three parts leaf-mould to one of ordinary soil.
Soil moisture: see "Dieffenbachia amoena" (No. 14).
Remarks: there are many beautiful named sorts including some practically cream, except for the midribs and margins.

---

16 FALSE ARALIA

Dizygotheca elegantissima (Aralia elegantissima):

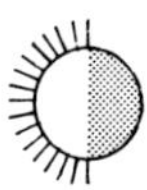

Family: Araliaceae. Name from Greek *dis*, twice, *zygos*, a yoke and *theka*, a crab, the anthers have double lobes.
Place of origin: New Caledonia; introduced in 1873.
Description: a slender evergreen shrub with elegant digitally compound leaves composed of 7 to 11 narrow, toothed leaflets of bronze-green. Small flowers in umbels but it seldom blooms in cultivation.
Use: as a tender greenhouse or room plant it is one of the most highly prized because of the elegance and delicacy of the leaves. It is however not easy to grow.
Propagation: by cuttings or layering. Both operations are difficult and must be carried out only in the greenhouse.
Environment and light: likes ample light, but not direct sun. Keep away from draughts and dry atmospheres.
Type of soil: equal parts sandy loam, peat and leaf-mould.
Soil moisture: water regularly when required, but sparingly. Do not let the water stagnate; provide good drainage to allow it to run away.

17 DRACAENA PALM

Dracaena deremensis:

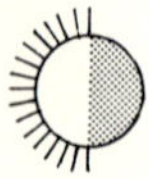

Family: Liliaceae. Name from Greek *drakaina*, dragon's blood; a red varnish used in the varnish industry is obtained from *D. draco.*
Place of origin: Tropical Africa.
Description: an upright plant, very leafy, the foliage long and strap-like, dark green edged with ivory or silver stripes and with greyish green centre. Flowers unpleasant smelling, in long panicles of many small red and white florets.

Flowering time: spring–summer.
Use: as an indoor plant.
Propagation: by air layers in July, when the lower part of the stem is stripped of leaves.
Environment and light: hardier than sometimes credited; likes a lot of light, but not direct sun, and ample warmth and humidity; keep away from draughts, and sudden changes in temperature, and do not move. Aim at minimum temperature of 50°F (10°C), but warmer if possible.

Type of soil: ordinary garden soil mixed with heathland soil and sand.
Soil moisture: water and spray regularly during summer, and less in winter. Do not let water stagnate on the leaves, as this causes yellowing.

---

18 FRAGRANT DRACAENA

Dracaena fragrans:

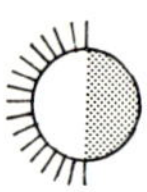

Family: Liliaceae.
Place of origin: Tropical Africa; introduced in 1768.
Description: the type species has broad green leaves but clones occur with gold leaf edges and central bands; others have green edges with gold centres. Flowers yellowish, in clusters, very fragrant.

Flowering time: sometimes in the spring.
Use: pot plant cultivated for its beautiful ornamental foliage. Used for hedging in West Indies.
Propagation: by air layers or cuttings.
Environment and light: well-lit place, out of the sun, away from draughts. Warm, humid conditions are ideal.
Type of soil: loose, light.

Soil moisture: water regularly in summer, spray leaves frequently, but much less in other seasons.
Remarks: use "small 'Dracaena' stumps" to obtain a handsome plant in an unusual way. It is enough to take part of a branch of this plant (found in shops), introduce it vertically into a glass receptacle with water, wedge it with pebbles at the bottom. Roots will appear followed by a healthy growth of leaves. Never change the water, just top it up.

19 RUBBER PLANT

Ficus elastica:

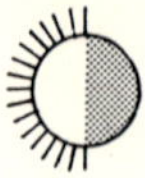

Family: Moraceae. Latin name for fig.
Place of origin: Malaya; introduced in 1815.
Description: the Rubber Plant is so-called because the stems and foliage contain a rubber-like latex. It has an upright stem with evergreen, leathery, alternate, stemmed, whole leaves which are dark, shiny green in colour, and ovate-elongated in shape, with pointed tips. For a period the leaves jut out horizontally and then become pendant. The young leaves appear wrapped in a bright red bract.
Use: as an indoor plant.
Propagation: by air layering, seed or cuttings rooted with bottom heat. 80°F (26·7°C).
Environment and light: likes light, but not direct sunlight. Keep in containers on the small side and feed plants in summer. Tolerant of low or high temperatures if they are not in draughts or constantly moved. 55°–60°F (12°–15°C) is ideal.
Type of soil: any good light, rich compost.
Soil moisture: immerse the pot in a receptacle full of water for a couple of hours when necessary so that the plant absorbs whatever it needs. Keep on dry side in winter with soil just moist, but water more plentifully in summer. Over-watering causes yellowing of leaves. Sponge foliage frequently with soft water containing a few drops of milk.

---

20 BANJO FIG; FIDDLE-BACK FIG; FIDDLE LEAF FIG

Ficus lyrata:

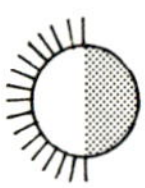

Family: Moraceae.
Place of origin: Tropical Africa; introduced in 1902.
Description: an imposing evergreen with large (12 in. (30 cm) long by 9 in. (22 cm) wide), thick and leathery leaves, smooth both sides and shaped like the body of a violin, dark green above but lighter beneath, with prominent midrib and veins. Very short leaf stalks. Like all *ficus* species, the stems and foliage contain a white sticky latex so avoid breaking these.
Use: impressive plant for offices, lofty rooms etc.
Propagation: by air layers in April.
Environment and light: likes a lot of light, but not direct sunlight. Avoid places with frequent draughts and keep well away from sources of heat. Temperature should not fall below 50°F (10°C).
Type of soil: leaf-mould or ordinary soil with leaf-mould and sand.
Soil moisture: advisable to immerse the pot in a receptacle not too full of water so the plant can absorb what it needs. Excessive moisture causes leaves to drop or premature yellowing. Immerse the pot for 2–3 hours as required, more in summer and in high temperatures. Syringe leaves daily in growing season.

21 FITTONIA

Fittonia verschaffeltii "Argyroneura":

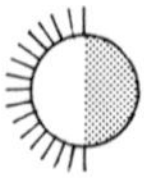

Family: Acanthaceae. Name commemorates two sisters, M. and E. Fitton, authors of the book *Conversations on Botany*.
Place of origin: Peru; introduced in 1867.
Description: a charming trailing plant with oval to round, simple leaves, 3–4 in. (7–10 cm) across, of soft green liberally veined with silver, giving them a netted appearance. Flowers insignificant and best removed.

Flowering time: during summer.
Use: as an indoor plant because of its beautiful leaves and the ease with which it is grown, or in moist shade under greenhouse benches.
Propagation: by cuttings rooted with bottom heat.
Environment and light: likes light, but not direct sun, with a good degree of humidity during the summer months. Very sensitive to draughts and dry atmosphere. Does not enjoy low temperatures.

Type of soil: proprietary loamless compost or prepared compost of loam (7 parts), peat (3 parts), sand (2 parts) with a little general fertilizer.
Soil moisture: water regularly to keep soil moist.

---

22 MARANTA

Maranta leuconeura "Erythroneura":

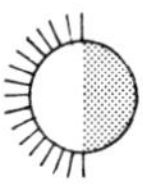

Family: Marantaceae. Name refers to the Venetian naturalist, B. Maranti, who lived in the sixteenth century.
Place of origin: Brazil; introduced in 1875.
Description: perennial, apparently stem-less plants with creeping rhizomes, entire, oblong-oval leaves with sheathing stems, emerald-green with crimson midribs and veins and patterning of lighter, yellowish green.

Use: as house plants, or can be grown in bottle gardens.
Propagation: by division of the rhizomes from the adult specimens in spring.
Environment and light: maintain a humid atmosphere during growing season by plunging container in bowl of damp peat. Needs a lot of light, but not direct sun. The atmosphere should be mild, not too dry and draught-free.

Type of soil: proprietary loamless compost or mixture of equal parts of sand, peat and leaf-mould.
Soil moisture: water freely spring to late summer, then sparingly.

23 MONSTERA; mistakenly called SPLIT LEAF PHILODENDRON; SWISS CHEESE PLANT

Monstera deliciosa:

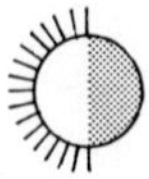

10

Family: Araceae. The name refers to the appearance of the leaves which are perforated and almost . . . "monstrous".
Place of origin: Mexico.
Description: a climbing evergreen (up to 12 ft. (3·6 m)) with huge, tough, dark green leaves which have deeply incised margins and large holes in the blades. Thick aerial roots hang down and will root into moist soil under favourable conditions. Flowers creamy arums followed by juicy, cone-shaped fruits with a delicious pear cum pineapple flavour.
Flowering time: summer.
Use: as an indoor and greenhouse plant, or in tropical climates, as a garden plant.
Propagation: by air layers or cuttings rooted in warm propagating frames, or seed.
Environment and light: humid, adequately lit, but not exposed to the sun, and well away from sources of heat.
Type of soil: rich but well drained. Feed occasionally.
Soil moisture: keep soil moist. Too much water causes leaves to turn yellow or go brown at tips.
Remarks: in the tropics the fruit pulp is used in ices and drinks.

---

24 SWORDFERN

Nephrolepis exaltata:

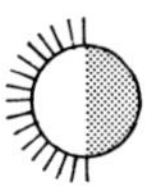

9

Family: Oleandraceae. Name from Greek *nephros*, kidney, *lepis*, scale, referring to shape of membrane covering the reproductive organs.
Place of origin: Tropics; introduced in 1793.
Description: rapid growing fern of $1\frac{1}{2}$–$2\frac{1}{2}$ ft. (45–75 cm) with pale green pinnate fronds.
Use: one of the most beautiful ferns for pot plant work, hanging baskets or shady corners in frost-free climates. Otherwise can be planted outside for summer only. Tenacious of life, neglected specimens reviving in a few weeks of nursing.
Propagation: from spores sown on fine, leafy soil in pots, stood in a saucer of water and covered with a sheet of glass until germination. Turn the glass daily. Also by division in spring.
Environment and light: humid, adequately lit, but well away from sources of heat and the direct rays of the sun.
Type of soil: leaf-mould, sand and loam, with a porous substratum.
Soil moisture: water generously, and do not let the soil dry out.

25 PEPEROMIA

Peperomia caperata:

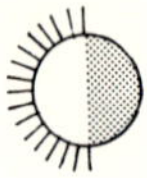

Family: Piperaceae. The generic name derives from the Greek and means "pepper-like".
Place of origin: Central and tropical South America.
Description: popular members of a large family with numerous, dark green, heart-shaped leaves which have deep corrugations with purplish shadings at their bases, and a grey-green sheen on the ridges. The leaf-stalks are pale pink. Flowers white in long spikes—like mice tails—sometimes branched.
Flowering time: late spring to early winter.
Use: as an indoor plant, because they are quite decorative and easy to grow.
Propagation: by leaf cuttings, inserting the stalks in sandy compost in a propagating frame kept at 60°F (15·6°C).
Environment and light: well-lit place in the house but away from sun.
Type of soil: two parts loam to one each of peat, leafmould and sand.
Soil moisture: never overwater or plants will rot; they have very small root systems. Allow compost to dry out between waterings but syringe the leaves regularly in hot weather to create humidity.

---

26 PHILODENDRON ELONGATUM

Philodendron hastatum:

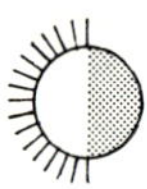

Family: Araceae. Name from Greek *phileo*, to love and *dendron*, tree, referring to the climbing habits of many species.
Place of origin: Brazil.
Description: a climbing evergreen with long, heart-shaped, leathery leaves with short stems and sheathing stipules. The aerial roots are produced at every stem node. Flowers arum-like, yellowish-white but rare in cultivation.
Use: as pot plant indoors or for greenhouse borders. In warm climates can be grown up poles or tree trunks.
Propagation: by tip cuttings, taken in early summer, 4–6 in. (10–15 cm) long with leaf attached. Root in equal parts of loosely packed loam, peat, leaf-mould, and coarse sand at 10°–15°F (21°–24°C).
Environment and light: well-lit, but not exposed to direct sun.
Type of soil: light and coarse, not close-packed.
Soil moisture: water generously at least twice weekly, spraying leaves more frequently, especially if the atmosphere is hot and dry.

27 CLIMBING PHILODENDRON
Philodendron scandens:

Family: Araceae.
Place of origin: tropical regions of America.
Description: a climbing species up to 6 ft. (2 m), with slender stems, long interroots and numerous adventitious roots. Leaves evergreen, heart-shaped, tapering to a sharp point, shining green, pinkish beneath.
Use: in pots with the trailing stems trained round a block of cork or cone of wire netting filled with live sphagnum moss. Can also be grown up walls and trellises.
Propagation: by cuttings.
Environment and light: well-lit, but never expose directly to the sun's rays. One of the easiest philodendrons, even tolerant of oil and gas fumes.
Type of soil: peaty soil with sand.
Soil moisture: syringe frequently and water as required. Large plants can be cut back in spring.

(10)

---

28 CANARY DATE PALM; CANARY ISLAND DATE PALM
Phoenix canariensis:

Family: Palmae. The ancient Greek name for date palm, used by Theophrastus.
Place of origin: Canary Islands; introduced in 1850.
Description: a tree type palm with trunk of up to 15 ft. (5 m), encompassed by scales and leafy crown composed of many slender, arching, green pinnate leaves, the lowest pinnate spiny. Flowers small and yellow but compounded in dense panicles. Dioecious. Fruits date like, oval, golden-brown.
Use: small specimens are well-suited for rooms and public buildings, tree-size specimens for parks and gardens, especially in regions with a Mediterranean climate.
Propagation: by seed sown in heat (64°–70°F (18°–21°C)) in early spring.
Environment and light: well-lit indoors, but not in direct sun; for outdoor specimens, in regions with a not so mild climate, avoid over-exposed places and protect with canvas or rush-matting etc. in winter.
Type of soil: any good but well-drained compost.
Soil moisture: indoors, water frequently but not excessively; outdoors, water generously.

(8) 

29 ALUMINIUM PLANT

Pilea cadieri:

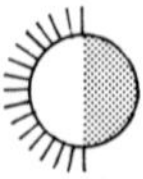

Family: Urticaceae. Name from Greek *pileas*, cap, referring to the shape of the female flowers.
Place of origin: Annan, Vietnam; introduced into Europe in 1938.
Description: the most popular member of a very large family of annual and perennial herb. The species makes a spreading, branching plant with oblong oval leaves about $2\frac{1}{2}$ in. (6 cm) long by $1\frac{1}{2}$ in. (3 cm) wide, dark green with silvery patches between the veins. Flowers rare, unisexual and insignificant.

Use: as an indoor plant because of its striking foliage.
Propagation: by cuttings in spring.
Environment and light: well-lit, but not in direct sun. Keep away from draughts.
Type of soil: ordinary garden soil with sand and peat added.
Soil moisture: water often, but sparingly. The soil should never be saturated or the leaves tend to rot.
Remarks: plants need frequent stopping or they become leggy.

---

30 ELKHORN; STAG-HORN FERN

Platycerium bifurcatum (P. alcicorne):

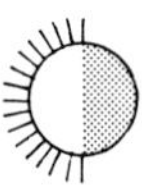

Family: Polypodiaceae. Name from Greek *platys*, broad and *keras*, horn, referring to shape of fronds.
Place of origin: Australia; introduced in 1808.
Description: an evergreen epiphytic fern with two sorts of fronds—rounded and flat sterile leaves which anchor and wrap themselves round the host and are downy when young, and forked fertile fronds which bear spores near their tips. The whole plant is a pleasant shade of green.

Use: planted in fork of a tree branch in warm climates or fastened to cork or wood and hung up in the home or greenhouse.
Propagation: by offshoots or spores.
Environment and light: can take strong light indoors, but part shade outside.
Type of soil: equal parts peat and sphagnum moss.
Soil moisture: needs moist atmosphere and water at the roots. Keep on the dry side in winter. Some growers leave them without water until they droop, then immerse them in a pail of water, continuing in this way indefinitely.

31 **RIBBON FERN; STOVE FERN**

Pteris cretica var. *crispata:*

Family: Pteridaceae. Name from Greek *pteron*, fern, referring to the leathery fronds (leaves).
Place of origin: S.W. Europe, Mediterranean Islands, Iran, India, Japan; introduced into Britain in 1820.
Description: a shade-loving fern with long wiry stems and 6–12 in. (15–30 cm) pinnate fronds with long narrow pinnules. Many varieties including *crispata*, the one illustrated, which has crisped, spreading fronds with a band of glaucous grey down the middle of each segment. Also variegated, crested and deeply cut forms.
Use: as a decorative indoor or greenhouse plant.
Propagation: by division in spring.
Environment and light: fairly light, but keep in constant shade.
Type of soil: a mixture made up of ordinary garden soil, peat and sand.
Soil moisture: water regularly so that the soil is always moist. With young plants spray the fronds frequently.

---

32 **BOWSTRING HEMP; MOTHER-IN-LAW'S TONGUE; SNAKE PLANT**

Sansevieria trifasciata "laurentii":

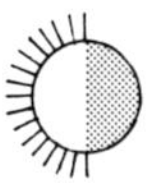

Family: Liliaceae. The name derives from that of Duke Raimondo di Sangrio, Prince of Sansevero. (1710–1771).
Place of origin: West Africa; introduced into Europe in 1904.
Description: a plant with flat-concave, radical, thick and hard leaves, sword-shaped, 12–16 in. (30–40 cm) in height, slightly grooved, dark-green in colour, with yellow leaf margins and inner green, grey and yellow variegations. Flowers fragrant, creamy, in long racemes.
Use: as a tough indoor plant, even when conditions are not favourable.
Propagation: by division of larger specimens in spring; leaf cuttings will root but will become plain green.
Environment and light: prefers plenty of light and air, but never expose to direct sunlight.
Type of soil: sandy compost.
Soil moisture: only water when the soil is dry, and water less often during the winter months—overwatering causes rotting.
Remarks: the leaves are a source of fibre used for fishing lines, nets, shoes, hats and mats.

33 IVY ARUM; POTHOS

Scindapsus aureus (now more correctly *Rhaphidophora aurea*):

Family: Araceae. Name from Greek *raphis*, needle and *phoras*, bearing—the fruits have needle-like points. Member of Bromeliad family.

Place of origin: warm regions of Asia and Australia.

Description: a perennial climber with heart-shaped, dark green, shiny leaves flecked with yellow (not golden as the name indicates). These become larger on older plants, especially where plants are grown up green wood or moss. Cultivars exist with rich yellow leaves ('Golden Queen') also green marbled with white ('Marble Queen').

Use: as an indoor plant because of the foliage, and rapid growth.

Propagation: by summer cuttings in a peat/sand mixture or layering throughout the year.

Environment and light: train up supports or across walls or round a moss-filled, wirenetting framework. Light place but away from direct sunlight. Winter temperatures around 50°–55°F (10°–12°C) minimum. Feed regularly in summer and repot occasionally.

Type of soil: proprietary peat-based mixture or mixture of sand, loam and peat or leaf-mould.

Soil moisture: water generously in the summer months, sparingly in winter.

---

34 CLUB-MOSS

Selaginella martensii:

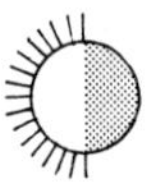

Family: Selaginellaceae. Name from Greek *selago*, the name of another mossy plant (*Lycopodium selago*).

Place of origin: Mexico.

Description: evergreen plants resembling mosses, with much branched stems 6–12 in. (15–30 cm) long with trailing root fibres from their undersides. Leaves bright green. There are numerous varieties, including some with variegated leaves.

Use: in bottle gardens or shallow pans indoors or in damp, humid, woodland places in warm, temperate climates.

Propagation: by layering the fronds on a damp mossy surface at any season or by cuttings.

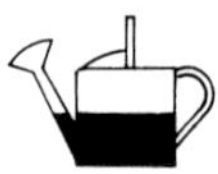

Environment and light: these plants need a warm, moist, close atmosphere; temperature around 65°F (18°C) is ideal. Placing glass over them helps sickly specimens. Avoid draughts and direct sun.

Type of soil: light soil kept open with peat, charcoal or broken up crocks.

8

Soil moisture: water frequently so that the soil is always slightly moist, but do not syringe.

INDOOR FLOWERING PLANTS

35 CHENILLE PLANT; RED-HOT CAT'S TAIL

Acalypha hispida:

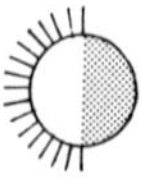

9

Family: Euphorbiaceae. Name from Greek *akalephe*, nettle which the leaves of some species resemble.
Place of origin: New Guinea; introduced in 1896.
Description: a shrub growing 10–15 ft. (3–5 m) with large, bright green, ovate leaves, pointed at the tips and with dentate edges. Flowers bright red borne on long drooping, tassel-like spikes.
Use: as an indoor plant because of its brightly-coloured blooms, but also as a garden plant in sheltered, frost-free and semi-shaded spots.
Propagation: by soft cuttings rooted in sandy soil in a warm frame in spring. 70°F (21°C).
Environment and light: this plant likes a lot of light, but must not be exposed to direct sun. Keep well away from sources of heat and draughts.
Type of soil: rich compost with peat or leaf-mould added.
Soil moisture: water sparingly but often, even daily, so that the soil—which should not be close-packed—is always just moist.

---

36 AECHMEA FASCIATA

Billbergia rhodocyanea:

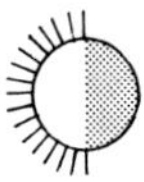

Family: Bromeliaceae. Name from Greek *aichme*, a point, referring to the still sepal points.
Place of origin: introduced in 1826.
Description: an evergreen epiphyte with rosettes of overlapping, grey-green leaves forming an open funnel at the centre. These have short points and silvery striations and are individually up to 18 in. (45 cm) long and 3–4 in. (7–10 cm) across. The flower scape is rosy-pink, individual blooms being blue at first, then rose and enclosed by spiny pink bracts.
Flowering time: spring, but greenhouse plants can flower at any time. The plant only flowers once.
Use: as an indoor plant.
Propagation: by detaching and rooting side shoots.
Environment and light: mild warmth, well ventilated, but draught-free and not directly exposed to sun.
Type of soil: lime-free, open textured soil. Equal parts of pine-needles, leaf-mould and peat with a little sand makes a suitable home-mix.
Soil moisture: water sparingly in winter, and more generously in spring and summer. Keep "vase" or funnel centre filled with rain water.

37 AFRICAN LILY; LILY OF THE NILE
Agapanthus africanus (A. umbellatus):

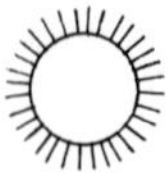

Family: Liliaceae. Name from Greek *agape*, love, and *anthos*, flower.
Place of origin: Cape Province; introduced into Europe in 1629.
Description: a perennial with fleshy tubers from a short, creeping rootstock. It is of compact habit with long, arching, strap-shaped radical leaves up to $2\frac{1}{2}$ ft. (75 cm) long. The blue or white tubular flowers are carried on large round heads (umbels). Height $2\frac{1}{2}$ ft. (75 cm).

Flowering time: all summer and into autumn.
Use: in temperate climates frequently grown in tubs, placed in key positions outside in summer, also in sunny sheltered beds, where the roots will tolerate several degrees of frost if covered with straw or leaves in winter.

Propagation: by division of the tubers in spring.
Environment and light: well-drained rich soil in full sun. Store tub specimens in frost-free shed for winter and do not water.

Type of soil: rich; turfy loam, rotted manure, leaf-mould and sand.
Soil moisture: water copiously in summer, very little in winter.

---

38 FLAMINGO FLOWER; PAINTER'S PALETTE
Anthurium andreanum:

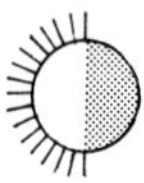

Family: Araceae. Name from Greek *anthos*, flower and *oura*, tail, referring to the shape of the flower spike.
Place of origin: Colombia; introduced in 1876.
Description: an evergreen plant of up to 18 in. (45 cm) with many tough, deep green, oblong cordate leaves on long green stems and waxy-red (occasionally white) palette-shaped flower spathes each with a 3 in. (7 cm), protruding, white spadix. This is the parent of many hybrids in shades of pink, red and cream.

Flowering time: very rarely except when forced in spring to late summer.
Use: as an indoor plant because of the bright colours.
Propagation: by division in early spring.
Environment and light: a constant temperature of 55°F (12·5°C) minimum gives the best results; if too low the leaves turn yellow. Give plants a good light, but not direct sun. Standing pots on pebbles with their base creates humidity in centrally-heated rooms.

Type of soil: three parts peat to one part chopped sphagnum moss with a little charcoal and loam. Pots should be one-third full of crocks for good drainage.
Soil moisture: water moderately in winter, freely in summer. Syringe leaves in hot weather.

39 ZEBRA PLANT

Aphelandra squarrosa:

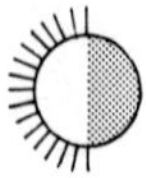

Family: Acanthaceae. Name from Greek *aphelea*, simple and *aner*, male; the anthers are single celled.
Place of origin: Brazil.
Description: a small, erect, evergreen shrub with handsome, shining green, elliptic leaves with slender points about 9 in. (23 cm) long with the main veins in ivory, giving a zebra effect. The yellow flowers are enclosed in deep yellow, red-edged bracts which turn green with age; the inflorescence crowded in 4-sided, terminal heads. Height 18 in. (45 cm).
Flowering time: autumn, but can be forced.
Use: an excellent indoor plant.
Propagation: by cuttings from side shoots taken with a heel and rooted in mixed sand and peat in a propagating bench with bottom heat. 65°–70°F (17°–21°C).
Environment and light: moist in good light but not direct sun. Avoid sudden changes of temperatures and draughts. Temperature of 58°F (15°C) ideal.
Type of soil: rich and porous.
Soil moisture: water regularly and fairly frequently more often if the atmosphere is dry.
Remarks: after flowering cut back to a good pair of leaves. When good side shoots appear, turn from pot, remove soil and repot in pot of same size.

---

40 SHRIMP PLANT

Beloperone guttata:

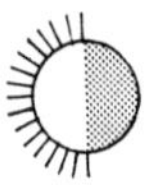

Family: Acanthaceae. Name from Greek *belos*, arrow and *perone*, buckle, referring to the arrow-shaped connective of the filament and anther.
Place of origin: Mexico; introduced in 1936.
Description: a small twiggy shrub of 2–3 ft. (75 cm–1 m) with oval, elliptical, bright green leaves and creamy flowers with conspicuous pinkish-brown bracts, the whole forming a 6 in. (15 cm) pendent spike. There is also a white flowered, green bracted form.
Flowering time: quite extended, and if not throughout the year, at least from spring to autumn.
Use: as a house plant esteemed for its long flowering season; or as a shady border subject in warm climates.
Propagation: by cuttings.
Environment and light: well-lit, but keep away from direct sun; minimum winter temperature 45°F (7°C).
Type of soil: garden soil, leaf-mould, manure
Soil moisture: water regularly as required, more generously in summer, but do not wet the inflorescences. If plants are too wet the foliage becomes discoloured.
Remarks: Shorten back after flowering and feed regularly during growing season.

41 SLIPPERWORT; POCKETBOOK PLANT

Calceolaria × herbeo-hybrida:

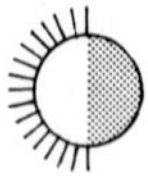

Family: Scrofulariaceae. The name derives from the form of the slipper-like corolla ("calceolus").
Place of origin: a hybrid from various cross-pollinations.
Description: comprises a group of half-hardy hybrids invariably treated as biennials. Tremendous variation; with large or small, slipper-like flowers, mostly in shades of yellow, red or orange spotted. They have a honey like scent. The large, slightly hairy leaves are soft and easily damaged so plants need plenty of room and careful handling. Various strains give plants from 6–18 in. (15–45 cm) tall.

Flowering time: spring–summer.
Use: as an indoor plant.
Propagation: by seed sown preceeding summer; temperature 64°F (18°C). The seed is very fine so sow thinly and cover pot with shaded glass until germination takes place, then pot on and keep plants fairly cool (outdoors if possible) until autumn.

Environment and light: well-aired and lit, not direct sunlight. Winter temperature 45°–50°F (7°–10°C).
Type of soil: any good potting soil.
Soil moisture: water regularly but sparingly.
Remarks: large specimens require staking. Plants suceptible to aphis, so spray at the first sign of trouble.

---

42 COLUMNEA; FLYING GOLD FISH PLANT

Columnea gloriosa:

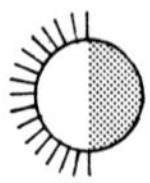

Family: Gesneriaceae. The name derives from that of the Roman patrician Fabius Colunna (1567–1640).
Place of origin: Central America; introduced in 1915.
Description: an evergreen epiphyte with slender, pendulous branches clothed for the whole of their length with opposite pairs of medium green, softly hairy, simple leaves. Bright scarlet, tubular flowers with yellow throats appear at every leaf-joint.

Use: ideal hanging basket plant or can be used on a pedestal so that the branches hang over its sides. Suitable for a greenhouse or light room indoors.
Propagation: by cuttings in spring to early summer, rooted in peat and sand; temperatures 64°–70°F (18°–21°C).
Environment and light: mild, not hot, and adequately lit, but not in direct sun.
Type of soil: proprietary peat-based compost.

Soil moisture: water frequently in the summer months and less often in winter. This plant requires a constantly humid atmosphere.
Remarks: repot every other year in mid-summer. Feed weekly in summer.

43 CROSSANDRA
Crossandra infundibuliformis:

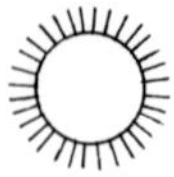

Family: Acanthaceae. Name from Greek *krossos*, a fringe and *aner*, male—the anthers are fringed.
Place of origin: India.
Description: a small evergreen shrub with glossy opposite, ovate leaves and showy salmon-pink flowers in four-cornered spikes.
Flowering time: autumn–winter, but by forcing in the greenhouse flowering may occur in other periods.

Use: as a small pot plant for homes or greenhouses; in tropical gardens becomes a long-blooming 3 ft. (1 m) bush.
Propagation: by seed, or cuttings taken in spring or summer and rooted in a mixture of peat and sand with bottom heat. Temperature 70°F (21°C).
Environment and light: well-lit and in a warm place. In the warmer months it may be put outside, but it must be well sheltered.

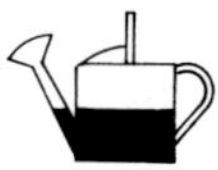

Type of soil: rich soil with peat.
Soil moisture: water regularly in summer but in winter only enough to prevent drying out.
Remarks: cut back after flowering.

---

44 CYCLAMEN; SOWBREAD
Cyclamen persicum: hybr.

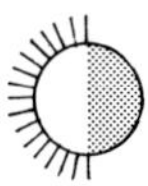

Family: Primulaceae. Name from Greek *kyklos*, a spiral, because the peduncle twists before ovary sheds its seeds.
Place of origin: E. Mediterranean; introduced in 1731.
Description: species has sweetly scented, elegant pink, rose or white flowers on slender stems which contract into spirals in fruit. Leaves simple, heart-shaped, smooth or cristate at the edges, green with silvery marbling. Rootstock is a flattened corm. Garden forms often scentless with larger flowers of pink, red, purple or white; sometimes double, undulating or with fringed margins and five backward-turned petals.

Flowering time: winter–spring.
Use: as an indoor plant.
Propagation: by seed sown the previous summer.
Environment and light: well-lit and well-aired, avoiding direct sun.

Type of soil: loam, leaf-mould and sand.
Soil moisture: the cyclamen prefers a high level of humidity rather than moist soil. Do not overwater.
Remarks: a diet of cyclamen corms is said to give a unique flavour to the pork products of Perigord. Used medicinally for colic and toothache.

9

45 SCARLET PLUME
Euphorbia fulgens:

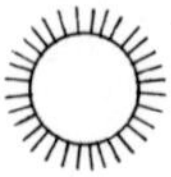

9

Family: Euphorbiaceae. Named after Euphorbus, physician to the King of Mauretania.
Place of origin: Mexico; introduced in 1836.
Description: a small, willowy deciduous shrub with arching green, slender branches rich in latex; alternate, narrow, well-stemmed, dark-green leaves. The flowers grow in axillary inflorescences surrounded by small orange-red bracts.
Flowering time: winter–spring.
Use: outdoors only in sub-tropical climates; elsewhere as an indoor plant for the elegance and colouring of the bracts.
Propagation: by young tip cuttings 3–4 in. (7–10 cm) long, dipped in charcoal to check flow of latex, then rooted in sand and peat with bottom heat in mid-summer. Temperature 65°–70°F (17°–21°C).
Environment and light: in the hot-house or in places with a good deal of sun. Avoid draughts or leaves drop. Likes warmth (55°–60°F (12·5°–15·6°C)).
Type of soil: any good soil potting compost.
Soil moisture: water generously whilst flowering, and then gradually reduce the amount of watering.
Remarks: cut back current season's growth after flowering to within 6 in. (15 cm) of stem bases.

---

46 CHRISTMAS FLOWER; POINSETTIA
Euphorbia (Poinsettia) pulcherrima:

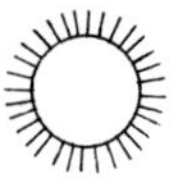

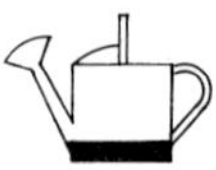

9

Family: Euphorbiaceae. Named after Dr J. R. Poinsett.
Place of origin: Mexico; introduced in 1830.
Description: a small shrub with caducous, large, dark-green, stemmed, oval-lanceolate leaves with 1–2 teeth on either side; one or two flowers are yellowish in terminal umbels surrounded by a ring of brilliant, bright-red bracts. Pink and white bracted forms are in cultivation. The Mikkelsen poinsettias, introduced in 1964, are best for pot work.
Flowering time: mid-winter and persists for months.
Use: as Christmas pot plants in northern hemisphere, or in tropical or sub-tropical gardens in full sun.
Propagation: by cuttings, dipping cut ends in charcoal to stop bleeding of latex. Root with bottom heat.
Environment and light: well-lit and sunny, not too dry.
Type of soil: rich compost (sand, loam and peat).
Soil moisture: water very carefully; the leaves drop if the soil is too wet.
Remarks: dwarfed plants (more convenient for room decoration) are obtained by watering the soil or spraying young plants with chemical dwarfing compounds, at present only available to commercial growers.

47 CAPE JASMINE; GARDENIA

Gardenia jasminoides:

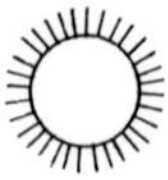

Family: Rubiaceae. Named after Dr Alexander Garden, Scots correspondent of Linnaeus (1730–1791).
Place of origin: China; introduced in 1763.
Description: evergreen shrub of 1–6 ft. (30 cm–2 m), according to conditions with oval or lanceolate, opposite, dark green and shiny leaves and white, powerfully scented flowers with spirally arranged petals. They turn to a chamois leather colour with age. The double forms are the most sought after, such as "Florida", shown here.

Flowering time: summer.
Use: as a garden plant in semi-tropical and tropical gardens, for cut flowers, or as a pot-plant.
Propagation: by cuttings.

Environment and light: in half-shade or full sun, in which case it requires generous watering and spraying.
Type of soil: any good potting compost but no lime. Proprietary peat composts also good.

⑧

Soil moisture: water freely so that the soil is always moist in summer but rather less so in winter.
Remarks: an essential oil, used in perfumery is obtained from the flowers, which are also used for scenting tea. Fruits yield a yellow dye sold in some parts of tropical Africa.

---

48 GUZMANIA

Guzmania cardinalis (probably a natural hybrid of *G. sanguinea*)*:*

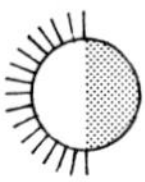

Family: Bromeliaceae. The generic name derives from that of the Spanish botanist, A. Guzmán.
Place of origin: Colombia.
Description: a handsome epiphyte, producing rosettes of evergreen leaves which are so arranged as to form a vase-like interior. This holds water and provides a convenient receptacle when watering in the home. Foliage bright green and narrow; flowering stems to 12 in. (30 cm) with clusters of golden florets at their tops, surrounded by conspicuous scarlet bracts.

Flowering time: in hot-house all year round by forcing.
Use: as an indoor plant for its long-lasting flowers, and decorative bracts.
Propagation: by offshoots from base of old plant but leave these until a reasonable size before detaching.
Environment and light: warm, airy conditions, but not in full sun; light should be filtered, and average humidity; good in high temperatures.

Type of soil: coarsely shredded peat, garden-soil and half-rotted leaf-mould.
Soil moisture: frequent watering and spraying in summer; less in winter. Use rain water.

49 GUZMANIA LINGULATA MINOR

Guzmania lingulata minor:

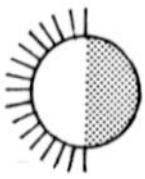

Family: Bromeliaceae. The name derives from that of the eighteenth-century Spanish naturalist, Anastasio Guzmán.
Place of origin: Central and South America.
Description: An epiphyte with long radical, stiff rosettes of leaves which are about 9 in. (22 cm) long, medium green and so arranged as to form a central "vase". From this comes a single inflorescence of small, tubular, whitish-yellow flowers, surrounded by rosettes of orange-red bracts which have touches of yellow.

Flowering time: as hot-house plants, flowering may be induced virtually all year round by forcing.
Use: as an indoor plant for the long-lasting and decorative blooms.
Propagation: by offshoots at the base of the plant. These grow very quickly and flower a year later.
Environment and light: warm, airy, with filtered light and average humidity.

Type of soil: coarse shredded peat, garden soil and partially rotted leaf-mould.
Soil moisture: frequent watering and sprinkling in summer months; less in winter.

---

50 JACOBINIA CARNEA

Jacobinia carnea:

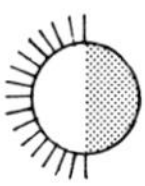

Family: Acanthaceae. Named after Jacobina, a town in Brazil.
Place of origin: Brazil.
Description: an upright shrubby plant with grey-green, oval, entire leaves and clustered heads of tubular, flesh-pink or rosy-purple flowers.
Flowering time: towards the end of summer.
Use: as an indoor or greenhouse plant.

Propagation: by cuttings rooted in small pots. Prick the tops out when the plants are 4–5 in. (10–13 cm) tall to encourage a bushy habit.
Environment and light: adequately lit, but not directly exposed to the sun's rays. Winter temperature 50°–55°F (10°–12·5°C).
Type of soil: equal parts of leaf-mould or peat and loam with enough sand to keep the compost open.
Soil moisture: water freely during the growing period but cut this down drastically once the plants have been pruned after flowering. They must have this rest period otherwise the results are poor.

51 KALANCHOE
Kalanchoe blossfeldiana:

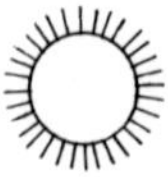

⑧

Family: Crassulaceae. The generic name derives from the Chinese name for a succulent plant.
Place of origin: Tropical Asia, southern regions of America and Africa.
Description: excellent flowering plant for winter decoration, about 12 in. (30 cm) with light green, fleshy leaves edged in red, broadly ovate with scalloped margins. Flowers borne in dense clusters from the upper leaf axils, rich scarlet, individually small and tubular.
Flowering time: although blooming naturally in spring or early summer, flowers can be induced at other seasons by restricting the light to eight or ten hours a day for two months. They flower three months later.
Use: as an indoor plant, but in mild climates may also be grown in the rockery, sheltered and in sun.
Propagation: by cuttings, and, less easily, by seeding.
Environment and light: plenty of light, and mild. Temperature 55°–60°F (12·5°–15·6°C).
Type of soil: any good well-drained soil.
Soil moisture: water quite frequently when in flower, then sparingly until new growth appears. Too much wet causes root rot.
Remarks: after flowering pinch the flowering points back to a good pair of leaves to keep the plant bushy.

---

52 MEDINILLA
Medinilla magnifica:

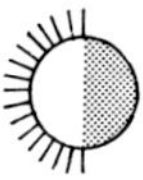

Family: Melastomataceae. Name derives from the Governor of the Marianna Islands, José de Medinilla.

Place of origin: Philippine Islands; introduced in 1888.
Description: an evergreen shrub about 6 ft. (2 m) in height with rich green, oval, opposite leaves, prominently veined and stalkless. Flowers in showy, 1 ft. (30 cm) drooping inflorescences consisting of many rosy-red flowers with yellow stamens and purple anthers, surrounded by large pink bracts.
Flowering time: early summer.
Use: as an indoor plant because of its magnificent flowers. These do not last long, except under special conditions of temperature and humidity.
Propagation: by layers or cuttings of half-ripe wood in spring in mixture of peat and sand with bottom heat.
Environment and light: well-lit, moist atmosphere.
Type of soil: compost of leaf-mould, peat and sand.
Soil moisture: water frequently, but not too generously. The soil should always be reasonably moist.
Remarks: prune back hard after flowering. Plants can be kept in same size pots for many years if top-dressed and fed during the growing season.

53 AZALEA; AZALEA INDICA

Rhododendron simsii (often incorrectly listed as *R. indicum*, which is a different species)*:*

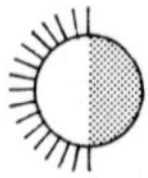

Family: Ericaceae.
Place of origin: China; introduced into Europe in 1810.
Description: well-known house plants, mainly derived from the Chinese—not Indian—*R. simsii*. Small evergreen shrubs with small, oval-oblong leaves and funnel-shaped flowers in clustered heads. There is a tremendous colour range from white, pink, salmon, crimson, magenta to orange.

Flowering time: winter and early spring, but can be forced or retarded to bloom at other times.
Use: as a long-flowering pot plant for the home or cool greenhouse.
Propagation: by half-ripe summer cuttings struck in a compost of equal parts sand and peat, with bottom heat. Rooting erratic but hormone rooting powders help, also mist propagators.

Environment and light: keep in light place indoors but away from direct sun. When risk of frost is past plunge pots in moist peat or soil in a shady place outdoors. Bring inside again early autumn. Repot if necessary after flowering.
Type of soil: proprietary peat composts.
Soil moisture: water regularly—azaleas need a lot of water. Also spray the foliage. Use soft water.

---

54 RHODODENDRON

Rhododendron ponticum: hybr.

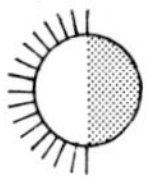

Family: Ericaceae.
Place of origin: garden hybrid; the type species comes from Asia Minor and was introduced into Europe circa 1763.
Description: most hybrid rhododendrons have been derived from about seven species, including *R. ponticum* and several from the Himalayas. The results are varied. There are tall and short hybrids, squat and thin, early and late bloomers in a wide range of brilliant colours. The evergreen leaves are simple, shiny and mostly oblong in shape.

Flowering time: late spring and early summer.
Use: as a garden plant to create great splashes of colour, or in patios and the like in large pots.

Propagation: by layering in mid-summer or by grafting scions on *R. ponticum* stock.
Environment and light: sun or light shade.
Type of soil: acid; peaty or leafy—no lime. Mulch roots with leaf-mould annually to keep them cool.

(5)

Soil moisture: water with rain water if tap water contains lime.

55 AFRICAN VIOLET
Saintpaulia ionantha:

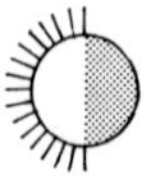

Family: Gesneriaceae. Named after Baron Walter von Saint Paul-Illaire (1860–1910).
Place of origin: Tropical East Africa.
Description: an evergreen plant of approximately 6 in. (15 cm) with long-stalked, simple, oval leaves, softly hairy to the touch and loose sprays of violet flowers with 5 unequal corolla lobes. Cultivated varieties with pink, white, red, mauve and deep purple flowers; bicolors, doubles and some with variegated foliage.

Flowering time: almost all year round.
Use: because of its long flowering period.
Propagation: by seed or leaf cuttings; the latter essential for named varieties. Seed needs germinating in considerable heat—70°–80°F (21°–26·7°C). Cuttings root readily in equal parts sand and peat.
Environment and light: bright light in cool climates, avoiding direct sun. Ideal temperatures around 55°F (12·5°C) at night to 70°F (21°C) in the day.

Type of soil: peat with some loam and sharp sand.
Soil moisture: moist essential. Plunge pots in moss or moist peat to maintain humidity and water as required—at the roots, not over the leaves.
Remarks: high temperatures and a dry atmosphere cause plants to shrivel. The "Diana" and "Rhapsodie" strains are particularly good.

---

56 CINERARIA
Senecio cruentus:

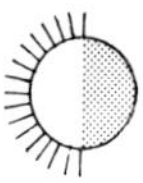

Family: Compositae.
Place of origin: Canary Islands; introduced in 1777.
Description: although perennial, florists' cinerarias are usually grown as annuals because they are at their best the first year from seed. They have large, palmate and pubescent leaves with wavy and toothed margins and large, massed heads of white, pink, red, blue or violet daisy flowers. Some varieties have rings of other colours in the blooms.

Flowering time: spring, but earlier when forced.
Use: Favourite home or greenhouse plants for spring flowering in cool climates. Also used for bedding, window boxes and the like, but are damaged by frost.

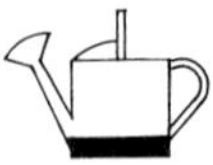

Propagation: by seed grown under glass in fairly cool conditions. Temperature 45°–60°F (7°–15·6°C).
Environment and light: indoors, good light but away from direct sunlight. Outdoors light shade.
Type of soil: good potting compost with good drainage to prevent collar-rot which causes plants to wilt even when the soil is moist. Feed during growing season.
Soil moisture: water if dry; over-watering causes rot.
Remarks: leaves are easily damaged so never crowd plants. Guard against aphides and leaf-miner.

(7)

57 GLOXINIA
Sinningia speciosa:

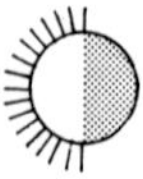

Family: Gesneriaceae. Name derives from that of Wilhelm Sinning (1794–1874).
Place of origin: Brazil; introduced in 1815.
Description: an upright herbaceous perennial with rosettes of large, short-stemmed, simple leaves, velvety to the touch with toothed margins. Flowers 5-lobed, tubular but flaring outwards at the margins. The type is purple but horticultural varieties are legion with red, pink, white and purple, plain or bicolor flowers.

Flowering time: summer.
Use: as an indoor or greenhouse plant.
Propagation: by seed, or especially good forms vegetatively from stem or leaf cuttings. These need a temperature of 70°F (21°C).
Environment and light: in well-lit places, but never in direct sunlight.
Type of soil: leaf-mould and peat with enough sharp sand to keep the mixture open.

Soil moisture: water regularly but sparingly. The soil should always be moist, but never sodden.
Remarks: after flowering watering should be reduced and then stopped. Dig up the tubers when the leaves have yellowed and keep until the following year in a cool, dry place. Start again in spring with bottom heat.

---

58 WHITE SAILS
Spathiphyllum wallisii:

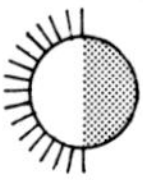

Family: Araceae. Name, Greek *spathe*, spathe and *phyllon*, a leaf, referring to the shape of the inflorescence.
Place of origin: Colombia.
Description: a perennial evergreen plant with long-stalked shiny lanceolate and arum-like flowers. These start life green, become white and then revert again to green with age. Height around 15 in. (6 cm) but more in tropics.

Flowering time: from spring onwards for several months.
Use: as an indoor plant, but as an outdoor shade plant as well in warm climates.
Propagation: by division in spring.

Environment and light: well-lit, but not in direct sun. Avoid sudden changes of temperature. This plant prefers constant warmth.
Type of soil: grow in well-crocked pots in a compost of equal parts loam, leaf-mould and sphagnum moss.

9

Soil moisture: water frequently, at least three times a week, in the plant's most active period, and less at other times. Spray the leaves frequently in summer.
Remarks: the variety "Mauna Loa" is highly scented.

59 MADAGASCAR PERIWINKLE

Vinca rosea, now more correctly *Catharanthus roseus* (Syn. *Lochnera rosea*):

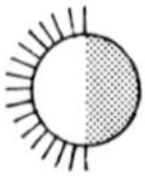

Family: Apocinaceae.
Place of origin: The Tropics; introduced into Europe in 1756.
Description: a widespread plant in the world's tropics with large, flat rose-pink or white flowers with red centres on 1–2 ft. (30–60 cm) leafy stems. Leaves oblong-ovate, entire, deep green and glossy.
Flowering time: almost all year round in mild climates; elsewhere in summer and autumn.
Use: as an indoor pot plant, or to decorate flowerbeds or borders. In the tropics grown in hot arid, as well as shady, places.
Properties: currently being used in the treatment of diabetes and certain types of cancer.
Propagation: usually grown as an annual from seed or by soft cuttings, taken in spring.
Environment and light: in full sun or half-shade outdoors; well-lit if the plant is indoors.
Type of soil: any good light potting compost.
Soil moisture: water regularly but sparingly.

---

60 FLAMING SWORD

Vriesia splendens:

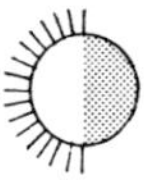

Family: Bromeliaceae. Named after W. H. de Vriese, a Dutch botanist.
Place of origin: Guyana.
Description: an epiphytic evergreen with leathery rosettes of bluish-green leaves, which have transverse bands of purple or claret-red and flattened rather striking spikes of yellow flowers with red bracts.
Flowering time: spring, but as a greenhouse plant there is no definite flowering period.
Use: ideal for centrally heated rooms, in pots or fastened (with moss round the roots) to a tree branch in a warm greenhouse.
Propagation: by seed or offshoots. The latter should be taken when they are about half the size of the parent plant and should be dried for a day before planting.
Environment and light: warm, well-aired, not in direct sun and away from draughts. Temperature 64°–70°F (18°–21°C).
Type of soil: light and porous. Equal parts sand and leaf-mould. Keep pots as small as possible.
Soil moisture: water freely in summer, less in winter. Soft water preferable.

SHRUBS AND BUSHES

61 BLACK WATTLE; MIMOSA; QUEEN WATTLE
Acacia decurrens:

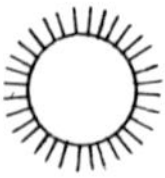

(9)

Family: Leguminosae. Name from Greek name for the Gum Arabic tree, *A. arabica*, derived from *akis*, a sharp point.
Place of origin: Australia; introduced into Europe in 1820.
Description: a large bush or tree, 20 ft. (7 m) or more, closely allied to *A. dealbata*. The compound leaves have numerous fern-like segments of rich green and the round, scented flowers, like small fluffy balls, are massed in large panicles.
Flowering time: winter and early spring.
Use: for its early and abundant flowers.
Propagation: by seed sown in spring in heat. Temperature 60°F (15·6°C). Selected kinds, half-ripe cuttings struck with gentle heat.
Environment and light: cool climates: plant in greenhouse borders, or tubs or large containers to restrict growth. Outdoors they may live for a few seasons in a sheltered corner, and can then be replaced. In sub-tropics and tropics grow in full sun.
Type of soil: any good lime-free potting soil for container plants. Outdoors any soils except the very chalky. Feed pot plants monthly in summer.
Soil moisture: water generously, especially in summer.

---

62 GOSSAMER SYDNEY ACACIA; SYDNEY WATTLE
Acacia longifolia:

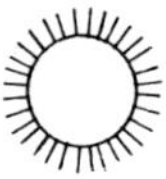

(9)

Family: Leguminosae.
Place of origin: Australia and Tasmania; introduced in 1792.
Description: a large evergreen shrub or small tree of 15–30 ft. (5–10 m) with willow-like, grey-green leaves and short axillary racemes of fragrant, golden yellow flowers.
Flowering time: early spring.
Use: as an ornamental plant, due to the striking and spectacular blossoms; suitable for greenhouses or outdoors in mild and semi-tropical areas.
Propagation: by seed or cuttings of half-ripe wood struck with the aid of a little bottom heat.
Environment and light: in full sunlight.
Type of soil: any good potting soil for container plants and feed occasionally in summer.
Soil moisture: water moderately in autumn and winter; in summer rather more freely.
Remarks: prune if necessary after flowering.

63 FULLMOON MAPLE; JAPANESE MAPLE
Acer japonicum:

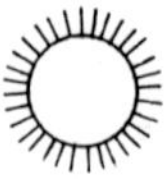

Family: Aceraceae. The genus *Acer* (from *acer* meaning harsh or hard) includes more than a hundred species.
Place of origin: Japan, Central China; introduced in 1864.
Description: slow-growing shrub or small tree, to 20 or 30 ft. (7–10 m) with soft green palmate leaves having 7–11 lobes, which colour to a rich crimson in autumn. The long stalked clusters of purplish-red flowers are followed by "key" like fruits with two wings.
Use: as a garden or park plant, best grown in sheltered positions away from cold and strong winds.
Propagation: by seed outside in autumn; named forms can be grafted in spring on rootstocks of the stock species.

Environment and light: places exposed to full sun, but also half-shade.
Type of soil: it is advisable to use a permeable soil with sand or gravel at the bottom for drainage.
Soil moisture: water constantly in the first years of life; later the plant will receive the necessary amount of water through its root system.

⑤

Remarks: numerous cultivars exist with differently shaped foliage, golden leaves and other diversities. The name Japanese Maple frequently applied to *A. palmatum*, but leaves have less fingers than *A. japonicum*.

---

64 BOTTLEBRUSH BUCKEYE
Aesculus parviflora (Pavia macrostachya):

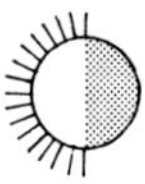

Family: Hippocastanaceae. Latin name for an oak but applied by Linnaeus to this genus.
Place of origin: S. United States, introduced into Britain 1785.
Description: a spreading shrub 8–15 ft. (3–5 m) high with smooth palmate leaves divided into 5 or 7 leaflets and erect 8–12 in. (20–30 cm) panicles of white flowers with long, pink, thread-like stamens. Fruits smooth with large seeds, but these rarely ripen in Britain.

Flowering time: summer.
Use: for parks or gardens, for avenues etc., in areas not subject to hard frost.
Propagation: by seed sown outside in autumn.

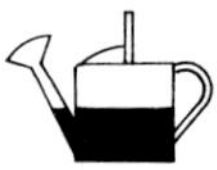

Environment and light: full sun to half-shade.
Type of soil: ordinary garden soil, preferably fresh and soft, with a little lime.
Soil moisture: water in dry periods until well established (usually after two seasons).

⑦

65 MIMOSA (U.S.); PINK SIRIS; SILKTREE
Albizia julibrissin:

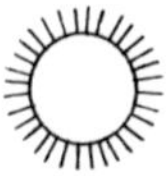

(8)

Family: Leguminosae. Generic name commemorates F. del Albizzi of Florence, who introduced *A. julibrissin* in 1749.
Place of origin: Subtropical Asia.
Description: the hardiest of some 100 species of deciduous trees and shrubs. The species makes a 40 ft. (13 m) tree with doubly pinnate leaves made up of 20 or 30 pairs of leaflets. Flowers in terminal mop-like clusters, noteworthy for their numerous long pink stamens.
Flowering time: summer.
Use: ideally only suitable for mild climates outdoors, but sometimes flowers well against a sunny wall following a hot summer in less temperate zones. Spring sown plants are sometimes used as sub-tropical bedding subjects for their foliage. They are then potted up and taken under cover for winter or discarded.
Propagation: by seed, sown in heat in spring.
Environment and light: in sun.
Type of soil: good garden soil.
Soil moisture: water as required.

---

66 BARBERRY; ROSEMARY BARBERRY
Berberis × stenophylla:

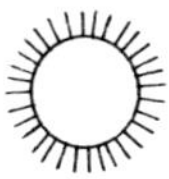

(5)

Family: Berberidaceae. Latinized version of Arabic name for the berries of *B. vulgaris*.
Description: a fine evergreen shrub of hybrid origin (*B. darwinii × empetrifolia*), growing to 8 ft. (2·5 m) with long, reddish, arching spiny branches carrying many small, linear leaves which are glaucous beneath and racemes of golden-yellow flowers. The purple berries have a glaucous bloom.
Flowering time: spring.
Use: to form hedges or enclosures, but also as decorative shrubs scattered here and there on lawns or in shrubberies.
Propagation: by half-ripe cuttings in late summer. Take these about 4 in. (10 cm) long and root them in peat and sand with slight bottom heat or a cold frame outdoors.
Environment and light: sun or light shade.
Type of soil: ordinary garden soil.
Soil moisture: to establish only.
Remarks: prune to shape after flowering. Hedges should be trimmed annually and take hard cutting.

67 BOUVARDIA

Bouvardia longiflora:

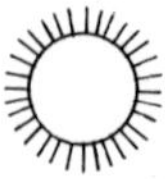

9

Family: Rubiaceae. The generic name commemorates Dr Charles Bouvard (1572–1658).
Place of origin: Mexico; introduced in 1827.
Description: Bouvardias are low growing, evergreen shrubs or herbs much valued in the tropics for their long flowering season. *B. longiflora* grows 2–3 ft. (60 cm–1 m) high with slender stems; smooth, oblong, opposite leaves which are wedge-shaped at the base and terminal corymbs of white, tubular, 4-lobed, fragrant flowers. Individually these resemble jasmine.
Flowering time: normally autumn and winter.
Use: as a greenhouse pot plant or in warm frost-free areas; as a garden plant or for cut flowers.
Propagation: by soft cuttings in spring rooted with bottom heat—70°F (21°C). They root in 3–4 weeks and should then be potted and grown on.
Environment and light: in greenhouses, keep in light shade during summer. Outdoors, keep in full light.
Type of soil: any good potting compost.
Soil moisture: water frequently and generously during summer and vegetative period, but keep soil barely moist after flowering until growth restarts in spring.
Remarks: cut plants hard back in spring, to within 1 in. (2·5 cm) of base. Renew every second year.

---

68 BUDDLEIA; BUTTERFLY BUSH

Buddleja (Buddleia) davidii (B. variabilis):

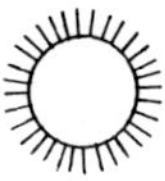

5

Family: Buddlejaceae. Named after Rev. Adam Buddle, English vicar and botanist (1660–1715).
Place of origin: Central and Western China; introduced into Europe by the French missionary David in 1864.
Description: a vigorous deciduous shrub of 12–15 ft. (4–5 m) with mid-green, lanceolate leaves, greyish beneath and slender panicles 12–15 in. (30–38 cm) long of closely packed, fragrant, lilac to purple flowers. White and crimson forms also in cultivation.
Flowering time: late summer.
Use: as summer flowering garden shrubs in various settings.
Propagation: by half-ripe cuttings in late summer rooted in sand/peat mixture in a cold frame or with gentle bottom heat.
Environment and light: full sun. Plant during dormant season.
Type of soil: very adaptable and tolerant of lime, good drainage advisable.
Soil moisture: not necessary after first establishment.
Remarks: to keep plants manageable prune previous year's shoots hard back in late winter to within a few inches of the old wood. Flowers on current year's growth.

69 CAROLINA ALLSPICE; COMMON SWEET-SHRUB

Calycanthus floridus:

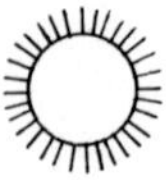

Family: Calycanthaceae. Name from Greek *kalyx* and *anthos*, flower; both calyx and corolla are the same colour.

Place of origin: North America; introduced into Europe in 1726.
Description: an aromatic deciduous shrub of 6–9 ft. (2–3 m) with opposite, oblong-oval leaves, pointed at their tips, soft and downy beneath and 2 in. (5 cm) fragrant flowers of reddish-purple. The dried wood and leaves are also aromatic. Leaf buds concealed by the bases of the leaf-stalks.
Flowering time: summer.
Use: to beautify gardens, both as an individual shrub, or in small clumps in areas subject to the lightest of frosts.
Propagation: by layers or basal suckers.
Environment and light: in full sun; necessary to ripen the wood.
(7)
Type of soil: any reasonably good open soil provided it is deep and moist.
Soil moisture: no special requirements.

---

70 CALIFORNIAN ALLSPICE; CALIFORNIA SWEETSHRUB

Calycanthus occidentalis (C. macrophyllus):

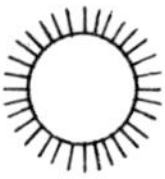

Family: Calycanthaceae.
Place of origin: California.

Description: discovered by David Douglas in 1831 this species is commoner than No. 69 in British gardens. The leaves are also larger and are smooth except for a slight downiness on the undersides. Flowers 2–3 in. (5–8 cm) across, purplish-red tinged with brown. The aromatic wood is sometimes used as a cinnamon substitute. Height 8–12 ft. (3–4 m). Differs from No. 69 by having exposed leaf buds.
Flowering time: summer.
Use: to beautify gardens, both as an individual shrub or in small clumps in areas subject to the lightest of frosts.
Propagation: by layers or basal suckers.
Environment and light: in full sun; necessary to ripen the wood.
Type of soil: any reasonably good open soil provided it is deep and moist.
(8)
Soil moisture: no special requirements.

71 COMMON CAMELLIA

Camellia japonica: hybr.

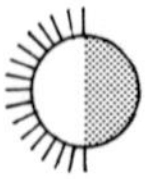

7

Family: Theaceae. Named after Georg Josef Kamel.
Place of origin: East Asia; introduced in 1739.
Description: evergreen flowering trees and shrubs with glossy green, leathery, short-stemmed leaves having dentate edges with pointed tips arranged alternately on the stems. Flowers large, 5-petalled, red in the type and single. Cultivars are legion with white, pink and red blooms, single and double.
Flowering time: winter and spring.
Use: as a garden plant for early blossom under practically frost-free conditions or can be grown in tubs or a cold greenhouse. Useful for cutting. (Other species hardy in colder climates.)
Propagation: by layers, air layers, bud cuttings, seed or ripe wood cuttings in late summer rooted with mild bottom heat.
Environment and light: in mid to partial shade. Roots must never dry out or become waterlogged.
Type of soil: lime-free, deep humus type such as peat and loam with well-decayed leaf-mould and some sand.
Soil moisture: water constantly in dry weather.
Remarks: repot tub specimens when growth is dormant. Protect outdoor blossoms with netting when frost threatens.

---

72 BASTARD JASMINE; JESSAMINE

Cestrum purpureum (C. elegans):

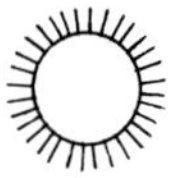

8

Family: Solanaceae. The generic term derives from Greek name for another plant of uncertain definition.
Place of origin: Mexico; introduced into Europe in 1840.
Description: a slender evergreen of 7 ft. (2·3 m) with downy pendulous shoots carrying simple, alternate, oblong-lanceolate, downy leaves and dense terminal panicles of 1 in. (15 cm) funnel-shaped purplish-red flowers with 5 pointed lobes.
Flowering time: summer, autumn.
Use: For a cool greenhouse, trained up pillars or rafters or grown as a wall shrub in sheltered, practically frost-free gardens. Warm climates, grow on walls, arches etc.
Propagation: by cuttings from half-ripe shoots in summer and rooted with slight bottom heat.
Environment and light: full sun or half-shade.
Type of soil: rich and light.
Soil moisture: water indoor specimens regularly, not more than twice a week.

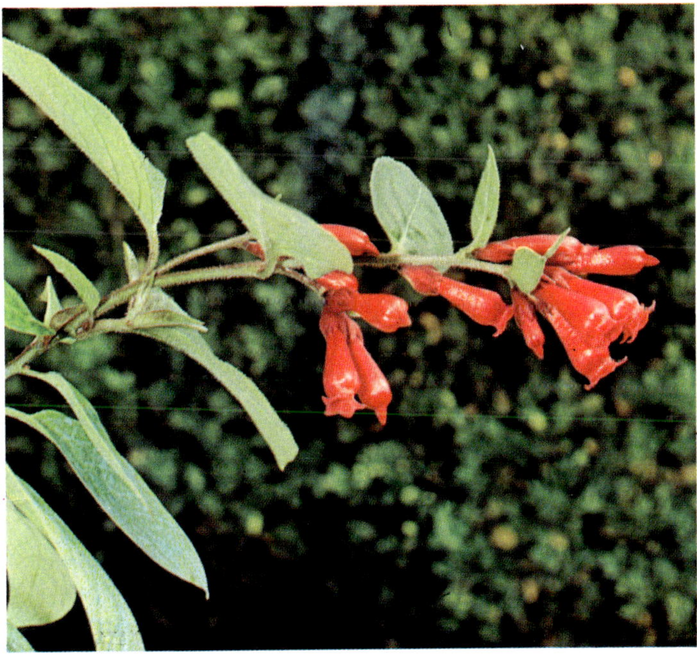

73 DWARF FAN PALM

Chamaerops humilis:

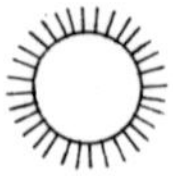

8

Family: Palmaceae. Name derived from Greek, *chamai*, dwarf and *rhops*, a bush, referring to the habit.
Place of origin: Mediterranean Italy, Spain, Sicily, Algeria, Morocco; introduced into Britain in 1731.
Description: the only native European palm and a dwarf species of 6–8 ft. (2–2·6 m). Suckers from the base, producing flat, fan-shaped leaves on long stems. These are split into 12–15 awl-shaped segments and the stems are spined. Flowers yellow in dense heads protected at the back when young by a large bract.
Flowering time: spring and early summer.
Use: ornamental garden or tub plant. Fibre from the leaves used for making brushes and ropes.
Propagation: by suckers or seed.
Environment and light: sunny and open. Only hardy in very mild localities, elsewhere must be overwintered under glass.
Type of soil: ordinary garden soil with a little sand.
Soil moisture: after the first vegetative period when it requires frequent watering, the Palm thrives in long dry periods.

---

74 WINTER SWEET

Chimonanthus praecox (C. fragrans; Calycanthus praecox):

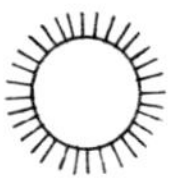

7

Family: Calycanthaceae. Name from Greek *cheima*, winter and *anthos*, to love.
Place of origin: China; introduced in 1766.
Description: a medium sized deciduous shrub of 5–8 ft. (2–3 m) (or taller if grown on a wall), with ovate-lanceolate leaves, rough to the touch and extremely fragrant, pale yellow flowers stained purplish-red inside.
Flowering time: mid-winter, in mild climates only, before the leaves.
Use: grown for its very early blooms.
Propagation: by layers or seed.
Environment and light: full sun, preferably against a fence or wall. Unless the wood is ripened, flowers are sparse.
Type of soil: Any good garden soil.
Soil moisture: no special requirements.
Remarks: new plants take several years to flower. Pruning: Thin out old wood occasionally, also weak and overcrowded shoots. Shorten back stronger twigs on wall specimens only; after flowering.

75 CLEMATIS

Clematis integrifolia:

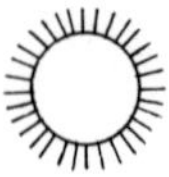

3

Family: Ranunculaceae. Old Greek name.
Place of origin: Balkans, Siberia; introduced in 1573.
Description: an herbaceous, semi-woody perennial about 2–3 ft. (60 cm–1 m) tall, with simple, stalkless, ovate, smooth leaves and solitary, bell-shaped, blue or violet (sometimes white) flowers 1–1½ in. (2–4 cm) across. Non-climbing. Can die to the ground in winter.
Flowering time: summer.
Use: herbaceous borders, garden beds and containers.
Propagation: by seed or division.
Environment and light: sun or light shade.
Type of soil: good garden soil; must be well-drained plus a little lime.
Soil moisture: keep roots moist in dry weather.

---

76 CLERODENDRUM

Clerodendrum bungei (C. foetidum):

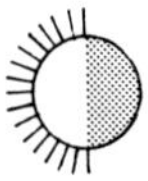

6

Family: Verbenaceae. Name from Greek *kleros*, chance, *dendron*, tree, referring to the variable medicinal properties of the family.
Place of origin: China; introduced to Europe by Fortune in 1844.
Description: a medium sized, suckering, deciduous shrub of 6–8 ft. (2–3 m) which even in temperate countries can be cut to the ground in winter. It usually recovers to send up more shoots in spring. Leaves large and heart-shaped, unpleasant smelling when bruised. Flowers fragrant, rose-pink, star shaped, in flat terminal heads 4–5 in. (10–13 cm) across.
Flowering time: late summer.
Use: as a summer flowering shrub for sheltered places.
Propagation: by division or cuttings rooted with bottom heat in spring.
Environment and light: sheltered place; light shade.
Type of soil: good rich, well-drained.
Soil moisture: water as required in summer.

77 **JAPANESE CLERODENDRUM; HARLEQUIN GLORY BOWER**

Clerodendrum trichotomum:

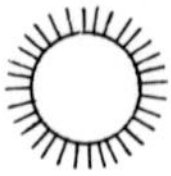

(7)

Family: Verbenaceae.
Place of origin: Japan, E. China; introduced into Britain in 1893.
Description: a bushy deciduous shrub of slow growth, ultimately reaching 10–15 ft. (3–5 m). The deep green, ovate leaves are downy beneath and smell unpleasant when crushed. Flowers star-shaped, white or pinkish in full terminal panicles 6–9 in. (15–23 cm) across. Berries exquisite shade of turquoise blue surrounded by persistent bright red calyces.
Flowering time: late summer.
Use: ornamental garden plant with beautiful flowers and fruits for temperate areas, free from sustained frosts.
Propagation: by seed or heel cuttings rooted in peat and sand with slight bottom heat.
Environment and light: sunny sheltered place.
Type of soil: good garden soil but must be well-drained. Plant spring or autumn.
Soil moisture: water freely in summer, less in winter.

---

78 **CABBAGE PALM; DRACENA (U.S.)**

Cordyline indivisa:

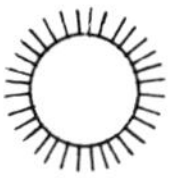

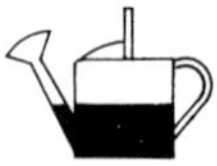

(8)

Family: Agavaceae. Name from Greek *kordyle*, a club, referring to the manner of the root growth. Sometimes called Dracaena to which it is related.
Place of origin: New Zealand.
Description: this plant has a stout upright trunk 10–25 ft. (3–8 m) tall topped by 3–6 ft. (1–2 m) long, dark green, sword-shaped leaves which have red or white midribs and veining. Flowers off-white, in huge panicles 2 ft. (60 cm) across. These have a rich hay-like scent and are followed by round purple berries.
Flowering time: summer.
Use: as an ornamental garden plant for light or frost-free climates. Small specimens can also be grown in tubs and wintered under cover.
Propagation: by suckers or by seed.
Environment and light: in full sun.
Type of soil: well-drained fertile soil.
Soil moisture: water regularly, but not too generously for tub specimens. Outdoors can usually fend for itself.

79 PINK FLOWERING DOGWOOD

Cornus florida "Rubra":

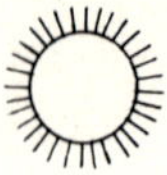

④

Family: Cornaceae.
Place of origin: Eastern United States; introduced into Europe c. 1730.
Description: *C. florida (Cynoxylon floridum)*, the type plant is a handsome deciduous shrub or small tree of 10–15 ft. (3–5 m) with opposite, broadly oval, 3–6 in. (7–12 cm) leaves, pale green beneath. Its crowded heads of insignificant greenish flowers are surrounded by four large white bracts. A tree smothered with these looks most effective. "*Rubra*" is similar but with red or pink bracts.
Flowering time: spring.
Use: for garden decoration, particularly amongst other shrubs.
Propagation: by seed sown when ripe, by suckers or half-ripe cuttings struck in gentle heat in summer.
Environment and light: positions not susceptible to spring frosts with plenty of summer sun to ripen the wood. This is not always possible in Britain; the plant does much better in the Eastern United States.
Type of soil: moist soil with leaf-mould or peat added.
Soil moisture: water frequently in dry seasons.
Remarks: the type is the state flower of Virginia. Plant new trees in autumn.

---

80 ANGEL'S TRUMPET

Datura suaveolens (Brugmansia suaveolens):

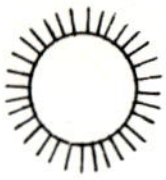

⑧

Family: Solanaceae; from an old Indian vernacular name.
Place of origin: Mexico.
Description: a tree or large shrub which will grow 10–15 ft. (3–4·5 m) high with large, flannel-like, ovate-oblong leaves of 6–12 in. (15–30 cm) and huge, pendulous, musk scented, trumpet-shaped flowers up to 10 in. in length. These are pure white at first but mellow to cream with age. The double flowered form is the most spectacular.
Flowering time: summer.
Use: frost prone, so use as accent plants in tubs (wintered indoors) or as isolated lawn specimens in warm climates.
Propagation: heel cuttings of 4–6 in. (10–15 cm), taken in early summer and rooted in a sand/peat mixture in a warm propagating frame.
Environment and light: in sunny places.
Type of soil: very rich and loose.
Soil moisture: water frequently, daily in summer.

81 CORNUS KOUSA; JAPANESE DOGWOOD

Dendrobenthamia kousa; Benthamia japonica:

Family: Cornaceae; from the Latin name for the Cornelian cherry *Cornus mas.*
Place of origin: Japan, Korea and Central China; introduced into Europe in mid-nineteenth century.
Description: large deciduous shrub or small tree up to 20 ft. (6 m) high with opposite, oval, leaves with slender points and rounded bases. Flowers small and inconspicuous, purplish-green like a button surrounded by four showy, creamy-white bracts. Fruits strawberry-like, scarlet.
Flowering time: summer.
Use: as an ornamental tree for gardens or parks.
Propagation: by seeds sown when ripe and kept in cold frame—they may take 18 months to germinate. Also by layers.
Environment and light: sunny.
Type of soil: moist—not recommended for poor, shallow, chalk soils. Add peat or leaf-mould to original soil.
Soil moisture: always keep moist at roots.

---

82 DEUTZIA

Deutzia scabra:

Family: Philadelphaceae. Named after Johan van der Deutz, Dutch naturalist (1783–1822).
Place of origin: Japan and China; introduced in 1822.
Description: deciduous flowering shrubs, esteemed for their early and dainty flowers. *D. scabra*, a bushy species, reaches a height of 6–10 ft. (2–3 m) and has opposite, ovate leaves and large paniculate clusters of white, 5-petalled flowers. There are also some double and rosy flowered forms.
Flowering time: summer.
Use: in shrubberies or with herbaceous perennials.
Propagation: by cuttings 3–4 in. (7–10 cm) long of the lateral shoots in mid-summer, rooted in sand/peat mixture in a cold frame, or with gentle heat.
Environment and light: full sun or light shade; avoid draughts.
Type of soil: good garden soil or potting compost.
Soil moisture: water when very dry.
Remarks: young growths can be damaged by late frosts. Prune occasionally by taking out worn-out branches to ground level. Flowers on wood of previous year so don't shorten side branches.

83 ENKIANTHUS CAMPANULATUS; REDVEIN ENKIANTHUS

Enkianthus campanulatus:

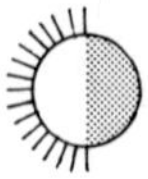

⑤

Family: Ericaceae. Name from Greek *enkyos*, pregnant and *anthos*, flower, referring to the swollen corolla.
Place of origin: Japan; introduced into Europe in 1880.
Description: an erect shrub, to 8 ft. (2·5 m), with varied qualities—red shoots, clusters of green elliptic leaves at their tops which turn brilliant red in autumn and masses of bell-shaped flowers of creamy-yellow with red veining.
Flowering time: early summer.
Use: as a garden adornment in light woodland conditions in mild climates.
Propagation: by seed and cuttings in late spring.
Environment and light: likes half-shade rather than fully exposed places, with constant humidity, out of the wind and draught-free.
Type of soil: acid or neutral, with added peat or leaf-mould. Plant in autumn or spring.
Soil moisture: water if required in summer.

---

84 COCKSCOMB; COCKSPUR; CORAL BEAN; CORAL TREE

Erythrina crista-galli:

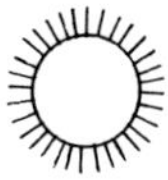

⑦

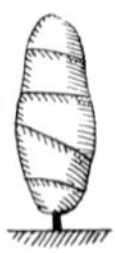

Family: Leguminosae. Name from Greek *erythros*, red.
Place of origin: Brazil; introduced into Europe in 1771.
Description: a small or average sized tree in very mild climates, or a shrub in cold climates; in the latter instance it is grown in pots and sheltered during the coldest times of year; has spiny branches and stems, and brilliant green leaves formed by three oval-shaped pinnules. The flowers, growing in magnificent terminal inflorescences, are a splendid vivid red in colour and look like waxen sweet peas.
Flowering time: summer.
Use: to beautify and decorate parks and gardens in sheltered spots or stood about in containers.
Propagation: by cuttings in warmth, in spring.
Environment and light: full sun in well-drained soil. In warm climates leave outside all year; in mild, it is usually cut to ground level by frost so protect crowns with straw, bracken or leaves. In cold climates, take under cover for winter.
Type of soil: garden soil with sand and peat added.
Soil moisture: water pot plants regularly to leave soil slightly moist; little or no water in winter.

85 EUPATORIUM SORDIDUM

Eupatorium ianthinum; Hebeclinium ianthinum:

Family: Compositae; old Greek name.
Place of origin: Mexico; introduced into Europe in 1849.
Description: an attractive plant which (except in subtropical gardens) usually needs the protection of glass. It droops when the temperature drops below 50°F (10°C). Woody stems of about 3 ft. (1 m) with opposite, short-stemmed, oval-lanceolate leaves and large, showy, terminal corymbs of mauve-purple, fragrant flowers.
Flowering time: winter–spring.
Use: in warm climates to decorate lawns and form small individual clumps. Greenhouse plant for borders and containers.
Propagation: by spring cuttings in a warm frame.
Environment and light: sunny, but the soil must always be fairly moist.
Type of soil: fresh and rich.
Soil moisture: water generously in hot weather and feed during the growing season.

---

86 EUPHORBIA

Euphorbia griffithii:

Family: Euphorbiaceae. Named after Euphorbus, physician to the King of Mauretania.
Place of origin: Himalayas.
Description: a perennial sub-shrub of 2–$2\frac{1}{2}$ ft. (60–75 cm) with lanceolate, mid-green leaves with pink midribs with small yellow flowers surrounded by brilliant orange-red bracts.
Flowering time: summer.
Use: for small individual clumps in borders.
Planting: the small plants obtained from cuttings are planted outdoors soon after they have taken root. Adult plants dislike being transplanted.
Propagation: by cuttings after flowering or by division.
Environment and light: does best in open sunny position if soil is moist.
Type of soil: ordinary garden soil or even poor soil.
Soil moisture: water in hot weather.

87 EVERGREEN EUONYMUS; EUONYMUS

Euonymus japonicus "Ovatus Aureas":

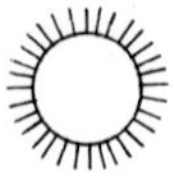

Family: Celastraceae. From the Greek *euonymos*, "of good name", referring rather surprisingly to its being poisonous to animals.
Place of origin: Japan; introduced into Europe in 1804.
Description: the type species comes from Japan but the form portrayed is the best of the golden variegated kinds. It is a slow but compact grower with tough, leathery, elliptical leaves with a broad irregular rich yellow margin, suffusing into the green centre. It needs sun to bring out the colour. The type has small greenish flowers and (rarely in cultivation) pink and orange fruits.

Use: not reliably hardy in cool climates but where it is can be used for hedging or shrubbery planting. Recommended for town and coastal areas.
Propagation: by cuttings rooted with a little bottom heat; these strike at almost any season; by layers.
Environment and light: sun.
Type of soil: good, well-drained loam.
Soil moisture: water if necessary.

(8)

---

88 FEIJOA; PINEAPPLE GUAVA

Feijoa sellowiana:

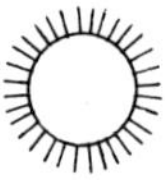

Family: Myrtaceae. Named after Don de Silva Feija, a Brazilian botanist.
Place of origin: Brazil, Uruguay; introduced into Europe in 1898.
Description: a large evergreen shrub or small tree of bushy habit with oval or ovate, opposite, rather leathery, grey-green leaves, felted beneath. Flowers with fleshy crimson and white petals and numerous crimson stamens. Fruits edible, egg-shaped, up to 2 in. (10 cm) with a strong aromatic flavour.

Flowering time: in the height of summer.

Use: needs a warm sheltered position in temperate climates where the winters are not too harsh. Elsewhere it can be grown in large pots which are taken under cover in the cold months. In the tropics cultivated as a fruit tree.
Propagation: by cuttings rooted with bottom heat in summer; by layers.

(7)

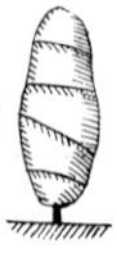

Environment and light: keep out of the wind, in sunlight or half-shade.
Type of soil: ordinary garden soil with a little sand.
Soil moisture: water intermittently, about once a week.

89 FLOWERING ASH; MANNA ASH
Fraxinus ornus:

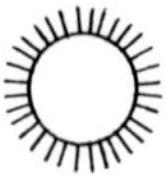

Family: Oleaceae. Classical Latin name.
Place of origin: Southern Europe, Asia Minor; introduced into Britain before 1700.
Description: this is the type species of a group known as flowering ashes because the inflorescences have showy panicles of white petalled flowers (other ashes have no petals). The blooms are also heavily scented. The species make a tree of about 50 ft. (17 m) with a rounded head, and leaves with 5–9 leaflets of dull green. Flowers in 3–4 in. (7–10 cm) panicles.
Flowering time: early summer.
Use: as garden or park plants.
Propagation: by seeding or division of suckers at the base of the mother plant.
Environment and light: full sun or half-shade.
Type of soil: good, moist loam.
Soil moisture: water frequently, at least in the tree's early life.
Remarks: Manna sugar is obtained by wounding stems.

(6)

---

90 CAROLINA SILVERBELL; SNOWDROP TREE
Halesia carolina (H. tetraptera):

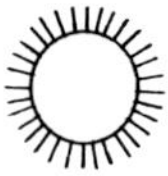

Family: Styracaceae. Named after the Rev. Stephen Hales, chemist and inventor (1677–1761).
Place of origin: S.E. United States; introduced into Europe in 1756.
Description: a large deciduous shrub or tree up to 30 ft. (9 m) with ovate-lanceolate leaves 2–5 in. (5–12 cm) long, grey downy beneath, less so above, taper pointed and minutely toothed. Flowers in clusters, pure white, drooping, bell-shaped on slender stalks.
Flowering time: early summer.
Use: in temperate climates not subject to heavy frosts, as individual specimens (or to form clumps) in gardens and parks.
Propagation: by seeding and layers.
Environment and light: sunny, sheltered places; but may also thrive in half-shade.
Type of soil: moist, well-drained, loamy.

(7)

91 HIBISCUS

Hibiscus rosa-sinensis:

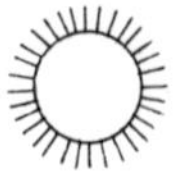

(10)

Family: Malvaceae. Greek name used by Dioscorides for Musk Mallow.
Place of origin: China; introduced into Europe in 1731.
Description: a magnificent evergreen shrub for frost-free areas. Grows 6 ft. (2 m) or more, with pointed oval leaves, coarsely dentate; the large flowers measure some 5 in. (13 cm) in diameter, and are bright red in colour, either single or double. The stamens and stigma protrude from the flowers.
Flowering time: in the height of summer.
Use: as a garden, terrace or balcony plant, or can be grown in large pots, wintered under cover.
Propagation: by cuttings.
Environment and light: in full sun.
Type of soil: well fertilized, loam, with sand and peat added.
Soil moisture: water frequently and generously, especially in the month prior to flowering.
Remarks: in Jamaica the species is known as Shoe Flower; the petals can be used to polish shoes.

---

92 ALTHEA; ROSE OF SHARON

Hibiscus syriacus (Althea frutex):

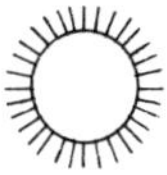

(5)

Family: Malvaceae. The Greek name for Mallow.
Place of origin: India and China; in Syria as a cultivated plant only; introduced in the late 16th century.
Description: a deciduous shrub attaining a height of 4–10 ft. (1–3 m) and 4–6 ft. (1–2 m) across. Rather erect branches with smooth, roughly oval, coarsely toothed leaves with three irregular lobes. Flowers large—3 in. (7 cm)—in pink, lilac, red, violet or white, sometimes blotched. Stamens and stigma not protruding.
Flowering time: late summer.
Use: as a garden or park plant, but also for terraces or balconies in large pots.
Propagation: by cuttings, or layers; rare sorts can also be grafted on common ones.
Environment and light: full sun; not for badly drained spots.
Type of soil: well fertilized, fresh, with sand and peat.
Soil moisture: water frequently and generously, especially in the month prior to flowering.
Remarks: very large specimens can be pruned back in early spring. The plant does better in warm climates than cold, but is nevertheless hardy in most temperate zones. Treat as a wall shrub in cooler areas.

93 OAKLEAF HYDRANGEA

Hydrangea quercifolia:

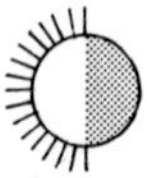

5

Family: Saxifragaceae. Name from Greek *hydro*, water and *angeion*, a jar, referring to the shape of the fruits.
Place of origin: S.E. United States; introduced into Europe in 1803.
Description: a deciduous shrub up to 6 ft. (2 m) of loose habit with broadly ovate, simple leaves having 5–7 sharp lobes, bearing some resemblance to those of the oak. These assume colourful autumnal tints. Flowers white, in erect terminal panicles, turning purplish as they fade.
Flowering time: summer.
Use: in gardens, flowerbeds, shrubberies etc., in mild climates.
Propagation: by cuttings, late summer in a sand/peat mixture in a propagating case; by layers.
Environment and light: in half-shade, in sheltered places. The species is tenderer than the Chinese hydrangeas.
Type of soil: ordinary garden soil provided it keeps moist. Mulch annually with well-rotted manure or compost.
Soil moisture: water frequently and generously in the growing season.

---

94 HOLLY

Ilex aquifolium:

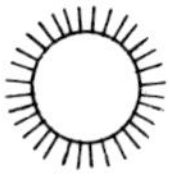

6

Family: Aquifoliaceae. From Latin *Quercus ilex*, holm oak.
Place of origin: Western and Southern Europe (including Britain), N. Africa to China.
Description: a well-known evergreen bush or small tree, which under good conditions can reach 80 ft. (28 m). Very leafy, the leaves thick and spiny, smooth and leathery, toothed and glossy. Small white flowers in axillary cymes, male and female on separate trees. Berries showy, bright red, round. There are countless varieties, with different leaf shapes, yellow or orange berries, weeping and variegated.
Flowering time: early summer.
Use: for hedges, boundary screens or as individual specimens. *Note:* to obtain berries at least one male plant must be in the vicinity. Not suitable for areas with prolonged and severe frosts.
Propagation: by seed.
Environment and light: sun or light shade.
Type of soil: moist but well-drained.
Soil moisture: water young plants whilst establishing.

95 HIMALAYAN INDIGO; INDOGO SHRUB
Indigofera gerardiana (I. dosua):

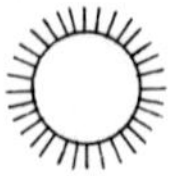

(7)

Family: Leguminosae. From Greek *indigo* and *fero*, to bear. Indigo is obtained from some species.
Place of origin: N.W. Himalayas; introduced into Europe circa. 1840.
Description: a 5 to 6 ft. (1·5–2 m) deciduous shrub, not reliably hardy in temperate climates so best grown against a wall or fence in cool regions, or in large containers. Very elegant pinnate foliage with numerous opposite leaflets and racemes of bright purplish-rose, pea-shaped flowers.
Flowering time: late summer to autumn.
Use: as a wall shrub or grouped in favoured areas.
Propagation: by seeds sown in spring.
Environment and light: sunny but sheltered from the wind.
Type of soil: light, with plenty of humus, or soil mixed with sand. It is advisable to fertilize the soil organically in autumn.
Soil moisture: water regularly, whilst establishing or in containers.
Remarks: cut hard back in spring to maintain shape. New shoots arise from the base.

---

96 CALICO BUSH; MOUNTAIN, SHEEP or SWAMP LAUREL
Kalmia latiflora:

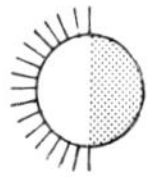

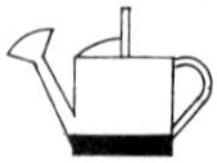

(4)

Family: Ericaceae. Named after Pehr Kalm (1715–1779), a pupil of Linnaeus.
Place of origin: Eastern North America; introduced into Europe in 1734.
Description: an evergreen shrub not more than 9–12 ft. (2·7–3·6 m) high, with alternate or sometimes verticillate leaves grouped in threes at the tips of the branches, oblong-lanceolate, stemmed, and a beautiful bright green in colour; pinkish-white, large parasol-shaped flowers on long peduncles in terminal corymbs.
Flowering time: early summer.
Use: garden plant both as an individual specimen, in clumps or to make splashes of colour.
Propagation: by layers or cuttings of semi-ripe young shoots in late summer, rooted in peat/sand mixture in a cold frame in shade.
Environment and light: half-shade.
Type of soil: Rhododendron conditions, soil fresh and peaty, but not calcareous or clayey, and always moist.
Soil moisture: if weather or soil becomes dry.
Remarks: remove spent flowers.

97 COMMON LABURNUM; GOLDEN CHAIN TREE
Laburnum anagyroides (L. vulgare):

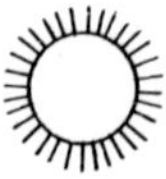

(5)

Family: Leguminosae.
Place of origin: Central and S. Europe.
Description: small, deciduous tree of 10–18 ft. (3–5·5 m) with dull green, slightly hairy, trifoliate leaves and pendulous racemes of yellow, pea-shaped flowers with a bean-like scent. There are many garden forms.
Flowering time: late spring and early summer.
Use: as an isolated specimen, but usually well-suited to forming avenues.
Propagation: by seed, or named hybrids must be grafted on seedling stocks in spring.
Environment and light: in regions with sufficiently mild climates it prefers sunny places; in warmer climates it likes open, half-shady places.
Type of soil: suited to virtually all types of soil, but better if the soil is fresh and moist, with a certain amount of peat.
Soil moisture: water quite frequently in summer so that the soil is always moist.

---

98 CRAPE MYRTLE
Lagerstroemia indica:

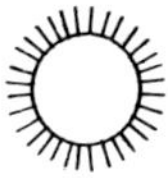

(7)

Family: Lithraceae. Named after Magnus von Lagerstroem (1696–1759).
Place of origin: China, Korea; introduced in 1754.
Description: a large deciduous shrub or small tree which requires plenty of sun to ripen its wood or it will not flower. Stem attractively mottled in grey, pink and cinnamon. Leaves opposite, alternate or in whorls of three, privet-like, smooth and mostly obovate. Flowers in showy terminal panicles, 6-petalled, pink to deep red with crinkled petals and numerous stamens.
Flowering time: summer.
Use: only suitable for areas receiving plenty of sun in summer; otherwise grow in conservatories or large containers in hot situations.
Propagation: by cuttings.
Environment and light: full sun.
Type of soil: fresh, not packed, mixed with some peat.
Soil moisture: water container plants regularly.
Remarks: the plant must be pruned towards the end of winter; trim the older branches and remove the weak ones which will not produce flowering shoots. It flowers on the current season's wood.

99 BAY LAUREL; SWEET BAY

Laurus nobilis:

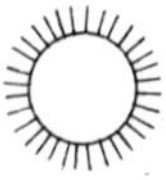

7

Family: Lauraceae.
Place of origin: Mediterranean region; introduced into Britain in 1562.
Description: evergreen shrub or tree with alternate, sharply lanceolate, short-stemmed, wavy-edged leaves, bright green in colour, glabrous and rather leathery, producing an aromatic scent caused by the essential oil-bearing glands; insignificant, yellowish flowers.
Flowering time: spring.
Fruit: berry-shaped, the size of a small olive, green at first and turning black as they ripen towards the late autumn.
Use: the Bay Laurel is well suited for shrubberies and hedges and as a tree for avenues in mild climates. It stands clipping well, so in colder areas can be grown in tubs as topiary specimens. Need wintering under cover.
Propagation: usually by seed; by cuttings and layering.
Environment and light: full sun to half-shade. In warm regions it also grows well in shady places.
Type of soil: ordinary garden soil with a little sand.
Soil moisture: water fairly frequently about twice a week, and more generously in summer.
Remarks: this is the "laurel" of the Ancient Greeks and the leaves are used to flavour food and medicine.

---

100 COMMON PRIVET

Ligustrum vulgare:

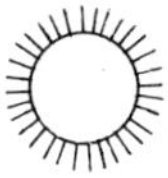

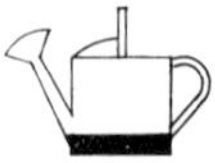

4

Family: Oleaceae. Latin name of plant.
Place of origin: Europe (including Britain), N. Africa.
Description: fast growing shrub, evergreen or semi-evergreen according to climate. Adaptable and shade tolerant. Leaves oval or elliptic, smooth, about 2 in. (5 cm) long and half as wide. Flowers small, dull white, in erect 1–2 in. (2·5–5 cm) panicles at the ends of the twigs, heavily scented. Followed by round, black, shiny fruits.
Flowering time: summer.
Use: for hedging or as individuals in semi-shaded shrubberies. The golden-leaved *"Aureum"* is the most garden worthy.
Propagation: by cuttings struck from ripe wood of current season's growth rooted in sandy compost in a frame in autumn.
Environment and light: in full sun or half-shade, sometimes also in shady places.
Type of soil: most garden soils.
Soil moisture: water in very dry weather.
Remarks: in cold climates the shrub usually loses its leaves.

101 LAUREL MAGNOLIA; SOUTHERN MAGNOLIA

Magnolia grandiflora:

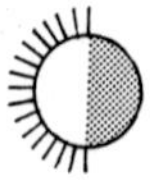

7

Family: Magnoliaceae. Named after Pierre Magnol (1638–1751), botanist at Montpellier, France.
Place of origin: S.E. United States; introduced into Britain in 1737.
Description: a magnificent evergreen tree growing to 80 ft. (27 m) in nature but more like 15–25 ft. (4·5–7·6 m) in Europe. In Britain it is best grown as a wall shrub. Leaves large and leathery, 6–10 in. (15–25 cm) long, less than half as wide, tapered and dark green above, rusty felted beneath. Flowers huge, 8–10 in. (20–25 cm) across, cup-shaped, creamy white with a strong fruity smell.
Flowering time: summer–autumn.
Use: as a wall shrub or specimen tree where conditions permit; it will not stand hard waters.
Propagation: by layering, but also by seed.
Environment and light: sun or half-shade.
Type of soil: lime-free, rich, deep and well-drained.
Soil moisture: in the first years of the plant's life water regularly, then generously in the summer months. When the plant has reached a certain size it should be left to adjust to the general climatic conditions, but do not let the ground become too dry. Not hardy north of zone 7.

---

102 OYAMA MAGNOLIA; MAGNOLIA SIEBOLDII

Magnolia parviflora:

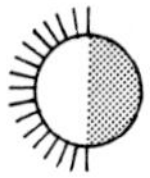

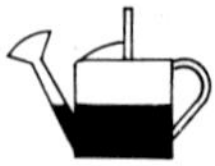

6

Family: Magnoliaceae. See *M. grandiflora.*
Place of origin: Japan and Korea; introduced into Europe in 1865.
Description: a small deciduous tree or large shrub of up to about 10 ft. (3 m) with slender branches; oblong-ovate leaves, dark green above, paler and downy beneath; white, fragrant, cup-shaped flowers 3–4 in. (7–10 cm) across, with 6 petals and many red stamens followed by pendent carmine fruits full of scarlet seeds.
Flowering time: early summer.
Use: to decorate gardens and parks.
Propagation: by layering.
Environment and light: in half-shade, in fairly sheltered places.
Type of soil: light, better if acid, mixed with a little sand, and capable of maintaining a certain degree of moisture. Dislikes lime.
Soil moisture: water to establish. Never let the soil dry out completely.

103 **MAGNOLIA; SAUCER MAGNOLIA**
Magnolia × soulangana:

Family: Magnoliaceae.
Place of origin: This is a hybrid obtained in 1826 by M. Soulange-Bodin of Paris by crossing *Magnolia denudata × Magnolia liliiflora.*
Description: one of the best and most popular magnolias for general garden use. The large tulip-shaped flowers are white, stained rose-purple inside but there are numerous forms, raised mostly from its seeds including one called *"Lennei"* with the colouring reversed. Grows to 30 ft. (9 m) or more.

Flowering time: spring.
Use: for garden or park decoration; tolerant of urban conditions and most soils but dislikes lime.
Propagation: by layering.

Environment and light: full sun or half-shade.
Type of soil: light, better when acid, capable of maintaining some moisture.
Soil moisture: water regularly during initial establishment. The soil should never dry out.

5

---

104 **MAGNOLIA STELLATA; STAR MAGNOLIA**
M. kobus var. *stellata:*

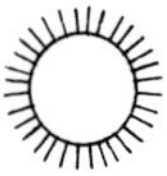

Family: Magnoliaceae. See *M. grandiflora.*
Place of origin: Japan; introduced into Europe in 1862.
Description: a much branched deciduous shrub to around 10 ft. (3 m), compact, slow growing with aromatic young bark. Leaves narrow oblong or obovate, tapering at the base to a short stalk. Flowers elegant, fragrant, many petalled (12–18), pure white ageing to pink. "Rosea" has pink flowers.

Flowering time: late winter or early spring.
Use: for open positions where the blooms can be enjoyed e.g., banks, borders, etc.
Propagation: by layering.

Environment and light: full sun or half-shade, but sheltered from high winds.
Type of soil: well-drained but moist loam.
Soil moisture: water enough to keep soil moist and from drying out.

6

105 **MAHONIA; OREGON GRAPE; OREGON HOLLY GRAPE**

Mahonia aquifolium:

Family: Berberidaceae. Named after Bernard M. Mahon (1775–1816), an American horticulturalist.
Place of origin: Western N. America; introduced into Britain in 1823.
Description: an evergreen shrub with tough pinnate leaves, with 5 to 9 stalkless leaflets, rich glossy green, turning purplish in winter. Flowers yellow in dense terminal racemes followed by decorative bunches of grape-like blue-black berries.
Flowering time: late winter and early spring.
Use: for ground cover or underplanting in shrubberies, game coverts, to make thickets.
Propagation: by seed sown as soon as ripe or by division in spring.
Environment and light: sun or shade; very adaptable, will tolerate wind.
Type of soil: any ordinary garden soil.
Soil moisture: only necessary to establish.

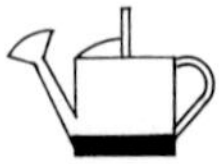

(5)

---

106 **OLEANDER**

Nerium oleander:

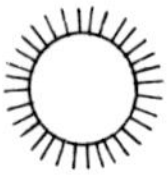

Family: Apocynaceae; classical Greek name.
Place of origin: Mediterranean; introduced in 1596.
Description: an evergreen shrub with long, slender, upright branches; opposite or ternate, single and entire leaves, lanceolate and leathery and grey-green in colour. Red, pink, peach, yellow and white flowers in terminal corymbs with single or double corollas formed by five petals turned somewhat to the right.
Flowering time: all summer.
Use: as individuals or to form clumps with variously coloured varieties. It is also suited for decorating entrance halls, gardens etc. Very popular in mild climates. In cold climates it should be grown in pots so it can be taken under cover during winter.
Propagation: by layers or cuttings in summer.
Environment and light: full sunlight.
Type of soil: ordinary garden soil.
Soil moisture: generous watering in the growing season.
Remarks: specimens grown in pots should have water added daily to the dish beneath the pot, so that the soil remains moist. Note that all parts of the plant are poisonous.

(7)

107 SWEET OLIVE ; *Osmanthus fragrans (Olea fragrans):*

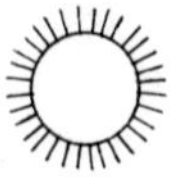

(8)

Family: Oleaceae. Name from Greek *osme*, fragrance and *anthos*, flower.
Place of origin: China, Japan; introduced in 1771.
Description: an evergreen shrub or tree with opposite and entire, or subtly dentate, lanceolate leaves, shiny on both surfaces and dark-green in colour. Flowers small but richly fragrant, white and 4-petalled in the leaf axils. The Chinese use them for scenting tea.
Flowering time: summer.
Use: a greenhouse shrub for all but very sheltered places in cool climates, when it may be tried as a wall shrub. In mild climates can be grown as a hedging subject or as individual specimen.
Propagation: by late summer cuttings in the shade under glass.
Environment and light: sunny or half-shade, but keep away from direct wind. It tends to suffer in hard winters in colder regions and should therefore be grown in sheltered places.
Type of soil: good open loamy soil.
Soil moisture: water if necessary to prevent flagging.

---

108 MOCK ORANGE; commonly called SYRINGA, a name which rightly belongs to the lilacs. *Philadelphus coronarius:*

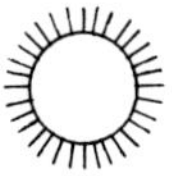

(4)

Family: Philadelphaceae. Name from Greek *filos*, friend and *adelfos*, brother.
Place of origin: the Caucasus; introduced in 1596.
Description: a robust deciduous shrub up to 12 ft. (3·6 m) high with angular branches, peeling as they age, ovate leaves, wedge-shaped at their bases and terminal racemes of yellowish-white, 4-petalled, heavily scented flowers. A variety called "Aureus" has golden yellow leaves.
Flowering time: summer.
Use: for the back of herbaceous borders, shrubberies or as specimen plants in lawns. Also as hedging.
Propagation: by cuttings from soft young wood rooted in bottom heat; by layers.
Environment and light: full sunlight or half-shade.
Type of soil: grows best in loam soil but very tolerant, succeeding even under rather dry conditions.
Soil moisture: water only when required.
Remarks: plants flower on short lateral twigs of previous season's growth so any pruning should consist of taking out old branches, but only when necessary for space reasons. Does not do well in the Tropics.

109 FORMOSA ANDROMEDA

Pieris taiwanensis:

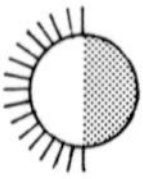

7

Family: Ericaceae. Name derived from Pierides, surname of the Muses.
Place of origin: Formosa; introduced into Europe in 1918.
Description: a compact evergreen shrub of 6–10 ft. (2–3 m) with yellowish-green young shoots. Leaves oblanceolate or oval, tapered at both ends, leathery and deep green and glossy above, pale green beneath. Flowers in a cluster of racemes at the end of the shoot, semi-erect, white flowers, urn-shaped and nodding—something like lily-of-the-valley.
Flowering time: early spring.
Use: in shrubberies, backs of rock gardens or along walks.
Propagation: by air layers, stem layers, seed.
Environment and light: cool, semi-shady places.
Type of soil: must be lime-free. Loam improved by addition of decayed leaves or peaty soil.
Soil moisture: water if necessary, in dry season.

---

110 PITTOSPORUM

Pittosporum tobira:

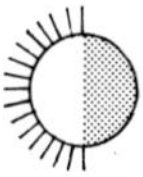

7

Family: Pittosporaceae. The name derives from the Greek and means resin-coated seeds.
Place of origin: China and Japan; introduced in 1804.
Description: a slow growing evergreen shrub or small tree with short branches and whorls of glossy, bright green, oval or obovate leaves amidst which occur bunches of tubular, 4-petalled, creamy-white flowers with a strong fragrance like orange blossom.
Flowering time: spring–summer.
Use: as a container plant wintered under cover in cold climates; or for hedging or as individual specimen shrubs in warm areas.
Propagation: by seed or half-ripe summer cuttings rooted in bottom heat or with a mist propagation.
Environment and light: in half-shade or full sun. Young plants, grown outdoors in cool areas subject to occasional frosts, should be protected during winter with plastic sheets and leaves around the base of the plant.
Type of soil: ordinary garden soil mixed with sand and peat.
Soil moisture: water regularly, and more generously in summer.

111 **POINCIANA**

Poinciana gillesii (now more correctly *Caesalpinia gillesii*):

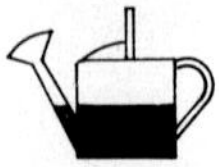

10

Family: Leguminosae. Genus named after Italian botanist Andrea Cesalpini (1524–1603).
Place of origin: Argentina; introduced into Europe in 1829.
Description: a deciduous shrub or small tree (to 36 or 40 ft.) (11 or 12 m) with glandular hairy shoots, handsome feathery leaves, doubly pinnate with numerous fine leaflets and terminal racemes, 12 in. (30 cm) or more in length, composed of 5-petalled, rich yellow flowers with long protruding scarlet stamens.
Flowering time: summer.
Use: as recommended for sub-tropical or tropical gardens or on sunny walls in mild, nearly frost-free areas. Alternatively, greenhouse borders or large containers stored away from frost in winter.
Propagation: by seed or layers; soft cuttings sometimes root in a warm propagating frame.
Environment and light: as a plant growing in hot climates it should be in full sun and well exposed.
Type of soil: garden soil with peat and sand.
Soil moisture: water frequently in dry weather.

---

112 **HARDY ORANGE; JAPANESE BITTER ORANGE**

Poncirus trifoliata (Citrus trifoliata; Aegle sepiaria):

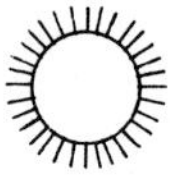

5

Family: Rutaceae. The name of the genus derives from the French "poncire", old word for orange.
Place of origin: N. China; introduced in 1850.
Description: a tough, slow growing, medium sized (6–9 ft. (2–3 m)) deciduous shrub with angular branches supporting stout spines and trifoliate leaves. Flowers resembling orange blossom and sweetly scented, waxy white with 4–5 petals and golden centres. Fruits round and small like small greenish yellow oranges. Sometimes used for drinks.
Flowering time: spring.
Use: as solitary specimens in key positions away from cold winds; also makes a formidable hedge. In really cold climates grow in tubs—put outside in summer, or in greenhouses.
Propagation: by seed or half-ripe cuttings rooted in a closed frame in sandy compost.
Environment and light: grows well in full sun or half-shade.
Type of soil: permeable, ordinary garden soil.
Soil moisture: water if required but not too generously (more often in summer).

113 **POMEGRANATE**
Punica granatum:

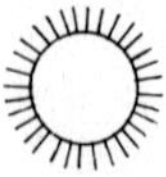

7

Family: Punicaceae. Name from Latin *punicum*, referring to an apple of Carthaginia.
Place of origin: Mediterranean region.
Description: a large shrub or under good conditions a small tree with oval, opposite, smooth, shiny green leaves which are coppery-red when young and showy tubular, scarlet flowers with crumpled petals. These are followed by large, round, leathery fruits filled with garnet-red seeds and yellowish pulp. Varieties with double red and double white flowers exist.
Flowering time: summer.
Use: for edible fruits (species only), as a wall shrub in cool climates or pot plant for terraces. In warmer climates, for hedging or as individual specimens.
Propagation: by layering in May, or by seed.
Environment and light: full sunlight.
Type of soil: ordinary garden soil.
Soil moisture: water pot specimens regularly 1–2 times a week in the hottest months, then reduce frequency.
Remarks: garden specimen always need considerable pruning in late winter.

---

114 **MINIATURE POMEGRANATE**
Punica granatum var. *nana:*

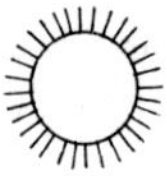

7

Family: Punicaceae.
Place of origin: Mediterranean region.
Description: a charming dwarf form of No. 113 with narrow, pointed, almost sessile, smooth and shiny leaves and orange-scarlet flowers followed by small round fruits with red and yellow striations.
Flowering time: summer.
Use: as a pot plant for terraces, patios, roof gardens and the like. Also for sunny sites outside in sheltered gardens in mild climates.
Propagation: by seed, cuttings or grafts on seedling stock of the type species.
Environment and light: full sun; in northern regions it should be grown in pots or tubs where it can be protected during the cold months.
Type of soil: ordinary garden soil.
Soil moisture: water pot plants regularly 1–2 times a week, more often during hot months.
Remarks: prune back hard in late winter where it thrives; in cool climates it is cut to ground level by frost.

115 FLOWERING CURRANT

Ribes sanguineum:

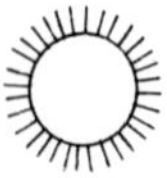

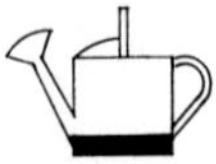

5

Family: Saxifragaceae. Name from the Arabic *ribas*, acid-tasting.
Place of origin: Western N. America; introduced into Europe in 1826.
Description: a popular early flowering shrub extensively planted in Britain and Northern Europe. Growing 4–10 ft. (1–3 m) high it has a characteristic smell when the heart-shaped, deeply lobed leaves are bruised. The flowers hang in dense racemes which droop at first and then become upright. The type is rosy-pink with white petals, "Pulborough Scarlet" is deep red and "Brocklebankii" has golden-yellow leaves.
Flowering time: spring.
Use: for shrubberies and planting in odd spots where the early flowers can be appreciated.
Propagation: by half-ripe cuttings in summer rooted with a little bottom heat or hardwood cuttings rooted outdoors in autumn.
Environment and light: sun or light shade; they flower better in sun.
Type of soil: any good garden soil, preferably on the damp side.
Soil moisture: water to establish.

---

116 ROSE ACACIA

Robinia elliottii (R. hispida "Rosea"):

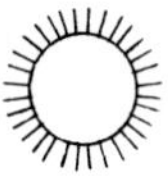

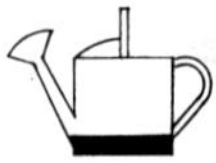

6

Family: Leguminosae. The generic scientific term commemorates J. Robin (1550–1629), gardener to Henry IV of France.
Place of origin: S.E. America; introduced into Europe in 1743.
Description: medium-sized suckering shrub with brittle branches, covered when young with glandular, bristly hairs. Leaves unequally pinnate with 7–15 leaflets, bristle tipped. Flowers in drooping racemes of 5 to 10, deep rose and 1 in. (2·5 cm) long. Many cultivars of which "Frisia" with bright golden leaves is outstanding.
Flowering time: early summer.
Use: in gardens, borders or against walls.
Propagation: usually grafted on *R. pseudacacia*; occasionally layered.
Environment and light: sun and a sheltered situation; branches easily broken by rough winds.
Type of soil: garden soil with sand.
Soil moisture: water if required.

117 SPANISH BROOM; WEAVER'S BROOM

Spartium junceum:

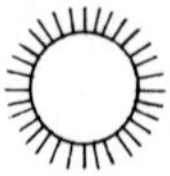

Family: Leguminosae. Name from Greek *spartion*, osier shrub (wicker).

Place of origin: Mediterranean region; introduced into Britain in 1548.

Description: a vigorous deciduous shrub with green, rush-like stems up to 8 or 9 ft. (2·5–3 m). Leaves small and inconspicuous, flowers large, pea-shaped, yellow and fragrant (occasionally double) in loose terminal clusters.

Flowering time: spring and summer.

Use: for garden decoration; good seaside shrub.

Propagation: by seed, potted as soon as large enough to handle, overwintered in first season under cover or in a sheltered place.

Environment and light: full sun; sometimes damaged by winter frosts and winds.

Type of soil: mainly calcareous with a little sand added.

Soil moisture: water sparingly twice or so every 8–10 days.

(7)

Remarks: Broom will not survive winters where the climate is too harsh. Remove dead flowers to prevent seeding.

---

118 SNOWBELL

Styrax obassia:

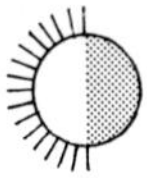

Family: Styracaceae; Classical Greek name.

Place of origin: Japan; introduced into Europe in 1879.

Description: a beautiful shrub or small tree of up to 20 or 30 ft. (6 or 9 m) with alternate, simple, large ovate to rounded leaves, which are downy beneath and long (6–8 in. (15–20 cm)) terminal, pendent racemes of fragrant, white, bell-shaped flowers.

Flowering time: early summer.

Use: as individual specimens or in gardens.

Propagation: seed, layers or cuttings.

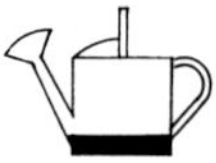

Environment and light: slight shade with shelter from strong winds. Not for very cold climates outdoors.

Type of soil: light, loamy or semi-peaty soil. Acid conditions.

Soil moisture: water if required in very dry seasons.

(7)

119 SNOWBERRY

Symphoricarpus albus (S. racemosus):

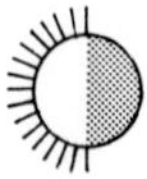

(3)

Family: Caprifoliaceae. Name from Greek *symphorein*, bear together and *karpos*, fruit, referring to the clustered fruit.
Place of origin: N.E. America; introduced into Europe in 1879.
Description: a slender shrub, deciduous, about 3 ft. (1 m) high with simple, oval leaves, smooth and short-stemmed, downy beneath and small pink flowers on slender spikes. These are succeeded by large, round, white berries.
Use: to make hedges, shrubberies and isolated clumps, to decorate slopes and rocky places etc., chiefly grown for the decorative fruits which persist in early winter.
Propagation: suckers form at the base of the plant; these are removed and become separate plants.
Environment and light: full sunlight, half-shade or shade.
Type of soil: no particular requirements.
Soil moisture: water if required.
Remarks: prune to shape in early spring.

---

120 LILAC

Syringa vulgaris:

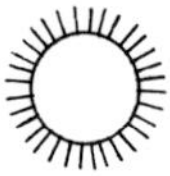

(4)

Family: Oleaceae. Name from Greek *syrinx*, flute. Lilac wood was used to make flutes.
Place of origin: mountains of E. Europe.
Description: *Syringa vulgaris* is the parent of numerous large flowered garden cultivars. These can be single or double, are all richly scented and the flowers in various shades of mauve or violet. There are also red, white and primrose-yellow sorts. The simple smooth leaves are ovate or heart-shaped, the flowers borne in dense, pyramidal panicles.
Flowering time: spring.
Use: in shrubberies, hedges, or as individual specimens. Also grown for cut flowers. Not for tropics.
Propagation: named varieties are frequently grafted on stocks of the species (*S. vulgaris*) or privet (*Ligustrum ovalifolium*). Also increased from heel cuttings using bottom heat or mist propagation.
Environment and light: full sun or partial shade.
Type of soil: fresh, ordinary garden soil, but clayey and fairly close-packed.
Soil moisture: water frequently the first season and remove buds. They take a year or two to re-establish after transplanting so never allow roots to dry out.

121 BRAZILIAN GLORYBUSH; SPIDER FLOWER

Tibouchina urvilliana (correct name for the plant known as *T. semidecandra* in cultivation; the true species is rarely seen):

9

Family: Melastomataceae.
Place of origin: Brazil; introduced into Europe in 1864.
Description: a beautiful large shrub with angled stems, short-stalked, velvety, mid to deep green, oblong-oval leaves with longitudinal veining and large (3–4 in. (7–10 cm)) vivid purple, 5 petalled flowers with long spidery purple stamens.
Flowering time: late summer and autumn.
Use: in greenhouse borders or large containers put out for summer but wintered inside, also for flower beds in tropical gardens.
Propagation: by soft cuttings rooted in spring in sandy soil in a propagating bench. Temperature 64°–70°F (18°–20°C).
Environment and light: good light but protected from direct sunlight if grown under glass; outdoors grow in sun.
Type of soil: rich; neutral or acid.
Soil moisture: plenty in growing season, just enough to keep soil moist in winter.
Remarks: prune annually to keep bush shapely.

---

122 JAPANESE SNOWBALL

Viburnum plicatum (V. tomentosum "Sterile"):

4

Family: Caprifoliaceae.
Place of origin: China and Japan.
Description: a beautiful deciduous shrub of 8–10 ft. (2–3 m) with neat green, ovate leaves and showy white "Snowball" flowers arranged in double rows along the length of the outward spreading branches. These persist for several weeks. The form, which has long been cultivated in the Orient, is sterile and was introduced by Robert Fortune in 1844, the type species (see No. 123) arriving some 20 years later. For this reason the name *V. plicatum* takes precedence over *V. tomentosum*.
Flowering time: early summer.
Use: for the fronts of shrubberies, along walks or as island specimens in grass.
Propagation: by half-ripe cuttings taken in summer and rooted with bottom heat; by layers.
Environment and light: full sun to half-shade.
Type of soil: any good garden soil provided it is moist in summer.
Soil moisture: water regularly in dry spells during summer months.

123 DOUBLE FILE VIBURNUM; VIBURNUM PLICATUM TOMENTOSUM

Viburnum tomentosum:

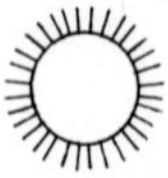

4

Family: Caprifoliaceae.
Place of origin: Japan, Formosa; introduced into Europe about 1865.
Description: this is the wild form of preceding and a spreading 6–9 ft. (1·8–2·7 m) shrub with oval, pubescent, green pleated leaves. The inflorescences sit in double rows along the tops of the branches, looking at a distance like frosted snow. The true flowers are small and creamy but surrounded by large and conspicuous, sterile white florets. Fruits red developing to black.
Flowering time: late spring and early summer.
Use: for hedges, walks, garden shrubberies.
Propagation: by layers or half-ripe summer cuttings rooted in sandy soil in mid-summer.
Environment and light: sun or half-shade.
Type of soil: good moist garden soil.
Soil moisture: water if necessary.

---

124 WEIGELA

Weigela (Diervilla) florida:

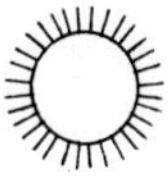

5

Family: Caprifoliaceae. Named after the German botanist Christian Ehrenfeld Weigel (1748–1831).
Place of origin: N. China; introduced into Europe in 1845.
Description: a deciduous spreading bush, growing to 6 ft. (2 m) with opposite, ovate-lanceolate, short-stemmed, prominently veined leaves and pink tubular flowers in clusters at the ends of short twigs along the arching branches. Cultivars exist with red and white flowers, purple foliage and also creamy leaf variegations.
Flowering time: summer.
Use: as a garden plant for shrubberies, borders, banks or large containers.
Propagation: by half-ripe summer cuttings rooted in sandy soil with bottom heat (60°F (15·6°C)).
Environment and light: sun or light shade.
Type of soil: well-drained but moist.
Soil moisture: water only in dry seasons.
Remarks: each year remove one or two of the older stems to ground level.

SUCCULENTS AND CACTI

125 AEONIUM

Aeonium canariense (Sempervivum canariense):

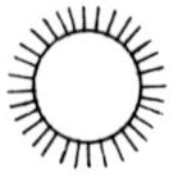

(8)

Family: Crassulaceae. Name from Greek *aionios*, eternal.
Place of origin: Teneriffe; introduced into Europe in 1699.
Description: an evergreen sub-shrub, up to 18 in. (45 cm), forming a large bowl-shaped rosette of velvety appearance on a short, thick stem. Basal leaves succulent and rounded, pointed at the tip; stem leaves sparse and oval shaped. Flowers many, on a branched inflorescence of up to 20 in. (50 cm), white or yellowish, with 7–9 petals.
Flowering time: late spring to mid-summer.
Use: outdoors, in very mild climates for rockeries, slopes etc.; or as an indoor or greenhouse plant.
Propagation: by cuttings in summer, calloused before insertion, or by seed.
Environment and light: outdoors in sunny positions; in pots, in well-lit places.
Type of soil: good garden soil, manure, washed sand, clay, in equal parts.
Soil moisture: only water when the soil is dry.

---

126 AGAVE VICTORIAE REGINAE

Agave victoriae-reginae:

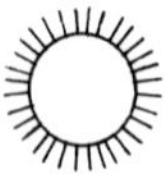

(10)

Family: Agavaceae. Name from *agauvos*, admirable, referring to the handsome flowers.
Place of origin: Northern Mexico; introduced into Europe in the second half of the nineteenth century.
Description: a noble plant with rosettes of leaves 2 ft. (60 cm) across. These are very closely packed and leathery, tapering to a point, dark green with conspicuous white lines along the entire edges which become imprinted on backs of leaves above. Flowers in close spikes of up to 12 ft. (3·6 m), yellowish green.
Flowering time: spasmodically and at any season. The rosette then dies and plant carries on from offshoots.
Use: its foliage outdoors in tropics and sub-tropics; elsewhere as container or greenhouse plant.
Propagation: by seed or sideshoots.
Environment and light: sunny if outdoors, in full sun if potted. In harsh winter climates the Agave must be taken under cover in the coldest time of year.
Type of soil: light and sandy with peat but well drained.
Soil moisture: if the plant is grown outdoors, practically no watering is necessary; if potted, water regularly throughout the year, and more generously in summer.

127 RAT'S TAIL CACTUS

Aporocactus flagelliformis:

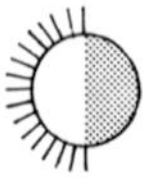

Family: Cactaceae. Name from Greek *aporos*, no way through, referring to the spiny habit.
Place of origin: from Mexico to Peru; introduced into Europe in the late seventeenth century.

Description: a free-flowering plant, not known in the wild but considered Mexican by many authorities. Flowers showy, 2–3 in. (5–7 cm) across, vermilion, at intervals on the long trailing, spiny stems. Red berries follow these, can be grown on its own roots but often grafted on a *Selenicereus* sp. to obtain upright (instead of pendulous) plants.
Flowering time: early summer.

Use: an excellent pot plant for decorating windows, hanging baskets, balconies, terraces in the warm months and to beautify the home and greenhouses in winter.
Propagation: by stem cuttings in summer.
Environment and light: in hot places in veiled sunlight in summer; in cold-houses well-lit and sunny in winter.

(9)

Type of soil: ordinary soil with peat and washed sand.
Soil moisture: in summer water generously as required; the whole plant should be left unwatered for two months or so after flowering. In winter water sparingly, preferably with a vaporizer; maintain a fairly humid atmosphere.

---

128 BISHOP'S CAP

Astrophytum myriostigma (Echinocactus myriostigma):

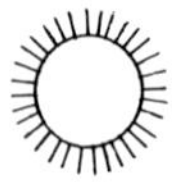

Family: Cactaceae. Name from Greek *astron*, star, *phyton*, plant, referring to the plant shape.
Place of origin: Mexico; introduced into Europe in circa mid-nineteenth century.

Description: a globular, spineless plant with (normally) 5 well-defined ribs and covered with small white spots. The amount of white varies. Yellow daisy-like flowers with brown tips on the outer ring of petals appear on top of the dome.
Flowering time: summer; the flowers last some six or seven days.

Use: as an indoor plant or under glass in winter; outdoors in summer in mild, temperate climates.
Propagation: by seed.
Environment and light: sunny outdoors; well-lit indoors.
Type of soil: garden soil, washed sand and one part made up of three parts ordinary soil to one of lime.

(8)

Soil moisture: water only when required and soil is dry.

129 STAR CACTUS

Astrophytum ornatum:

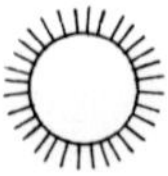

9

Family: Cactaceae.
Place of origin: Mexico.
Description: a plant with a greyish green stem dotted with white, almost spherical, then cylindrical, with 8 fairly large ribs. The 2 in. (5 cm) spines are borne in groups of 5–11. Flowers lemon-yellow. The plant is considered by some botanists to be a natural hybrid between *A. myriostigma* and an *Echinocactus* species.
Flowering time: summer.
Use: suited to indoors, and hot houses in winter. May be kept outside in summer.
Propagation: by spring sown seeds or cuttings, calloused before insertion, in spring or summer.
Environment and light: in full sun outdoors; well-lit indoors or in the greenhouse.
Type of soil: well crocked pots and any good sandy compost.
Soil moisture: in summer water regularly each week; in winter, according to temperature and local conditions. In any event only water when soil is dry.

---

130 CURIOSITY PLANT; PERUVIAN TORCH

Cereus peruvianus monstrosus:

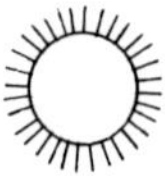

8

Family: Cactaceae. Name from Latin *cereus*, a wax taper; some species have columnar stems and are called torch thistles.
Place of origin: south-east coast of South America.
Description: an arborescent plant with a bright green, sometimes glabrous stem, with 6–9 compressed ribs; 5–10 spines, short, brown or black; large white flowers surrounded by brownish red sepals and fleshy, edible fruits. The form portrayed is a cristate variety, slow-growing but always retaining its grotesque habit.
Flowering time: early summer.
Use: as an ornamental plant outdoors in mild regions; indoors elsewhere. Must be wintered away from frost.
Propagation: by cuttings in spring or summer, calloused before insertion, in sand with bottom heat.
Environment and light: sunny outdoors; well-lit or sunny in pots or greenhouses.
Type of soil: mixture of sand and leaf-mould.
Soil moisture: water when required in summer, and hardly at all in winter.

131 CLUB MOSS CRASSULA

Crassula lycopodioides:

7

Family: Crassulaceae. Name from the Latin *crassus*, thick; the foliage is thick and fleshy.
Place of origin: S.W. Africa.
Description: an unusual succulent, resembling a club moss, with up to 12 in. (30 cm), stringy, branching stems sheathed by 4 rows of tiny, scale-like, oval, pointed, closely set leaves. The minute, whitish, sessile flowers are situated in the upper leaf-axis.
Flowering time: spring–summer.
Use: for small rock-gardens in fairly mild places, otherwise as an indoor or greenhouse plant.
Propagation: by stem cuttings rooted in sandy soil with bottom heat.
Environment and light: give a sunny position where temperature does not fall below 40°–45°F (4°–7°C) minimum.
Type of soil: fairly rich but well-drained, sandy compost.
Soil moisture: water in moderation and only as required.

---

132 ECHEVERIA

Echeveria:

8

Family: Crassulaceae. Named after Athanasio Echeverria Godoy, a botanical artist (1787–1797).
Place of origin: the genus embraces some 150 species, most of which come from Mexico.
Description: fleshy indoor or greenhouse plants grown for their symmetrical rosettes of fleshy leaves. These usually have a waxy bloom easily destroyed by rough handling. The bell-shaped flowers occur on branching stems in winter or early spring and are brownish-red, yellow, reddish-yellow or white.
Flowering time: winter or early spring.
Use: often used for summer bedding in mild climates. Planted outside when frosts are finished, especially carpet-bedding. Also for pots and containers.
Propagation: by leaf cuttings or root offsets.
Environment and light: sun or light shade, according to climate. Minimum winter temperature 40°–45°F. (4°–7°C).
Type of soil: garden soil, rich compost, washed sand and clayey earth (in equal parts).
Soil moisture: water freely in summer but not over the leaves; very little in winter.

133 **ECHINOCACTUS**

Echinocactus ingens var. *grandis:*

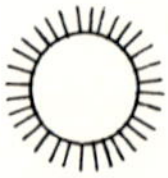

9

Family: Cactaceae. Name from Greek *echines*, hedgehog, referring to its spiny appearance.
Place of origin: Mexico.
Description: plants with globular stems, sometimes cylindrical, slightly depressed at the top, with fairly marked ribbing and small areas highlighted by a kind of yellowish down on which there are quite conspicuous tough, differently coloured spines. The flowers appear at the top of the stem in the slightly depressed area and are yellow. Young plants distinct with broad horizontal bands.
Flowering time: summer.
Use: in sub-tropics they may decorate slopes or rocky banks in the garden, but they are usually indoor or hothouse plants.
Propagation: by seed.
Environment and light: full sun or hot, well-lit places.
Type of soil: good garden soil and washed sand in equal parts.
Soil moisture: water and sprinkle regularly, and use vaporizer, in summer; less often in winter, but do not let the ground dry out completely.

---

134 **GOLD BALL CACTUS; GOLDEN BARREL CACTUS**

Echinocactus grusonii:

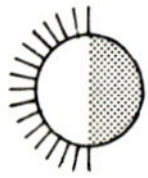

9

Family: Cactaceae.
Place of origin: Mexico.
Description: grown for its attractive golden spines which cover the whole rounded plant which may attain a diameter of up to 3 ft. (1 m). Flowers yellow at the top of the plant but seldom produced in cultivation. Fruits thin-skinned, egg-shaped and woolly.
Flowering time: early summer.
Use: will survive outdoors only in sub-tropics, otherwise a fine indoor or hothouse plant.
Propagation: by seed.
Environment and light: well-lit with slightly veiled sunlight.
Type of soil: mixture of ordinary garden soil and two parts of washed sand.
Soil moisture: in summer water regularly, but do not saturate; in winter less often, and keep the atmosphere reasonably humid.

135 **ORCHID CACTUS**
Epiphyllum: hybr.

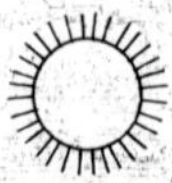

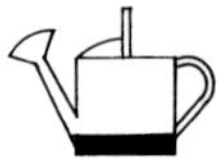

Family: Cactaceae. Name from Greek *epi*, upon and *phylos*, a leaf; the flowers were once thought to grow on the leaves which are, in fact, flattened stems.
Place of origin: Tropical America.
Description: epiphytic cacti are much esteemed for their large, showy, long-tubed flowers of brilliant pink, red, mauve, yellow, orange or white. Some are scented. Branches flattened, leaf-like, sometimes 3-angled, occasionally spined.
Flowering time: spring–summer.
Use: as a garden plant in well-exposed sunny places in sub-tropics; pot plant for terraces, balconies and indoors.
Propagation: by cuttings calloused before insertion in sandy soil with bottom heat or by seed.
Environment and light: sunny if grown outdoors, half-shade if grown in pots in summer; in winter pots must be protected indoors or in the greenhouse and kept lightly shaded.
Type of soil: rich but light—leaf-mould and sand.
Soil moisture: some watering and sprinkling in summer; just a little sprinkling in winter; need more water than desert cacti.

---

136 **CROWN OF THORNS**
Euphorbia milii (E. splendens):

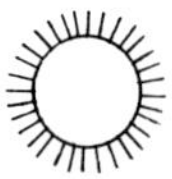

Family: Euphorbiaceae. Named after Euphorbus, physician to the King of Mauretania.
Place of origin: Madagascar.
Description: a spiny succulent shrub, up to 3 ft. (1 m) high, long tapering spines, oblong-oval leaves at the tops of the branches, thin, bright green and branching cymes of bright red flowers.
Flowering time: throughout the summer.
Use: outdoors only in tropical or sub-tropical climates where it is used for hedging; otherwise to decorate terraces, balconies and verandas in summer, indoors and greenhouses in winter.
Propagation: by cuttings, allowed to callouse before planting, in spring or summer.
Environment and light: full sun in tropical gardens; very well-lit indoors or in warm greenhouses.
Type of soil: very permeable made up of ordinary garden soil, rich compost and washed sand.
Soil moisture: needs a certain amount of water in spring or autumn, slightly more in summer, and, given a fairly humid atmosphere, hardly any in winter.

137 EUPHORBIA VIROSA

Euphorbia virosa:

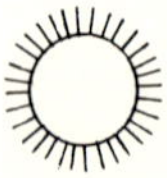

(8)

Family: Euphorbiaceae.
Place of origin: Southern Africa. Cape Province.
Description: a spiny shrubby species up to 5 ft. (1·5 m) in height, its main stems partly buried but with a number of ascending branches, bluish-green with 5–8 angles and spines in pairs. Flowers inconspicuous, yellowish; fruits, reddish.
Flowering time: late spring–early summer.
Use: in areas with frost-free winters the plant may stay outdoors in the sun and is good for decorating terraces, balconies or small rockeries. Elsewhere, a good indoor or greenhouse plant.
Propagation: by cuttings dried for a week before insertion in a sand-peat mixture with bottom heat; by seed.
Environment and light: in sun outdoors; indoors, in a well-lit place, even if not in direct sunlight. Winter temperature 45°–50°F (7°–10°C).
Type of soil: well-drained, coarse sand and loam with a little bonemeal.
Soil moisture: water a reasonable amount, but not in winter.

---

138 FISH HOOK CACTUS

Ferocactus horridus:

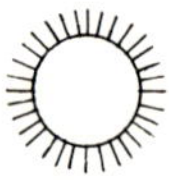

Family: Cactaceae. From Latin *ferox*, ferocious, referring to the formidable spines.
Place of origin: Mexico.
Description: a large and formidable rounded cactus with 13 broad ribs bearing groups of 8–12 white, slender, spreading outer spines and 6–8 reddish central spines. One in each group is flat and hooked and may be up to 6 in. long.
Flowering time: summer, winter.
Use: ornamental and hothouse plant.
Propagation: by seed.
Environment and light: in hothouses or indoors behind glass, well-lit.
Type of soil: sandy garden soil with plaster and brick chippings.
Soil moisture: water occasionally in winter and summer; the water should be quickly absorbed but the soil should not dry out completely.

139 OX-TONGUE

Gasteria verrucosa (Aloe verrucosa):

Family: Liliaceae. From the Greek *gaster*, belly, referring to the swollen flower bases.
Place of origin: South Africa.
Description: an attractive stemless succulent whose much thickened, succulent leaves are arranged in two ranks. They are 4–6 in. (10–15 cm) long, rough to the touch due to raised greyish-white spots and have grooved upper surfaces. The small drooping and swollen red flowers are individually about 1 in. (2·5 cm) and are carried along 2 ft. (60 cm) stems.

Flowering time: late spring to mid-summer.
Use: in warm regions a fine garden plant, elsewhere a pot plant, wintered indoors but more frequently kept all year in a greenhouse or light room.

Propagation: by careful division, occasionally by cuttings or seed.
Environment and light: plenty of light outdoors, even if not in direct sun; as much light as possible indoors or in the greenhouse.

9

Type of soil: ordinary garden soil, washed sand and clayey earth.
Soil moisture: water regularly in dry weather in the hot months; watering is reduced thereafter, and stopped altogether in winter.

---

140 CHIN CACTUS

Gymnocalycium:

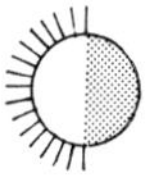

Family: Cactaceae.
Place of origin: S. America.
Description: strongly ribbed cacti normally grown for their flowers, which are freely produced and unusually large for the size of the plant. The pink specimen illustrated is a freak form without chlorophyll, which accordingly cannot live on its own roots. These are commonly grafted on other catii, a technique first practised by the Japanese. Popular as house plants but not as a rule long-lived.

Flowering time: summer.
Use: as an indoor plant.
Propagation:
Environment and light: well-lit, not in direct sun; the sun's rays should be filtered where possible.
Type of soil: ordinary garden soil, rich compost and washed sand.
Soil moisture: water enough to keep plant going.

141 GYMNOCALYCIUM
Gymnocalycium saglionis:

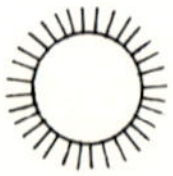

Family: Cactaceae. Name from Greek *gymnos*, naked, *kalyx*, bud; the flower buds are naked.
Place of origin: Argentine, Bolivia.
Description: a large, round cactus up to 12 in. (30 cm) across with numerous domed ridges with woolly centres, each having 7 to 12 curved browny-black spines which turn white with age. Flowers pinkish-white with red stamens.

Flowering time: early summer.
Use: in summer as an indoor or outdoor plant; in winter as an indoor or hothouse plant.
Propagation: by seed.
Environment and light: in summer plenty of sun in mild climates; minimum winter temperature 40°F (4·5°C).
Type of soil: garden soil, rich compost and washed sand.

Soil moisture: in summer water regularly as required, but do not let water stagnate; in winter water much less often, and preferably sprinkle.
Remarks: a fine, easy cactus.

---

142 HEURNIA
Heurnia schneideriana:

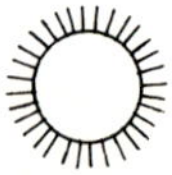

Family: Asclepiadaceae. Named from Justin Heurnius (1587–1652), the first collector of Cape of Good Hope plants. The mis-spelling is due to an error on the part of the namer, Robert Brown.
Place of origin: Nyassaland (now Malawi), Mozambique.
Description: a succulent plant, akin to *Stapelia*, with light green stems up to 8 in. (20 cm) long and 5–7 angled. The bell-shaped flowers are pale brownish outside and velvety black within.

Flowering time: summer.
Use: hothouse or indoor plant; sometimes, in sub-tropical gardens and in fairly mild winters may be grown in rockeries.

Propagation: by cuttings calloused before insertion and rooted with bottom heat in sandy compost.
Environment and light: outdoors in full sun; indoors or in the hothouse in plenty of light.
Type of soil: ordinary garden soil, leaf-mould, washed sand and clay.
Soil moisture: water a fair amount in summer, very little in winter.

9

143 ICE PLANT

Lampranthus coccineus:

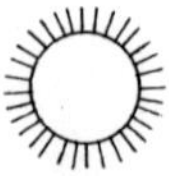

(9)

Family: Aizoaceae. From Greek *lampros*, shining, *anthos*, flower.
Place of origin: South Africa.
Description: beautiful perennial succulent making a spreading plant 1–$1\frac{1}{2}$ ft. (30–45 cm) in height with masses of bright red daisy flowers in spring. Leaves rounded, fleshy and grey-green in colour.
Flowering time: mid spring to early summer.
Use: in places with mild winters it is grown in the garden to decorate flowerbeds, or else in pots or flowerboxes. Does not tolerate frost.
Propagation: by cuttings, planted at the end of summer or in March in sandy soil.
Environment and light: in full sun.
Type of soil: ordinary garden soil mixed with sand; the mixture must be good and permeable.
Soil moisture: if the plant is grown outdoors hardly water at all; if grown in a pot or flowerbox, water regularly 2–3 times a month, more frequently in the tropics.

---

144 GOLDEN LACE CACTUS

*Mammillaria elongata (*now more correctly *Leptocladodia elongata):*

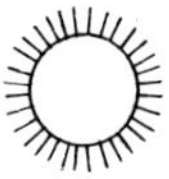

(8)

Family: Cactaceae. Name from Greek meaning thin-branched.
Place of origin: eastern Mexico.
Description: columnar cacti with upright, cylindrical stems forming clusters up to 6 in. (15 cm) high. The plants are covered with numerous rosettes of short yellowish spines, tipped with brown but not over prickly. Flowers white or yellowish-white.
Flowering time: May.
Use: in general, if very mild winter climates where it can live perennially outdoors are excluded, this Mamillaria is grown in pots, and put outside in the summer months; otherwise it is used as an indoor or hothouse plant.
Propagation: by seed or division of the buds which grow at the base of the mother plant.
Environment and light: sunny, half-shade.
Type of soil: dry, permeable, sandy.
Soil moisture: water freely in summer so that soil is moist but never waterlogged. In autumn and winter keep fairly dry.

145 MAMMILLARIA

Mammillaria geminispina:

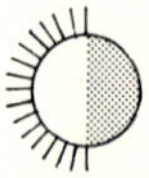

9

Family: Cactaceae. From Latin *mammilla*, nipple referring to the shape of the plant.
Place of origin: Mexico; introduced into Europe in first half of 19th century.
Description: a ball-like cactus which grows in clusters; ribless with 16–20 short white bristles, plus 2–4 long, black-tipped spines at each woolly areole. Flowers dark red, at the tops of the stems.
Flowering time: late spring to mid-summer.
Use: as an indoor or hothouse plant; can live outside in summer.
Propagation: by seed.
Environment and light: outdoors in half-shade; elsewhere well-lit.
Type of soil: clayey, sandy, good permeability.
Soil moisture: water a reasonable amount as required in summer; sprinkle very little in winter, but do not let soil dry out completely.

---

146 OLD LADY CACTUS; OLD LADY MAMMILLARIA

Mammillaria hahniana:

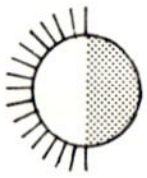

9

Family: Cactaceae.
Place of origin: Mexico.
Description: a pretty cactus with clusters of flat-topped, ball-shaped stems up to 4 in. (7 cm) across. The whole plant is covered with silky white spines and the freely produced flowers are crimson with yellow stamens. Grown for its spines.
Flowering time: summer.
Use: as an indoor or hothouse plant; during summer may live outdoors.
Propagation: by seed or offsets.
Environment and light: outdoors in half-shade; elsewhere well-lit.
Type of soil: clayey, sandy with good permeability.
Soil moisture: water a reasonable amount and sprinkle, but very sparingly in winter, although the soil should never dry out completely.

147 SOUR FIG

Mesembryanthemum acinaciforme (now more correctly *Carpobrotus acinaciformis*):

9

Family: Aizoaceae. Name from Greek *karpos*, fruit, *brotos*, edible.
Place of origin: S. Africa; introduced into Europe in early eighteenth century.
Description: perennial succulents with long trailing stems and oblong, fleshy, triangular-sided leaves grouped in pairs along their length. Flowers brilliant rose-magenta with yellow stamens, daisy like and 4 in. (7 cm) across. The ripe gooseberry-sized fruits have soft juicy centres with lots of seeds, like miniature figs. Jam and other preserves are made from them in South Africa.
Flowering time: throughout the summer.
Use: to trail over rocks and walls in hot places; very drought resistant and do well near the coast.
Propagation: by cuttings.
Environment and light: full sun. Tolerate light frosts so can be grown outside in climates like California, S.W. England and the Mediterranean area.
Type of soil: very well drained—they rot in cold wet.
Soil moisture: given that this plant is generally grown outdoors, water little or not at all.

---

148 INDIAN FIG

Opuntia ficus-indica:

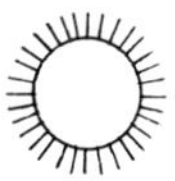

9

Family: Cactaceae. Old Greek name for another plant growing around Opus, an ancient town in Greece.
Place of origin: tropical America; introduced into Europe in the sixteenth century.
Description: makes a large bushy plant from 3–14 ft. (1–4 m) high with oblong, fleshy, flattened joints; small spineless areoles and large bright yellow flowers.
Flowering time: summer.
Use: much cultivated in tropics and sub-tropics for hedging, also to decorate gardens, particularly rockeries with large stones. Only grows where winters are mild enough. Young pot-grown specimens will survive the winter under cover.
Propagation: by cuttings.
Environment and light: full sun; if potted, veiled sunlight.
Type of soil: ordinary garden soil with a lot of sand and clay; should be very permeable.
Soil moisture: water a lot in summer, more during flowering; then reduce and water little in winter.
Remarks: cultivated in tropics for the fruits which are variously known as Tunas, Indian figs or prickly pears. These are eaten fresh or dried.

149 PRICKLY PEAR

Opuntia vulgaris (O. monacantha):

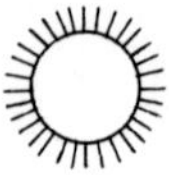

Family: Cactaceae.
Place of origin: Brazil, Uruguay, Argentine.
Description: a strong-growing cactus of up to 6 ft. (2 m) with flattened, oblong pads on jointed stems; white woolly areoles carrying yellowish or deep brown spines and many large golden-yellow or reddish flowers about 3 in. (7 cm) across.

Flowering time: early summer–early autumn.
Use: to beautify banks, rocky slopes etc.; also grown in pots as young specimens. Grows in places with relatively mild winters, including parts of northern Italy (lakes).
Propagation: by seed or stem cuttings.
Environment and light: in full sunlight or, if potted, veiled sunlight. Minimum winter temperature 40°F (4·4°C).

Type of soil: permeable, garden soil with plenty of sand and clay.
Soil moisture: water quite a lot in summer, and more generously during flowering; then gradually reduce the amount.

---

150 PORTULACA; ROSE MOSS; SUN PLANT

Portulaca grandiflora:

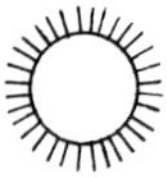

Family: Portulacaceae. Latin name for *P. oleracea*, used by Pliny.
Place of origin: Argentine, Brazil; introduced into Europe in 1827.
Description: herbaceous plant with fleshy, cylindrical, sparse leaves, greyish-green in colour, glabrous or velvety; fairly large flowers with 5 petals, $1\frac{1}{2}$–2 in. (4–5 cm) in diameter, very decorative and brightly-coloured (red, yellow, orange, purple, white etc.); there are also forms with double or semi-double flowers.

Flowering time: summer.
Use: to decorate rock gardens, steep places such as banks, slopes; also in containers, window boxes etc.

Propagation: in cool climates treat as half-hardy annuals. Raise under glass, plant out when no more risk of frost and scrap at end of season.
Environment and light: full sun.
Type of soil: loam, leaf-mould and sand; good drainage and not too rich.
Soil moisture: water regularly in the hottest months; much less in spring and autumn.

(6)

151 EASTER CACTUS

Rhipsalidopsis gaertneri (Epiphyllum gaertneri; Schlumbergera gaertneri):

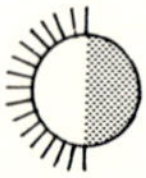

10

Family: Cactaceae. Name meaning "like Rhipsalis" another genus.
Place of origin: Tropical America, Brazil.
Description: an epiphytic plant with spreading or pendent jointed, flattened stems, with crenate margins and a few weak bristles; starry scarlet flowers at the tips of the branches.
Flowering time: late spring.
Use: indoor or hothouse plant; in summer may stay outdoors and decorate terraces and balconies.
Propagation: normally by cuttings. The plants can be grown on their own roots or grafted on other cacti.
Environment and light: well-lit when indoors or in the greenhouse, with sunlight filtered through glass; fresh and shady places when outside.
Type of soil: very permeable, acid, with one-third washed sand, and two-thirds leaf-mould.
Soil moisture: water occasionally, more often in the hottest months (about every ten days or so).

---

152 CRASSULA FALCATA; RED TREASURE; SCARLET PAINT BRUSH

Rochea falcata:

9

Family: Crassulaceae. Named after Daniel de la Roche (1743–1813), a Swiss physician.
Place of origin: South Africa; introduced into Europe in early eighteenth century.
Description: an attractive evergreen succulent with showy flat heads of scarlet flowers on 12 in. (30 cm) stems. These last for 3 or 4 weeks. Leaves broad, fleshy, stem-clasping, greyish-green and curved sideways "like a sickle".
Flowering time: summer.
Use: for bedding in tropical and subtropical gardens. Elsewhere mostly as a pot plant for summer blooming.
Propagation: by stem or leaf cuttings; by seed.
Environment and light: full sun or part shade—the latter essential in the tropics.
Type of soil: permeable, made up of ordinary garden soil, rich compost, washed sand and clayey earth.
Soil moisture: water plentifully in summer, much less in winter.

153 BURRO'S TAIL; DONKEY TAIL

Sedum morganianum:

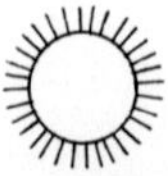

8

Family: Crassulaceae. Old name derived from *sedo*, to sit; many species grow "sitting" on walls and rocks.
Place of origin: the genus *Sedum* includes about 200 species from the temperate regions of the northern hemisphere, from Central America to Peru.
Description: a fleshy, drooping succulent with trailing stems up to 3 ft. (1 m) long, densely packed with glaucous-green, 1 in. (15 cm), lanceolate, incurved leaves and terminal corymbs of red flowers.
Flowering time: spring to autumn.
Use: ideal for hanging baskets in greenhouses, sun lounges and the like.
Propagation: by cuttings rooted with bottom heat after drying; sometimes single leaves root.
Environment and light: in full sunlight or if indoors or in the greenhouse, in well-lit places.
Type of soil: ordinary garden soil mixed with washed sand and clayey earth.
Soil moisture: water a certain amount, as required.

---

154 CARRION FLOWER; GIANT STAPELIA

Stapelia gigantea:

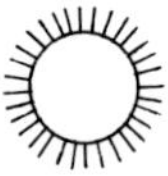

9

Family: Asclepiadaceae. Named after Johannes Bodaeus van Stapel (d. 1636).
Place of origin: South Africa.
Description: a succulent with finger-like stems forming large clumps but no leaves. The star-shaped flowers occur near the bases of these stems and open to flat, tapering, light fawn segments heavily rippled with crimson-purple striations. They may be 12 in. (30 cm) or more across and are the largest in the genus. They have a most unpleasant smell—only apparent if the blooms are sniffed.
Flowering time: late summer to mid-autumn.
Use: as a greenhouse or indoor plant. Sometimes in particularly sheltered mild-wintered regions it may be grown outdoors in rockeries.
Propagation: by stem cuttings which must be calloused before rooting in sandy soil with bottom heat.
Environment and light: sun or light shade in hot climates, but light and sun in colder areas.
Type of soil: well-drained soil with compost.
Soil moisture: not very much at any time, but certainly allow a rest period in winter.

CLIMBING AND SPREADING PLANTS

155 BIRTHWORT; CALICO PIPE
Aristolochia brasiliensis:

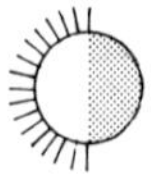

10

Family: Aristolochiaceae. Name from Greek *aristos*, best and *lochia*, birth, from its medical use in childbirth.
Place of origin: Brazil; introduced into Europe in 1838.
Description: a vigorous tropical climber of up to 30 ft. (9 m) with smooth, kidney-shaped leaves with deep sinuses and 5–7 in. (12–17 cm) pale purple flowers heavily striated and netted with dark purple. These have a curved perianth tube at the back—like the bowl of a pipe. The species needs warm greenhouse treatment but hardier kinds exist such as *A. macrophylla* (Dutchman's pipe) which is suitable for a cool house.
Flowering time: spring–summer.
Use: for climbing up pillars, trellises etc. in warm greenhouses or tropical gardens.
Propagation: by late summer cuttings rooted in a propagating case with bottom heat.
Environment and light: shady or protected by trees.
Type of soil: loam with decayed manure some sand.
Soil moisture: water generously in summer months, less in other seasons depending on climatic conditions.
Remarks: prune back hard after flowering to keep under control.

---

156 BOUGAINVILLEA; PAPER FLOWER
Bougainvillea glabra:

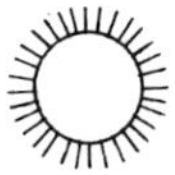

10

Family: Nyctaginaceae. Named after Louis Antoine de Bougainville who sailed round the world 1767–69.
Place of origin: Brazil.
Description: a vigorous spiny climber with thick oval leaves and showy clusters of small white flowers surrounded by brilliant cerise bracts. Varieties with orange, lemon and pink bracts exist, also a double and variegated leaved form.
Flowering time: spring, also early autumn.
Use: as a showy and long-flowering conservatory plant in a warm greenhouse, either in pots or borders; to cover walls, trees etc. outside in warm temperate and tropical gardens.
Propagation: by stem cuttings rooted with bottom heat in summer.
Environment and light: outdoors in full sun, with quite high temperatures. Where winters are harsh the plants should be taken into the greenhouse.
Type of soil: rich, loamy soil in borders; in pots, in a loam, leaf-mould and sand compost (equal parts).
Soil moisture: water generously in the growing season.
Remarks: pot specimens should be pruned back

157 MYSORE-THORN
Caesalpinia sepiaria:

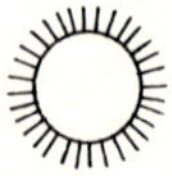

9

Family: Leguminosae. Named after the Italian botanist A. Cesalpino (1519–1603).
Place of origin: India; introduced into Europe in 1857.
Description: a prickly, scrambling shrub of up to 15 ft. (4·5 m) with bipinnate leaves having numerous oblong leaflets and erect racemes of canary-yellow, cup-shaped flowers.
Flowering time: spring.
Use: mainly to make fine dividing hedges, and for covering trellises, walls etc. in warm climates; elsewhere in warm greenhouses or conservatory borders.
Propagation: by seed in spring; cuttings are difficult to root.
Environment and light: full sun in an airy situation.
Type of soil: well-drained. Loam, sand and leaf-mould or peat.
Soil moisture: outdoors, water to establish only; generously under glass.

---

158 TRUMPET CREEPER
Campsis × tagliabuana:

8

Family: Bignoniaceae. From Greek *kampe*, bent; the stamens are curved.
Description: a collective name given to a group of hybrids between *C. grandiflora* and *C. radicans*, of which one called "Madame Galen" is outstanding. Vigorous deciduous climbers of 20 ft. (6 m) or more, with opposite, pinnate leaves and trumpet-shaped, orange-scarlet flowers in huge, showy inflorescences.
Flowering time: late spring to the height of summer.
Use: to cover walls, arbours etc.
Propagation: by seed, but the more practical method is by spring cuttings or layers in late summer.
Environment and light: full sun, or at least well-lit places.
Type of soil: loose, rich and well-drained.
Soil moisture: water a certain amount in warm temperate climates in summer; only where essential in cooler climates.
Remarks: in frost-prone areas grow in sheltered situations; in cold regions, under glass.

159 VIRGINS' BOWER

Clematis flammula:

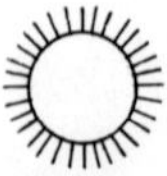

6

Family: Ranunculaceae.
Place of origin: S. Europe; cultivated in England since late sixteenth century. Greek name for a miscellany of climbing plants.
Description: a strong growing deciduous climber of 12 ft. (3·6 m) or more which forms a dense tangle of cinnamon coloured stems, clothed in green bi-pinnate leaves which are evergreen in mild climates. Flowers white, 4-sepalled, almond scented, small but most abundant, in loose panicles all over the plant. These are succeeded by silky seedheads.
Flowering time: late summer to autumn.
Use: to drape trees, summerhouses and the like; for clothing walls and unsightly hedges.
Propagation: by layers or internodal cuttings taken in summer and struck with bottom heat.
Environment and light: full sun to half-shade for the leafy, flowering part of the plant; the base prefers shade which can be made artificially by surrounding it with species without very developed root systems whose foliage acts as protection.
Type of soil: rich loamy, well-drained but cool. Likes lime.
Soil moisture: water to establish.

---

160 CLEMATIS HENRYI

Clematis lanuginosa "Henryi":

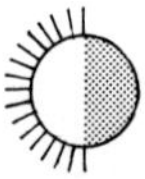

4

Family: Ranunculaceae.
Place of origin: China.
Description: a climbing cultivar with 12–20 ft. (3·6–6 m) stems, according to conditions; composite leaves with oval-elliptic segments, pointed with slightly cordate bases; flowers 6–8 in. (15–20 cm) across, creamy-white with pointed sepals and dark stamens.
Flowering time: early summer and again late summer to early autumn.
Use: to decorate gardens and terraces, and cover arbours, railings, walls, pillars etc.
Propagation: by layers in summer or early autumn or cuttings with bottom heat in spring.
Environment and light: sunny to half-shade; it is best if the base of the plant is not directly exposed to the sun.
Type of soil: cool and moist but well-drained.
Soil moisture: water frequently and generously, daily, and not less than every other day.
Remarks: pruning optional. Leave alone or if too rampant cut hard back in early spring.

161 JACKMAN'S CLEMATIS

Clematis × jackmanii:

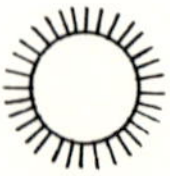

⑤

Family: Ranunculaceae.
Place of origin: Great Britain.
Description: a spectacular hybrid raised by Messrs Jackman in their Woking nursery in 1860. Strong and vigorous it will grow 9–12 ft. (2·7–3·6 m) high with pinnate leaves and masses of large (4–6 in. (10–15 cm) under good conditions), velvety flowers borne singly or in threes.
Flowering time: mid-summer to autumn.
Use: to decorate gardens and terraces, cover arbours, railings, walls and pillars. Also looks attractive planted with climbing roses—the two intertwine—since it flowers when the roses are over.
Propagation: by internodal cuttings in summer, rooted with bottom heat; by layers.
Environment and light: sunny to half-shade. The foot of the plant should never be directly exposed to the sun for too long.
Type of soil: well-drained moist, rich soil; likes lime.
Soil moisture: water frequently but only in dry weather.
Remarks: prune hard back (to within 18 in. (45 cm) of the ground) in early spring to maintain quality and quantity of flowers. Unpruned specimens often contract mildew and the flowers become very small.

---

162 CLEMATIS "BEAUTY OF WORCESTER"

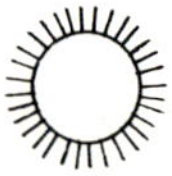

⑤

Family: Ranunculaceae.
Description: an attractive cultivar with large violet-blue flowers, 5–7 in. (12–17 cm), with contrasting creamy stamens. These are frequently double in the first flowering, with single blooms later in the season. Height 6–8 ft. (2–2·5 m).
Flowering time: late spring to early autumn.
Use: to decorate gardens and terraces, cover arbours, railings, walls, pillars etc.
Propagation: by layers between June and July, or spring cuttings. Also grafted commercially.
Environment and light: sun to half-shade. The base of the plant should be in shade, the shoots in sun. Sun necessary for flowers.
Type of soil: fresh, permeable, organic, well-fertilized, mixed with sand and peat.
Soil moisture: water frequently in summer; keep soil moist and cool.
Remarks: no pruning required beyond occasional removal of old flower growths (immediately after blooming) to keep habit tidy.

163 ANEMONE CLEMATIS; MOUNTAIN CLEMATIS
Clematis montana:

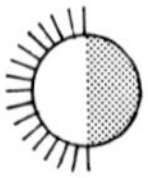

(6)

Family: Ranunculaceae.
Place of origin: Himalayas; introduced into Europe in 1831.
Description: a very vigorous climber under good conditions which will drape trees and arbours with cascades of blossom. It is deciduous with trifoliate smooth leaves and 2–3 in. (5–7 cm), pure white, 4 or 5 sepalled flowers with central bosses of golden stamens, in bunches on long stems. There are sweet scented forms and others with rose-pink flowers or bronzed foliage.
Flowering time: late spring to early summer; one form "Wilsonii", mid-summer.
Use: for growing over trees, ugly buildings, hedges etc. or training up posts, walls, arbours and the like.
Propagation: by cuttings or layers.
Environment and light: from half-shade to shade for the lower part of the plant; leaves and branches in full sun.
Type of soil: rich, cool and moist.
Soil moisture: water to establish or in periods of drought.
Remarks: prune to shape, if required, immediately after flowering.

---

164 OLD MAN'S BEARD; TRAVELLER'S JOY
Clematis vitalba:

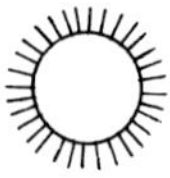

(4)

Family: Ranunculaceae.
Place of origin: S.W. and Central Europe (including Britain); N. Africa.
Description: a rampant climber of 20 ft. (6 m) or more in height found naturally in chalk districts, often smothering roadside trees and hedges with its rope-like stems, pinnate leaves and masses of small, faintly scented, greenish-white flowers with conspicuous stamens. The latter are followed by attractive silky seedheads.
Flowering time: late summer.
Use: should only be planted where there is plenty of room—to cover ugly features or clothe old tree-trunks etc.
Propagation: by layers in July.
Environment and light: very adaptable but likes lime and does well on chalky soil. Full sun or partial shade.
Type of soil: fresh, rich in organic matter with added heath-mould.
Soil moisture: water to establish.
Remarks: prune regularly to keep in bounds and shape.

165 **CREEPING FIG**

Ficus pumila (F. repens):

Family: Moraceae. The Latin name for edible fig.
Place of origin: China, Japan; introduced into Europe in 1721.
Description: an evergreen climber that clings to wall in the same manner as ivy (*Hedera*) and of which only the juvenile foliage is seen—as illustrated. Leaves small, entire, heart-shaped and pointed, deep green and in opposite pairs. Adult foliage—borne only in warm climates and when plant is free-standing—much larger and more leathery.
Use: for decorating shady greenhouse walls and bench supports in temperate and cool climates. In tropics and subtropics can be used outside to drape walls and buildings.

Propagation: by cuttings rooted in a warm propagating case.
Environment and light: half-shade or total shade in sheltered draught-free spots. Can only be grown where the winters are not too harsh.

(8)

Type of soil: mixture of earth, sand and peat.
Soil moisture: water regularly about once a week, quite sparingly.

---

166 **GLORIOSA LILY; GLORY LILY**

Gloriosa rothschildiana:

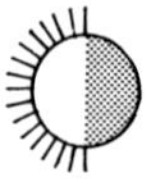

Family: Liliaceae. From the Latin, *gloriosus*, glorious.
Place of origin: Tropical Africa.
Description: a climbing lily of 6 ft. (2 m) or so with tuberous roots, ascending by means of "finger tip" tendrils at the end of the smooth, green, lanceolate leaves. Flowers very showy, with 6 waxy-edged, 3–4 in. (7–10 cm), crimson petaloid segments, which bend backwards to reveal their yellow bases and long extruding stamens.

Flowering time: summer.
Use: grown up tree trunks, over balconies and railings in the tropics; elsewhere in large pots, trained up twiggy sticks or wires or in greenhouse borders.

Propagation: by offsets of the tubers when plant is dormant.
Environment and light: in tropical gardens, light shade. Elsewhere, as pot plants, good light, sun or light shade. Not frost tolerant.

(10)

Type of soil: very rich, loam and peat with a little sand.
Soil moisture: water when needed in summer.
Remarks: tubers very brittle so handle with care. Plants must be rested in winter; lay pots on their sides to dry out and restart in spring.

167 IVY
Hedera helix "Gold Heart":

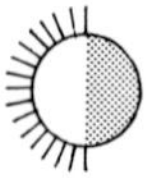

Family: Araliaceae. Old Latin name; ivy was the plant of Bacchus, god of wine.
Place of origin: garden origin.
Description: a striking, small-leaved ivy sometimes wrongly called "Jubilee". It is characterized by a conspicuous dash of golden-yellow at the centre of each lobed, heart-shaped leaf. Climbs by means of adventitious roots.
Use: not as hardy as the type species *H. Helix* but survives outside in areas not subjected to sustained or severe frosts. Makes an attractive pot plant for inside or out.

Propagation: by spring or summer cuttings rooted in sand and peat with mist propagator or gentle bottom heat.
Environment and light: half-shade to shade.
Type of soil: ordinary garden soil with a little peat added.
Soil moisture: water regularly, not too much, so that the ground is always moist.

(7)

---

168 MORNING GLORY; BLUE DAWN FLOWER
Ipomoea learii (Pharbitus learii):

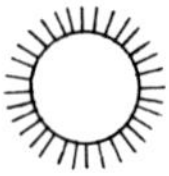

Family: Convolvulaceae. Name from Greek, *ips*, worm, *homoios*, similar to.
Place of origin: Tropical and subtropical America; introduced in 1839.
Description: a vigorous evergreen tropical climber with fine funnel-shaped flowers produced in clusters throughout the summer. These are bright blue at first and become magenta with age and only last for a day. Leaves cordate, entire, variable and frequently 3-lobed.

Flowering time: summer–autumn.
Use: for greenhouse borders or trained round twigs or wire supports in large pots for sun lounges and the like. Outdoors, in frost-free climates, can be used to cover fences, tree trunks, arbours etc.

Propagation: often treated as annual in cold climates, seed being sown under glass in early spring. Also possible to increase from cuttings rooted in sandy compost in a propagating case with bottom heat.
Environment and light: full sun.
Type of soil: no special requirements.
Soil moisture: water frequently but quite sparingly, daily in the height of summer.

(10)

169 COMMON WHITE JASMINE; sometimes called JESSAMINE

Jasminum officinale:

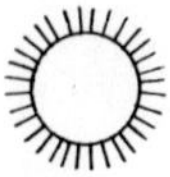

Family: Oleaceae. Name from the Persian-Arabic *yâsmin*, "white flower".
Place of origin: Persia, Himalayas; introduced in 1548.
Description: a deliciously fragrant, deciduous or semi-evergreen (according to climate) climber with pinnate leaves composed of 5, 7 or 9 leaflets, and terminal clusters of small, pure white, tubular flowers with 4 or 5 spreading lobes. Under good conditions growth is rapid, up to 6 ft. (2 m) in a season and ultimately 30–40 ft. (9–12 m).

Flowering time: summer and early autumn.
Use: for growing against walls in cool temperate climates, such as the North of England; in warmer areas in the open to mask pillars, summer houses etc. Can also be grown in pots if pruned each spring.

Propagation: by cuttings of half-ripe wood rooted with bottom heat or mist.
Environment and light: warm and sunny.
Type of soil: good garden soil.
Soil moisture: water regularly but sparingly, according to whether the plant is outdoors or pot-grown.
Remarks: prune as and when required. A perfume is made from the flowers.

(7)

---

170 CHINESE JASMINE

Jasminum polianthum:

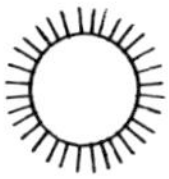

Family: Oleaceae. See No. 169.
Place of origin: China; introduced into Europe in 1891.
Description: a delightful winter blooming climber, but not frost tolerant. It is a robust grower, up to 10 ft. (3 m), evergreen with pinnate leaves composed of 5 or 7 leaflets and axillary, many-flowered (30–40) panicles of penetratingly sweet white flowers.

Flowering time: winter to early spring under glass but often in early spring and summer when grown outdoors.
Use: outdoors to cover walls, arbours and the like in frost-free climates; elsewhere in conservatories, sun lounges etc. in soil borders or large pots.

Propagation: by half-ripe cuttings rooted in a light compost with bottom heat.
Environment and light: sunny and warm.
Type of soil: light with plenty of humus and a little sand.
Soil moisture: water as required—regularly if in pots.
Remarks: this plant needs drastic pruning after flowering, so that next year's flowering on the young branches is more plentiful.

(8)

171 YELLOW JASMINE

Jasminum "Revolutum":

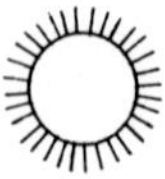

8

Family: Oleaceae.
Place of origin: Himalayas; introduced into Europe in 1656.
Description: a cultivar of *J. humile*, a variable species often known as Italian yellow jasmine and represented in gardens by several introduced forms. The plant illustrated makes a small to medium, evergreen (or nearly so) semi-shrub with deep green leaves composed of 5–7 leaflets and deep yellow, slightly fragrant flowers in clusters.
Flowering time: summer.
Use: as an individual plant or in clumps on lawns in mild to warm climates. Elsewhere, in pots or greenhouse borders, kept frost-free in winter.
Propagation: by cuttings rooted with bottom heat or the cultivar is sometimes grafted on the hardier *J. fruticans.*
Environment and light: warm and sunny.
Type of soil: light with humus and a little sand added.
Soil moisture: water pots or greenhouse borders regularly, but sparingly, once a week.
Remarks: prune to shape, keeping centres of bushes clear.

---

172 SWEET PEA

Lathyrus odoratus:

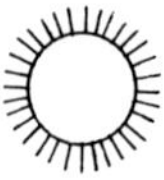

5

Family: Leguminosae. From the Greek, *lathyros*, pea.
Place of origin: Italy, Sicily; introduced in 1700.
Description: a well-known and much loved annual climber, esteemed for its large and shapely, richly fragrant flowers. The species is practically extinct but cultivars are legion with white, yellow, pink to red and crimson, mauve and purple flowers, often with 6 or 7 blooms on a stem. There are also low growing, hedge types like "Knee-hi" and "Jet-Set" (both about 3 ft. (1 m)) and "Dwarf Bijou" (12–15 in. (30–45 cm)) suitable for the fronts of borders. The plants climb by means of tendrils and normally must be staked.
Flowering time: late spring to autumn if old blooms are regularly removed—otherwise they go to seed.
Use: mostly in borders or for cutting.
Propagation: by seed in pots in spring or the previous autumn, planted out when all risk of frost is past.
Environment and light: rich soil and plenty of sun.
Type of soil: rich loam with decayed manure or compost at the bottom of the trench and mulches of same in the growing season. Feed in summer.
Soil moisture: water regularly and copiously in summer.

173 YELLOW HONEYSUCKLE
Lonicera implexa:

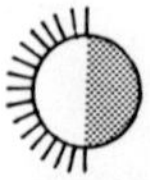

Family: Caprifoliaceae.
Place of origin: Mediterranean region; introduced into Britain in 1772.
Description: evergreen climber of up to 8 ft. (2·5 m) with smooth shoots, oval-oblong leaves, glaucous beneath and whorls of yellow flowers flushed with pink at the ends of the shoots.
Flowering time: summer.
Use: to decorate arbours, walls, railings, pillars etc.
Propagation: by layers between the end of spring and early summer; by cuttings in spring or summer.
Environment and light: half-shade or total shade. Rather tender in cold wet climates.
Type of soil: fresh earth made up of wood-loam with peat and a little sand.
Soil moisture: water only when necessary.

⑦

---

174 SWEET HONEYSUCKLE
Lonicera japonica:

Family: Caprifoliaceae.
Place of origin: Japan, Korea, China; introduced into Europe in 1806.
Description: an extremely vigorous climber of evergreen habit, to 30 ft. (9 m) or more. Stems hollow, hairy, leaves ovate to oblong, occasionally wavy-edged and $1\frac{1}{2}$–$3\frac{1}{2}$ in. (4–9 cm) long and half as broad. Flowers very sweetly scented, in pairs from the leaf-axils of the young shoots, two-lipped but changing to yellow with age. Fruits black.
Flowering time: late spring–early summer.
Use: a fine climbing plant, suited to covering arbours, walls, railings, treetrunks.
Propagation: by layers or cuttings.
Environment and light: cool, semi-shady or in sun if soil is moist.
Type of soil: any type is suitable, but best if fertile and porous.
Soil moisture: water only in drought periods to keep soil damp.
Remarks: this plant has become a pest in parts of eastern U.S.A. so should be used with caution in that country. Rarely troublesome in Europe.

④

175 TRUMPET HONEYSUCKLE

Lonicera sempervirens:

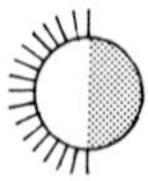

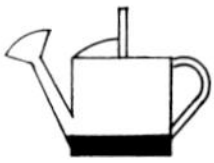

7

Family: Caprifoliaceae.
Place of origin: Eastern N. America; introduced into Europe in 1656.
Description: an evergreen or semi-evergreen high-climbing honeysuckle with ovate or oblong leaves, slightly downy beneath, the upper ones perfoliate or united in pairs. Flowers rich orange-scarlet, long tubed, in whorls at the end of the shoots; scentless.
Flowering time: spring–summer.
Use: against walls and pillars in suitable climates, but tender and needing cold greenhouse treatment in areas subjected to much frost.
Propagation: by layers at the end of spring, cuttings in summer, seed in autumn.
Environment and light: cool, semi-shady positions.
Type of soil: almost any type of soil, best if fertile and porous.
Soil moisture: water to establish.
Remarks: this is the honeysuckle growing up the pillars of George Washington's home at Mount Vernon.

---

176 BALSAM PEAR

Momordica charantia:

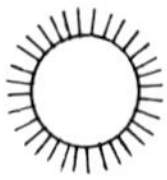

Family: Cucurbitaceae. Name from the Latin *mordeo*, to bite; the seeds appear to have been bitten.
Place of origin: S.E. Asia, Tropical Africa; introduced into Europe in 1710.
Description: a variable climbing member of the cucumber family grown for its warty fruits. It has simple tendrils, conspicuously lobed leaves, yellow, 5-petalled flowers and oblong, slender and pointed warted fruits. These are yellowish or copper-colour when ripe and open to disclose white or brown seeds with scarlet arils.
Flowering time: early to mid-summer.
Use: to cover walls, arbours etc., treetrunks and so on.
Propagation: by seed raised in warmth (55°–60°F (13°–15°C)), potted and grown on, then planted out when all risk of frost is past. Treat as an annual.
Environment and light: full sun.
Type of soil: loose, light, rich and permeable.
Soil moisture: water regularly and generously in summer.

177 VIRGINIA CREEPER

Parthenocissus quinquefolia:

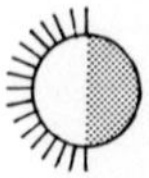

3

Family: Vitaceae. Name from the Greek *parthenos*, virgin, *kissos*, ivy; from place of origin. *Note*, the state of Virginia was named after Elizabeth I, the Virgin Queen.

Place of origin: Eastern N. America; introduced into Europe in 1629.

Description: a self-clinging creeper which can reach considerable heights, with long-stalked leaves composed of 5 oval leaflets. These are dull green but turn brilliant shades of scarlet and orange in autumn prior to leaf-fall. Blue-black fruits follow the insignificant greenish flowers.

Flowering time: early summer.

Use: to cover walls, trees, buildings etc. In nature it often reaches the tops of lofty trees but is never as rampant in Europe.

Propagation: by cuttings or layers in autumn.

Environment and light: can be full sun, half-shade or total shade.

Type of soil: well fertilized garden soil.

Soil moisture: water to establish.

---

178 BOSTON IVY

Parthenocissus tricuspidata:

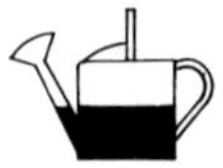

4

Family: Vitaceae.

Place of origin: Japan, Korea, China; introduced in 1868.

Description: a vigorous, self-clinging vine with numerous tendrils, long-stemmed, shining green leaves, varying in shape from almost entire, rounded or heart-shaped to 3-lobed. These turn crimson and scarlet in autumn. Deciduous. Much planted in Europe.

Flowering time: early summer.

Use: an excellent plant for covering walls, house-fronts etc.

Propagation: by cuttings and layers.

Environment and light: from half-shade to total shade.

Type of soil: deep, but with no particular features.

Soil moisture: water regularly when the plant is still young and has a poorly developed root-system.

179 PASSION FLOWER

Passiflora caerulea:

8

Family: Passifloraceae. Name given by early missionaries to S. America, who saw in the flower many features relating to the Crucifixion.
Place of origin: S. Brazil; introduced into Europe in 1699.
Description: although the hardiest of the Passion Flowers, capable of being grown outside in mild temperate areas such as the South of England, West coast of Scotland, the Mediterranean area, Florida and California, this species usually does best in temperate climates when grown in a frost-free greenhouse or sunroom. It is quite rampant when well suited with 5–7 lobed, smooth leaves and large 7 in. (20 cm), striking, slightly fragrant, white and blue flowers. The blue and white filaments between petals and stamens are particularly arresting.
Flowering time: summer–autumn.
Use: to decorate balconies, terraces, arbours, walls etc.
Propagation: by seed in spring or by cuttings.
Environment and light: full sun.
Type of soil: loose and very sandy.
Soil moisture: water frequently and generously, less in winter.

---

180 LEADWORT; PLUMBAGO

Plumbago capensis:

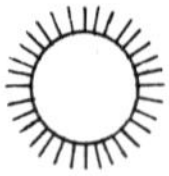

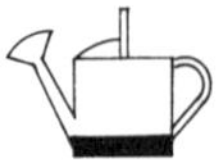

9

Family: Plumbaginaceae. Name from the Latin *plumbum*, lead; it was once believed to be an antidote to lead poisoning.
Place of origin: South Africa; introduced into Europe in 1818.
Description: a tender, climbing perennial, evergreen under warm conditions, with small oblong leaves, the older ones having whitish scales beneath, as do the stems. Terminal spikes of pale-blue, 5-lobed flowers. Pink and white varieties exist.
Flowering time: all summer.
Use: for training up greenhouse walls, rafters, pillars etc. In tropics sometimes fashioned into hedges or used to cover buildings, tree trunks and the like; also as a pot plant.
Propagation: by cuttings.
Environment and light: in full sun. Being a species originating from mild climates, it must be protected and taken under cover in colder regions.
Type of soil: well fertilized ordinary garden soil.
Soil moisture: water regularly, not too often.
Remarks: cut back fairly hard after flowering and allow to go through the winter fairly dry.

181 GIANT POTATO VINE; COSTA RICAN NIGHT-SHADE

Solanum wendlandii:

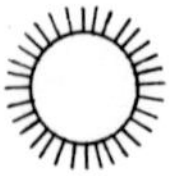

Family: Solanaceae. Old Latin name for a member of this family, probably *S. nigrum.*
Place of origin: Costa Rica; introduced into Europe in 1882.
Description: a vigorous prickly climber which can reach 20 ft. (6 m) under good conditions. Bright green leaves, very variable even on the same plant from simple and lanceolate to trifoliate or subdivided into 4–6 pairs of pinnules. Flowers $2\frac{1}{2}$ in. (6 cm) across, like those of the potato, bluish-lilac in 6 in. (15 cm) trusses at the ends of the drooping branches.
Flowering time: mid-summer.
Use: to cover arbours, walls, to form espaliers against walls etc. In pots and greenhouse borders.
Propagation: cuttings of side shoots rooted under glass in sandy soil with bottom heat.
Environment and light: warm and sunny; in exposed places, it is advisable to protect the base of the plant in winter but really this species is only suitable outdoors in practically frost-free climates.
Type of soil: fresh, loose and deep, made up of two parts compost to one of heath-mould and sand.
Soil moisture: water generously in summer.

---

182 BLACK-EYED SUSAN; THUNBERGIA

Thunbergia alata:

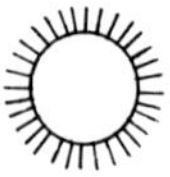

Family: Acanthaceae. Named after Carl Peter Thunberg.
Place of origin: Tropical Africa.
Description: a slender, slightly downy plant which can climb 8–10 ft. (2·5–3 m) in one season. Usually grown as an annual, although perennial in warm climates. Leaves opposite, ovate-heart-shaped; flowers 5-lobed, flat, 2 in. (5 cm) across, orange yellow with chocolate-brown centres and curved tubes behind. Varieties with white centres and lighter or deeper petal shades exist.
Flowering time: summer to mid-autumn.
Use: as house or conservatory plants in pots or containers where they can be made to climb up twiggy peasticks or wire frames. In tropics and sub-tropics can be used to cover railings, balustrades and the like.
Propagation: by seed sown in warmth, potted and grown on. Allow about three plants to a 5 in. (12 cm) pot or grow in baskets.
Environment and light: well-lit.
Type of soil: ordinary garden soil, fertilized; add a little sand to aid drainage.
Soil moisture: water regularly, more often in summer; never allow water to stagnate.

183 CHINESE STAR-JASMINE
Trachelospermun jasminoides:

Family: Apocynaceae. Name from Greek *trachelos*, neck, *sperma*, seed.
Place of origin: China and Japan; introduced into Europe in 1846.
Description: evergreen climber of up to 20 ft. (6 m) with smooth, tapering, oval-lanceolate, shiny, opposite leaves up to 3 in. (7 cm) long and very fragrant, white flowers about 1 in. (2·5 cm) across in axillary and terminal sprays. Stems exude a milky juice when cut.
Flowering time: mid-summer.
Use: under practically frost-free conditions, as a wall shrub or to cover balustrades; elsewhere as a greenhouse shrub, prized for its scented flowers.
Propagation: by cuttings.
Environment and light: full sun, preferably, but in half-shade in hot places.
Type of soil: compost mixed with wood-loam or heath-mould.
Soil moisture: specimens in the ground should be watered sparingly (e.g. greenhouse borders etc.), those in pots, more often.

---

184 CHINESE WISTERIA
Wisteria sinensis:

Family: Leguminosae. Named after Caspar Wistar.
Place of origin: China; introduced into Europe in 1816.
Description: a noble climber, reaching 60 ft. (18 m) or more feet under good conditions. Flowers fragrant, mauve to deep lilac in long, pendulous 8–12 in. (20–30 cm) racemes before the foliage. Leaves pinnate, 10–12 in. (25–30 cm) long with 9–11 oval to oblong leaflets. Seed pods long, like runner beans but velvety. There are also white, dark purple and double flowered cultivars.
Flowering time: early summer.
Use: to cover walls, arbours, railings, to decorate balconies and terraces.
Propagation: by layers.
Environment and light: full sun.
Type of soil: ordinary, deep garden soil; mulch roots to keep them cool.
Soil moisture: water regularly when the plant is young.
Remarks: plants can be trained into free-standing standards by careful pruning and giving support in early days. Climbers: prune in winter to keep within bounds and shorten leafy shoots in mid-summer.

GARDEN FAVOURITES

185 BEAR'S BREECH

Acanthus spinosus:

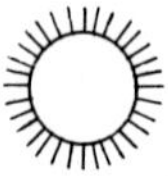

(8)

Family: Acanthaceae.
Place of origin: Southern Europe; widespread from 1629 onwards.
Description: an herbaceous perennial with handsome, shining deep green leaves rising directly from the ground. These are deeply lobed and spiny. Flower spikes up to 3 ft. (1 m), rosy-white with flaring lips and purplish-green hoods, the blooms sessile with spines below each on the main stem.
Flowering time: mid-summer to early autumn.
Use: for borders or to form clumps in fairly shady spots. As accent plants in key situations; flower spikes can be dried for winter arrangements.
Propagation: by root cuttings, seed or division.
Environment and light: light shade in hot areas, but elsewhere flourishing in full sun.
Type of soil: any good well-drained soil; too much moisture in winter can kill.
Soil moisture: water regularly.
Remarks: this is the plant which inspired the design of the Greek Corinthian columns in the 5th century B.C.

---

186 FERN-LEAVED YARROW

Achillea filipendulina:

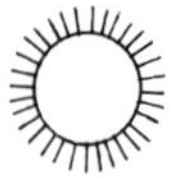

(3)

Family: Compositae. Named after Achilles, hero of the Trojan wars.
Place of origin: The Caucasus; introduced into Europe in 1803.
Description: an easily grown perennial with deeply cut, grey-green, fern-like foliage and large (3–4 in. (7–10 cm)) flat umbels of small mustard-yellow flowers on 3–4 ft. (1–1·2 m) stems. These can be dried for winter decorations.
Flowering time: mid-summer to early autumn.
Use: for border decoration and for cutting.
Propagation: by division in spring.
Environment and light: full sun to half-shade.
Type of soil: any well-drained soil; they are very tolerant of drought.

187 POPPY ANEMONE
Anemone coronaria:

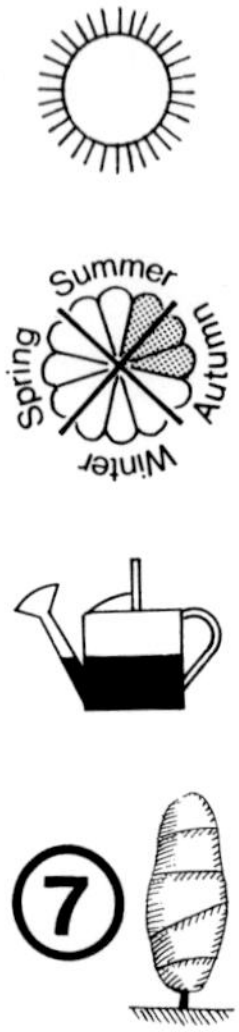

Family: Ranunculaceae. Name believed to be derived from the Greek, *anemos*, wind.
Place of origin: Greece and Eastern Mediterranean region; introduced into Britain in 1596.
Description: beautiful members of the buttercup family with large (2–3 in. (5–7 cm)) flowers on 6–12 in. (15–30 cm) stems. The blooms are variable in white, mauve, purple or scarlet with central boss of stamens. Mixed strains include the single "St. Brigid" and semi-double "de Caen" hybrids. Leaves deep green, deeply cut into narrow segments.
Flowering time: spring, but by successive planting can be induced to bloom throughout the summer. Florists force great quantities for the winter market.
Use: primarily as cut flowers but can also be grouped in rockery pockets and borders. As pot plants in rich soil with decayed manure and sand and protected.
Propagation: by seed or division of the tubers.
Environment and light: full sun.
Type of soil: plant in autumn in rich soil in an open, well-drained and sheltered position, setting the tubers 3 in. (7 cm) deep and 6 in. (15 cm) apart. In mild temperate climates lift after flowering, divide and store in dry sand in a cool place until autumn replanting.

---

188 JAPANESE ANEMONE
Anemone hupehensis (A. japonica):

Family: Ranunculaceae.
Place of origin: China; introduced into Britain in 1844 by Robert Fortune from plants found growing in Shanghai and said at that time to have come from Japan—hence the name *A. japonica*, often applied to this species.
Description: a useful late-flowering border plant which does well in shady situations. Roots fibrous; stems stiff, branching and 2–3 ft. (·6–1 m) tall with unequally lobed, toothed leaves and five sepalled pinkish-mauve flowers with central bosses of golden stamens. Cultivars with white, deep red and double flowers exist.
Flowering time: late summer to mid-Futumn.
Use: for borders, between shrubs and for cutting.
Propagation: by root cuttings or division.
Environment and light: light shade or sun provided the roots can be kept moist throughout the growing season.
Type of soil: well-drained but moist; leaf mould or peat moss help produce the right conditions.
Soil moisture: water frequently, at least every other day, during the vegetative period, not too generously. The earth should always be fairly moist.

189 COLUMBINE

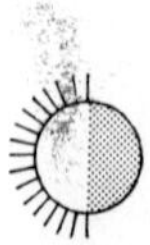

Aquilegia × hybrida:

Family: Ranunculaceae. Name from Latin *aquila*, eagle, referring to the curved spurs at back of flowers.
Place of origin: temperate northern regions.
Description: a race of long spurred hybrid columbines derived from *A. canadensis, A. chrysantha* and other species. Colours vary from white to pink, crimson, purple and yellow; many bicoloured. These are carried on 1–2 ft. (30–60 cm) branching stems and have long spurs behind the sepals and petals. The leaves are dark green or blue-green and deeply lobed.
Flowering time: spring–summer.
Use: to decorate semi-shady corners.
Propagation: by seed sown in spring or by careful division. In moist soil self-set seedlings usually carry on the race.
Environment and light: partial shade best, but will take sun if roots are moist.
Type of soil: ordinary soil if moist.
Remarks: in America humming birds often visit columbines for their nectar. Does not do well in tropical conditions. In areas of deep frost mulch with straw.

---

190 BUTTERFLY WEED

Ascelpias tuberosa:

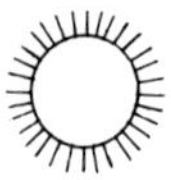

Family: Asclepiadaceae.
Place of origin: United States and Southern Canada; introduced into Europe in 1690.
Description: A delightful plant with 5–10, 1–2 ft. (40–80 cm) stems, carrying brilliant orange flower hoods 4–8 in. (1·25–2·50 cm) across, individual flowers are small waxy and fragrant and in character from mid-summer to early autumn. They are followed by canoe-shaped seed pods, full of silky seeds, leaves slender, 2–4 in. (5–10 cm) long and hairy.

Use: flowers excellent for cutting and seed pods in dried bouquets; patches of colour in summer borders.
Propagation: sown from seed in spring; slow to get going; once started leave undisturbed.

Environment and light: full sun.
Type of soil: well-drained sandy soil; the long top roots go down deeply and so can withstand drought.
Soil moisture: water regularly.
Remarks: resents disturbance so leave alone when happily established. Roots used as a medicine for pleurisy in India.

191 BLACKBERRY LILY; LEOPARD FLOWER
Belamcanda chinensis:

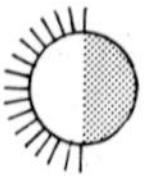

8

Family: Iridaceae. Latinized version of the East Asiatic local name for the plant, *balamtandum*.
Place pf origin: China; introduced into Britain in 1823.
Description: a tuberous-rooted herbaceous perennial allied to *Iris*, growing up to 3 ft. (1 m) tall with sword-shaped basal leaves and flowers in loose clusters. Individually these are about 2 in. (5 cm) across with six orange segments, spotted with red and brown.
Flowering time: early summer.
Use: for flower-beds, borders and isolated clumps.
Propagation: by spring division or seed.
Environment and light: sheltered place. Give winter protection in cool temperate climates; elsewhere grow in pots, overwintered away from frost.
Type of soil: rich sandy loam.
Soil moisture: water regularly, but not too generously.

---

192 CARPATHIAN HAREBELL; TUSSOCK BLUEBELL
Campanula carpatica:

4

Family: Campanulaceae. Name diminutive of the Latin *campagna*, bell, referring to the shape of the flower.
Place of origin: E. Europe, Carpathians; introduced in 1774.
Description: a beautiful, clump-forming perennial with leafy, branching stems of 9–18 in. (22–45 cm). Lower leaves roundish-ovate or heart-shaped on long stems; upper ovate and short-stalked. Flowers bell-shaped, up to 2 in. (5 cm) across on long naked, wiry stems in varying shades of violet, blue, purple or white.
Flowering time: throughout the summer.
Use: valued for its long flowering season; borders or rock gardens.
Propagation: by seed (which will not come true) or by division in spring.
Environment and light: a very accommodating plant for most soils; full sun or light shade.
Type of soil: garden soil, best if calcareous.
Soil moisture: water frequently and quite generously, so that the soil is always moist. Not good for sub-tropical conditions.

193 MILKY BELLFLOWER

Campanula lactiflora:

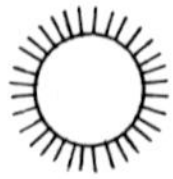

Family: Campanulaceae.
Place of origin: the Caucasus; introduced into Europe in 1814.
Description: a handsome perennial with large loose panicles of milky-white or occasionally pale blue, open, bell-shaped flowers about $1\frac{1}{2}$ in. (4 cm) across. These are borne on 4–6 ft. (1·2–1·8 m), branching leafy stems; the latter ovate-lanceolate, sessile, sharply toothed and pointed.

Flowering time: mid-summer to early autumn.
Use: for backs of borders or in thin grass in light woodland areas, wild gardens etc.
Propagation: by seed towards the end of summer and division of the larger clumps.

Environment and light: sun or light shade.
Type of soil: ordinary garden soil, best if calcareous.
Soil moisture: water regularly in dry weather and more often in summer.
Remarks: cutting the plant back for half length in early summer reserves the plant's energies for strong flowering later. Do not disturb established plants for 3–4 years. Will not thrive north of zone 5 or south of zone 8.

(6)

---

194 BACHELOR'S BUTTON; BLUE-BOTTLE; CORNFLOWER

Centaurea cyanus:

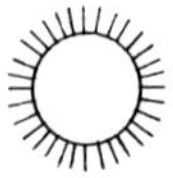

Family: Compositae. From Greek *kentauras*, centaur.
Place of origin: Europe including Britain; naturalised in N. America.
Description: a slender branching annual, 1–2 ft. (30–60 cm) high, woolly-white when young; leaves linear, entire, 3–6 in. (7–15 cm) long; flowers in round heads at tops of stems; blue, purple, pink or white—outer ray florets long.

Flowering time: mid-summer.
Use: mostly for cutting, but can also be grouped in annual borders and the like and there are dwarf strains —6 in. (15 cm)—for window boxes etc.
Propagation: by seed in spring.

Environment and light: full sun.
Type of soil: loose, light, permeable and fertile.
Soil moisture: water to establish and in dry summers.

(5)

195 OX-EYE DAISY
Chrysanthemum leucanthemum:

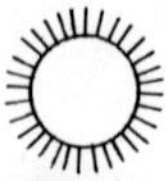

Family: Compositae. From Greek *chrysos*, gold and *anthos*, flower.
Place of origin: Europe including Britain.
Description: a robust perennial with stiff upright stems about 2 ft. (60 cm) high, terminating in large daisy flowers, white with yellow discs. Stem clasping leaves oblong pinnatifid at base; basal leaves obovate and stalked.

Flowering time: late spring and all summer.
Use: for growing in grass in wild gardens, on slopes, in rough borders, also for cutting.
Propagation: by seed in spring or division in autumn and spring.

Environment and light: full sun to half-shade.
Type of soil: ordinary garden soil, rather loose and light.
Soil moisture: water regularly.
Remarks: known as "dog-daisies" in country parts of Britain.

5

---

196 SPIDER FLOWER
Cleome spinosa:

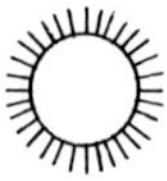

Family: Capparidaceae. Name derivation unknown.
Place of origin: Tropical America; introduced into Britain in 1817.
Description: strongly scented annual, sticky to the touch, 2–4 ft. (60 cm–1 m) high; leaves 5–7 lobed, leaflets oblong-lanceolate. Flowers white, flesh, rose-pink—or purple in newer cultivars in large and showy racemes. These have long (2–3 in. (5–7 cm)) extruding stamens.

Flowering time: summer.
Use: in annual beds or in groups in mixed borders.
Propagation: by seed raised under glass in early spring; put seedlings outside when all risk of frost is past.
Environment and light: usually full sun, but where the temperature is high also in half-shade.
Type of soil: ordinary garden soil, best if light and rich.
Soil moisture: water regularly to keep plant growing. The water must never stagnate at the foot of the plant, and the ground must never be soaked.

197 COREOPSIS; TICKSEED
Coreopsis grandiflora:

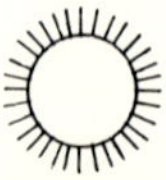

(5)

Family: Compositae.
Place of origin: S. United States; introduced into Europe in 1826.
Description: a smooth, leafy perennial 1–2 ft. (30–60 cm) tall with 2–3 in. (5–7 cm), bright yellow daisy-type flowers. Leaves 3–5 parted into lanceolate lobes; some of the lower leaves entire and spoon-shaped. Sometimes in double form.
Flowering time: late spring to late summer.
Use: for borders and flowerbeds, sometimes for cut flowers.
Propagation: by seed or spring division. Old clumps should be divided every third year or so.
Environment and light: full sun.
Type of soil: ordinary garden soil, not even very fertile. Must be well-drained especially in winter. Too much wet at that time can rot the roots.
Soil moisture: water if necessary in the hot months.

---

198 PAMPAS GRASS
Cortaderia selloana (C. argentea; Gynerium argenteum):

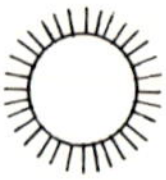

(6)

Family: Gramineae.
Place of origin: South America; introduced into Europe in 1848.
Description: a noble grass for key situations, widely grown on account of its stately habit. Forms huge mounds of tough, saw-edged, grassy leaves, 3–9 ft. (1–3 m) long and huge silky panicles of flowers at the tops of 6–8 ft. (2–2·4 m) even larger in hot countries). These are usually silvery-white or pink and can be dried for winter arrangements.
Flowering time: early to mid-autumn.
Use: as isolated specimens, to decorate flowerbeds, and for cut flowers.
Propagation: by division in spring.
Environment and light: full sun.
Type of soil: any soil—wet or dry.
Soil moisture: water to establish twice a week.
Remarks: try to obtain female plants as these have the best flower heads. In early spring burn over the clump to get rid of old leaves etc. and hibernating insects.

199 COSMOS

Cosmos bipinnatus:

Family: Compositae. From the Greek *kosmos*, ornament.
Place of origin: Mexico; introduced into Europe in 1799.
Description: a half-hardy annual, up to 3 ft. (1 m), with pinnate leaves cut into many narrow segments; large rose, purple or white flowers with yellow discs. Double varieties and varieties with yellow or orange flowers have been developed.
Flowering time: early summer–mid autumn.
Use: to decorate garden entrances, flowerbeds near walls, railings etc. An excellent cut flower.
Propagation: by seed grown in warmth in early spring and seedlings planted outside when all risk of frost is past.
Environment and light: full sun and moist soil if possible. Not frost hardy.
Type of soil: ordinary garden soil.
Soil moisture: water in very dry weather.

---

200 DAHLIA

Dahlia hybrid:

Family: Compositae. Named after Dr Anders Dahl.
Place of origin: Mexico; introduced in 1789.
Description: a large and complex genus of about 20 species and countless cultivars. Broadly speaking they are herbaceous perennials with tubers, opposite and composite leaves, flowers in fairly large capitula, single, double, or semi-double, in a wide variety of shapes and splendid colours.
Flowering time: mid-summer to mid-autumn.
Use: for formal bedding, isolated clumps in mixed borders, containers and as cut flowers.
Propagation: from soft cuttings rooted under glass in spring in light sandy compost and with bottom heat; then potted on and planted out when all risk of frost is past. Also from seed and division of tubers.
Environment and light: full sun.
Type of soil: rich garden soil with plenty of humus.
Soil moisture: water generously in growing season.
Remarks: in frost-free climates tubers can be left out in winter in well-drained soil. Elsewhere lift the tubers in autumn, dry and clean and store them in damp peat or soil in a frost-free place. In spring bring tubers into warmth (60°F (15·6°C)), water and use sprouting shoots as cuttings.

201 DELPHINIUM

Delphinium: hybr.

3

Family: Ranunculaceae. Name from Greek *delphis*, a dolphin, referring to shape of annual species (now placed in *Consolida*).
Place of origin: the genus includes some 250 species from Europe, Asia, Africa and America.
Description: the term "Delphinium hybridum Hort." covers countless varieties obtained through cultivation. They are herbaceous, annual, biennial and perennial plants, 6 in. to 6 ft. (15 cm–1·8 m) in height, with alternate, deeply divided leaves, and showy flowers in spikes or racemes, with fairly long spurs and brightly coloured, from white to skyblue, violet, red, pink and purple. Single or double flowers. Individual blooms have long spurs at the backs of the flowers; the *elatum* hybrids with contrasting dark or light coloured "eyes".
Flowering time: summer.
Use: in herbaceous borders or as accent plants, also (although the blooms are not long lived) for cutting.
Propagation: by cuttings or division in spring; seed gives variable results.
Environment and light: full sun.
Type of soil: rich soil with humus and mulches in summer.
Soil moisture: water generously when necessary. The ground should be damp, but never saturated.

---

202 AFRICAN DAISY; CAPE MARIGOLD; STAR OF THE VELDT

Dimorphotheca sinuata (D. durantiaca):

10

Family: Compositae. "Dimorphoteca" means a plant which produces two different kinds of seed.
Place of origin: South Africa; in Europe since 1774.
Description: a half-hardy perennial with thick radical leaves, entire, alternate and rough to the touch with cut edges; flowers large and showy, deep orange with darker centres. Yellow, salmon, apricot and white varieties are available.
Flowering time: summer.
Use: for container cultivation, annual and mixed borders and for cutting.
Propagation: by seed sown under glass in early spring; seedlings put outside when risk of frost is past. Seed can also be sown outdoors late spring where plants are to flower but flowers will be smaller and later. In tropics and frost-free areas plants can also be increased by spring division.
Environment and light: full sun.
Type of soil: ordinary garden soil, permeable, with a little sand added.
Soil moisture: water to establish and in very dry seasons. Do not let water stagnate or ground become too moist.

203 GLOBE THISTLE
Echinops ritro:

Family: Compositae. From Greek *echinos*, a hedgehog, *ops*, appearance, referring to the shape of the flower heads.
Place of origin: southern Europe, introduced into Britain in 1570.
Description: a robust perennial with much divided, spiny edged and lobed leaves, downy on the undersides and round; flower heads contain many small steely blue florets.
Flowering time: summer–early autumn.
Use: good for dryish borders or to decorate rockeries, banks and well-exposed slopes.
Propagation: by division or root cuttings.
Environment and light: sun or shade.
Type of soil: ordinary garden soil mixed with sand for good drainage.

③

---

204 ERYNGO; SEA HOLLY
Eryngium alpinum:

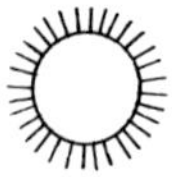

Family: Umbelliferae. Old Greek name.
Place of origin: Europe; introduced into Britain in 1597.
Description: a charming member of the carrot family with showy teasel-like flowers of metallic blue, framed by long and lacy, bluish, spiny bracts. The deeply heart-shaped, toothed, basal leaves are long stalked with the upper ones almost sessile and palmately lobed. Stems $1\frac{1}{2}$–2 ft. (45–60 cm).
Flowering time: summer–early autumn.
Use: for grouping in borders, large rockeries and as cut flowers.
Propagation: by root cuttings in autumn or winter, inserted in sand and kept in a cool but frost-free place; also by division or seed.
Environment and light: full sun.
Type of soil: ordinary rather dryish garden soil.

⑥

205 CALIFORNIA POPPY
Eschscholzia californica:

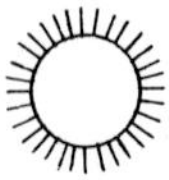

Family: Papaveraceae. Named after the Estonian botanist Friedrich Eschscholtz (1793–1831).
Place of origin: California; introduced into Europe in 1790.
Description: a brilliant annual with large—2 in. (5 cm) —orange, 4-petalled flowers and grey-green, 3 pinnatifid leaves. With many linear segments. There are numerous hybrids, tall and short, single and double in various colours—orange, yellow, rosy-purple, carmine and creamy-white etc.
Flowering time: summer–mid-autumn.
Use: valued for their long flowering season; grouped in annual or mixed borders, edging flower beds; for containers and as cut flowers.
Propagation: by seed sown where plants are to flower in spring.
Environment and light: full sun.
Type of soil: any well-drained soil; tolerates lime.

⑤

---

206 BLANKET FLOWER; GAILLARDIA
Gaillardia aristata:

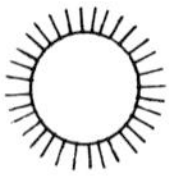

Family: Compositae. Named in 1786 after Gaillard de Marentonneau, a French magistrate and patron of botany.
Place of origin: Western N. America; introduced into Europe in 1812.
Description: an herbaceous perennial with erect 2 ft. (60 cm) stems, lanceolate or oblong, toothed leaves and yellow and red, large (3–4 in. (7–10 cm)), daisy-like flowers. It has produced many colourful hybrids in deep red, crimson and cream, tangerine and other shades.
Flowering time: early summer–late autumn.
Use: for borders and beds and as cut flowers.
Propagation: by division in spring or root cuttings.
Environment and light: full sun. Only reliably hardy in well-drained soil and areas of very light frost. Protecting the roots in winter with straw or leaves helps but winter wet is the real enemy.
Type of soil: well-drained, otherwise they rot in winter.

③ 

207 GAZANIA; TREASURE FLOWER
Gazania nivea:

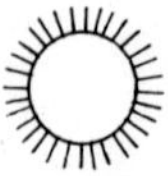

9

Family: Compositae. Named after Theodore of Gaza (1398–1478) who translated Theophrastus' botanical works from Greek into Latin.
Place of origin: South Africa; in Europe since 1892.
Description: a perennial plant with radical leaves, hoary both sides, mostly entire and spatulate, rolled at the edges, grey-green uppermost, tomentose, almost snow-white beneath; flowers in orange yellow capitula on peduncles which are shorter than the leaves; central disk of the capitulum surrounded by a brown ring which marks the end of the ligules.
Flowering time: summer–early autumn.
Use: on dry walls, as pot plants, edging flowerbeds, decorate rockeries etc.
Propagation: by cuttings or seed.
Environment and light: needs full sun or flowers will not open; well-drained, warm site.
Type of soil: loose and sandy.
Soil moisture: water only to establish.
Remarks: many colourful hybrids exist in pink, bronze, gold and ruby shades, usually with bold contrasting or toning shades as central zones or markings. The plants are only hardy in frost-free climates, so to perpetuate stocks they must be lifted—or increased from cuttings—and overwintered under glass.

---

208 BARBERTON DAISY; TRANSVAAL DAISY
Gerbera jamesonii:

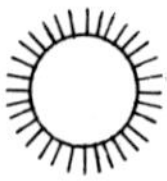

9

Family: Compositae. Named after Traugott Gerber.
Place of origin: Natal, Transvaal; introduced in 1887.
Description: a handsome, S. African perennial with tufts of radical, pinnatifid, rather leathery leaves, short-stemmed. Flowers like huge daisies on long stalks (1–1½ ft. (30–45 cm)), in yellow, flame or orange in nature but varying to pink, white, cream and crimson in cultivation.
Flowering time: summer.
Use: for cool greenhouse borders or large flowerpots in frost-prone areas; for flower beds in tropics and subtropics; for long flowering season; as cut flowers.
Propagation: by seed or side shoots taken with a heel, struck with bottom heat in a propagating frame.
Environment and light: foot of a warm wall in areas that are almost frost-free, the roots being covered with bracken or leaves in winter. Full sun. Plants are naturally deep rooting so give adequate depth.
Type of soil: well-drained loam or sandy soil with organic material. Feed several times in growing season.
Soil moisture: water frequently but sparingly, do not let water stagnate, because this may cause foot-rot.

209 COLVILLE GLADIOLUS

Gladiolus × colvillei:

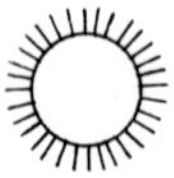

Family: Iridaceae. From the Latin diminutive of *gladius*, sword, referring to the foliage.
Place of origin: a garden hybrid between *Gladiolus cardinalis* and *G. tristis*; introduced in 1823.
Description: a charming small gladiolus of about 18 in. (45 cm) with long, narrow and sword-like foliage; flowers red or pink, often with a deeper central blotch, in few flowered spikes. The white form is called "The Bride".

Flowering time: summer but forced plants can be made to flower in winter.
Use: a popular florist's flower much grown for the cut flower trade. Can also be used in pots for home or greenhouse or planted in small sunny borders.
Propagation: by small cormlets which grow at the base of the parent corms.
Environment and light: full sun. Rather tender, so best cultivated as a cool greenhouse or frame plant in frost prone or cold countries.

Type of soil: garden soil with sand and peat added.
Soil moisture: water sparingly, 2–3 times a week. The water must not stagnate or the corms will rot.
Remarks: corms are normally lifted and rested for winter and replanted again in early spring.

---

210 GLADIOLUS

Gladiolus × gaudavensis hybrids:

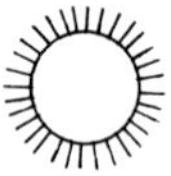

Family: Iridaceae. See No. 209.
Place of origin: South Africa. Of garden origin, derived from several S. African species.
Description: well-known summer-flowering plants with corms and broad sword-shaped leaves and handsome sessile flowers on full, often one-sided spikes. Colours rich varying from white and yellow to pink, red, crimson, mauve and purple; often bi-coloured. Height variable but usually $3\frac{1}{2}$–$4\frac{1}{2}$ ft. (1–1·3 m).

Flowering time: summer–early autumn or by forcing.
Use: for cut flowers and flowerbeds.
Propagation: from young cormlets round the mother corm.
Environment and light: full sun.
Type of soil: ordinary soil with sand and peat. Feed.
Soil moisture: water regularly and sparingly.
Remarks: plant the corms in sandy soil (or drop sand into the planting hole), 3 in. deep in spring. Lift after the first frost, hang plants up to dry, clean and store for winter in damp peat and sand. Flower spikes are heavy so stake the plants early.

211 STRAWFLOWER
Helichrysum bracteatum:

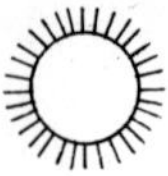

Family: Compositae. Name from Greek *helios*, sun; *chrysos*, golden.
Place of origin: Australia; introduced into Europe in 1799.
Description: a half-hardy annual (occasionally perennial) of 2–4 ft. (60 cm–1·3 m). Stems slightly hairy and branching with narrow sessile leaves and solitary flower heads at the end of each branch, composed of many pink or yellow bracts surrounding a golden disc. There are varieties with red, violet, pink, white and scarlet flowers and all retain their colour when dried.
Flowering time: summer–early autumn.
Use: as an annual for borders and flowerbeds, but primarily as cut flowers, for winter decoration.
Propagation: by seed raised under glass in frost-prone areas and planted out when conditions allow.
Environment and light: full sun.
Type of soil: any well-drained garden soil.

---

212 ROSE MALLOW
Hibiscus militaris:

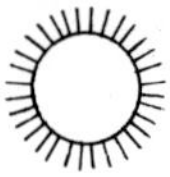

9

Family: Malvaceae. Name from Greek *hibiskos*, marsh mallow.
Place of origin: S.E. United States.
Description: herbaceous perennial of 2–4 ft. (60 cm–1·3 m), with heart-shaped, toothed, 3 lobed leaves, downy beneath and 3–5 in. (7–12 cm) showy flowers, bell-shaped in the leaf axils. These may be rose-pink or creamy white.
Flowering time: late summer–early autumn.
Use: to decorate gardens, parks, terraces and balconies.
Propagation: by careful division in spring, or spring cuttings rooted with bottom heat in a propagating case.
Environment and light: full sun. Hardy in warmer parts of Britain, elsewhere must be wintered under glass.
Type of soil: good fertile garden soil or a mixture of loam, sand and peat (equal parts) with a little fertilizer for container plants.
Soil moisture: water pot plants frequently and generously, especially in the month before flowering.

213 HYDRANGEA

Hydrangea macrophylla "Hortensia":

5

Family: Saxifragaceae. Name from Greek *hydro*, water, *angeion*, a vessel referring to the cup-shaped fruits.
Description: the familiar mop-headed Hortensia hydrangeas are of hybrid origin, mainly derived from the Japanese *H. macrophylla* and have large, round heads of sterile flowers, large petalled in shades of pink and red, white, blue and mauve or sometimes a combination of shades. They grow at the tops of upright woody stems, in height from 4–6 ft. (1·2–1·8 m). Leaves smooth, entire, oval-elliptic with toothed edges.
Flowering time: summer–autumn.
Use: for flowerbeds, shrubberies, terraces etc. Fine for tubs and containers; small specimens as indoor plants.
Propagation: by cuttings in late summer.
Environment and light: sun or light shade.
Type of soil: moist and rich. In chalk soils flowers tend to pinks and red. Acid soils are best for blue and mauve varieties. Blueing powder or aluminium sulphate (applied in water every 7–10 days in growing season) bring out the blue colourings and counteract the lime.
Soil moisture: frequently and generously in hot weather.
Remarks: remove old flower heads. In spring thin out weak shoots and prune back flowering shoots nearly to the old wood.

---

214 TRUMPET FLOWER

Incarvillea grandiflora:

6

Family: Bignoniaceae. Named after Fr. Pierre d'Incarville, French missionary in China who introduced many plants to Europe (1706–1757).
Place of origin: W. China; introduced into Britain in 1898.
Description: herbaceous perennial with radical, pinnate leaves and stout stems carrying 1 or 2 large (4 in. (10 cm)), funnel-shaped, 2 lipped flowers of rich rosy-red with white throat markings and yellow tubes.
Flowering time: late-spring–summer.
Use: borders, flowerbeds, rockeries.
Propagation: by seed (which takes 3 years to reach flowering size, or careful division in spring or autumn.
Environment and light: full sun to half-shade, but not in places which are too cold. During winter in colder regions it is advisable to protect the plant with dry leaves etc.
Type of soil: light, warm, well-drained, deep and rich.
Soil moisture: water to establish and in dry weather.

215–216 **BEARDED IRIS**

Iris germanica (I. barbata):

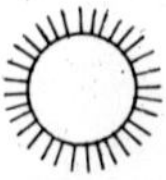

⑤

Family: Iridaceae. Named after Iris, the Greek goddess of the rainbow.
Description: hybrid bearded irises are now divided into 3 classes: dwarf, intermediate and tall. Their origin is uncertain although variable forms are found in S. Europe and they have been cultivated for centuries. The tall bearded (2 kinds illustrated here) are the most popular and grow 27 in. (68 cm) to 4 ft. (1·2 m) tall with large, variously coloured flowers up to 6 in. across. The taller kinds need staking. The rootstock is rhizomatous, the leaves sword-shaped, sheathing each other at the base, with parallel veining. Flowers often fragrant, in self colours or variations of several shades and always have prominent gold "beards" at the top inside of the talls. Colours white, pink, red, yellow, violet, mauve, purple and pale blue.
Flowering time: early summer.
Use: for grouping in herbaceous or mixed borders, cultivating in beds by themselves for brilliant effects in their season; generally to create splashes of colour; also for cut flowers.
Propagation: by division of the rhizomes directly after flowering. Established clumps should be divided every third year or so or the flowers deteriorate.
Environment and light: full sun.
Type of soil: light well-drained soil with manure added during initial digging. These irises like lime.
Soil moisture: water only in periods of drought.
Remarks: rhizomes should be planted horizontally and barely covered with soil. They soon make firm roots.

217 FRINGED IRIS; IRIS JAPONICA

Iris japonica (I. fimbriata):

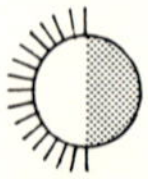

Family: Iridaceae.
Place of origin: China, Japan; introduced into Europe in 1792.
Description: this iris (belonging to a group known as the Evansia section) has distinct, orchid-like flowers of lilac or white, 2–4 in. (5–10 cm) across with fringed falls and standards; the falls are blotched or spotted with yellow or orange. Leaves persistent, dark green, broad and close together in a fan-shaped formation. Underground stolons enable the plant to form sizeable clumps when well suited. Height $1–1\frac{1}{2}$ ft. (30–45 cm).
Flowering time: spring–early summer.
Use: for borders near buildings, small flowerbeds; also possible as a pot plant.
Propagation: by division in autumn or spring.
Environment and light: cool, lightly shaded corner in a sheltered position as the species is not very hardy and may need winter protection in cold climates. Prefers mild Californian type conditions or makes a fine pot or border plant for cool or slightly heated greenhouses.
Type of soil: moist but well-drained with plenty of humus.
Soil moisture: water when necessary.

---

218 SPANISH IRIS

Iris xiphium:

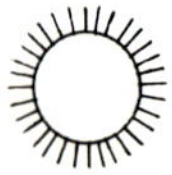

Family: Iridaceae.
Place of origin: Spain, Portugal; introduced into Britain in 1596.
Description: these are the florist's bulbous irises commonly forced in early spring as cut flowers. The true Spanish irises however are generally eclipsed by the so-called Dutch irises—descendants of Spanish irises crossed with an early flowering form of *I. xiphium*. Colours vary from white to yellow to sky-blue, purple and violet, often with yellow blotches on the falls. Leaves narrow, appearing in autumn—bulbs, therefore, should be planted late in autumn so as to delay this growth and protect it from winter cold.
Flowering time: late spring–early summer; or earlier, by forcing.
Use: mainly as cut flowers, because of early flowering, but also for borders and flowerbeds.
Propagation: by division of bulblets.
Environment and light: full sun to half-shade. Light, warm, well-drained.
Type of soil: ordinary calcareous garden soil.
Remarks: lift the bulbs annually after the foliage withers and store until replanted.

219 CORN LILY

Ixia:

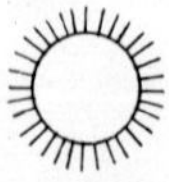

7

Family: Iridaceae. Greek name used by Theophrastus for bird-lime, but here referring to the plant's sticky sap.
Place of origin: South Africa; introduced into Europe in 1792.
Description: South African plants with small corms producing spikes of dainty star-like flowers on thin wiry stems. Height around 1 ft. (30 cm). Individual blooms variously coloured with 6 perianth segments. Leaves linear, somewhat swordshaped.
Flowering time: late-spring–early summer.
Use: for sunny borders or as a cool greenhouse plant in pots in cool climates. Hot countries—outdoors in beds etc. and for cutting.
Propagation: by division of bulbs.
Environment and light: full sun; in northern regions the plants are planted out in rather sheltered places, and are cultivated in places where the climate is not too harsh.
Type of soil: well-drained, sandy loam and leaf-mould.

---

220 JACOBINIA

Jacobinia suberecta:

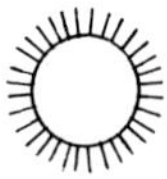

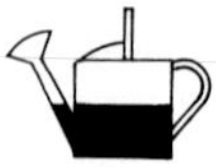

10

Family: Acanthaceae. Named after S. American town of Jacobina.
Place of origin: Uruguay, introduced into Europe in 1909.
Description: herbaceous perennial of low spreading habit with ovate, silvery, velvety leaves which are entire and sessile and compact clusters of 1–10 orange-red, 2-lobed, tubular flowers.
Flowering time: summer.
Use: only suitable for growing outside in tropical places; elsewhere cultivated in pots or baskets in warm rooms or greenhouses.
Propagation: by cuttings after flowering, under glass.
Environment and light: sunlight or well-lit places.
Type of soil: leaf-mould, garden soil, sand and peat.
Soil moisture: water frequently in hot weather; practically not at all in winter.

221 LION'S EAR

Leonotis leonurus:

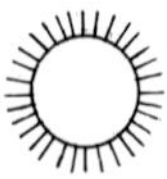

Family: Labiatae. Name from Greek *leon*, a lion, and *otis*, ear; the corolla is supposed to resemble the shape of a lion's ear.
Place of origin: South Africa; introduced into Europe in 1712.

Description: a shrub growing 3–7 ft. (1–2 m) tall, squarish stems; opposite, oblong-lanceolate, short-stemmed dentate leaves and whorls of bright orange-red, nettle-like flowers, each 2–2½ in. (5–7 cm) long.
Flowering time: early autumn to winter.
Use: in tropical gardens, as shrubs in mixed borders. In milder climates, in large pots taken under cover in winter or in sunny beds, protected in winter; also for greenhouse borders or pots under glass.

Propagation: by cuttings rooted under glass with bottom heat.
Environment and light: full sun.
Type of soil: good, fertile loamy soil; well-drained.
Soil moisture: water pot plants generously in summer.

(10)

---

222 BLAZING STAR; GAYFEATHER

Liatris spicata:

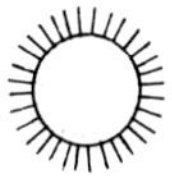

Family: Compositae. Derivation of name unknown.
Place of origin: East and South United States; introduced into Europe in 1732.
Description: a stout herbaceous perennial with alternate, slender, lanceolate, bright green leaves and stout 2 ft. (60 cm) spikes of sessile, lilac to purplish red flowers like miniature shaving brushes. The top flowers on these open first, unusual for spiky plants.

Flowering time: late summer–mid-autumn.
Use: for cut flowers, borders, flowerbeds, isolated clumps.
Propagation: by division in spring in the north, in autumn in the south; by seed sown soon after harvesting in light compost or pots—outdoors in mild climates.

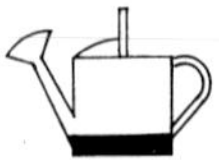

Environment and light: full sun; but if the place is excessively hot the plant does better in half-shade.
Type of soil: good garden soil mixed with sand; make sure of good drainage. Does well in poor soil but better in moist ground.
Soil moisture: water if necessary, in hot weather.

(5)

223 FLAX; PERENNIAL FLAX
Linum perenne:

4

Family: Linaceae. The Latin name for "flax".
Place of origin: South-eastern Europe, including Britain.
Description: a dainty herbaceous perennial, with slender 1–$1\frac{1}{2}$ ft. (30–45 cm) stems, clothed with sessile, lanceolate, linear leaves and many pale blue, 5-petalled flowers. White, pink and deep blue forms exist.
Flowering time: early to mid-summer.
Use: for borders, flowerbeds, small clumps in rock gardens.
Propagation: by seed or cuttings taken in summer and rooted in a close propagating frame.
Environment and light: full sun.
Type of soil: fertile garden soil, with porous sand added to heavy clays so that water drains easily.
Soil moisture: water to keep soil fairly moist.
Remarks: until cotton became available in the 18th century flax was the most important vegetable fibre in Europe and was widely grown as a crop. The seeds are the source of linseed oil.

---

224 CARDINAL FLOWER
Lobelia cardinalis:

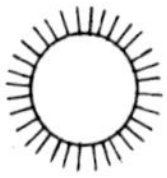

4

Family: Campanulaceae. Named after the Flemish botanist and physician to James I, Mathias de l'Obel.
Place of origin: N. America; introduced in 1626.
Description: a smooth, herbaceous perennial of 1–2 ft. (30–60 cm) with oblong-lanceolate, crimson leaves and spikes of scarlet flowers with unequal lips.
Flowering time: mid-summer–mid-autumn.
Use: growing near water features; for summer bedding either alone, in clumps, or mixed with annuals.
Propagation: by cuttings rooted in a close propagating frame in spring; by division or seed.
Environment and light: full sun.
Type of soil: moist, peaty.
Soil moisture: water regularly to keep the soil moist.
Remarks: often killed off in cold wet winters so always keep a few stock plants under glass in a frame or greenhouse as insurance against disaster.
English name refers to Queen Henrietta Maria of England who is said to have "laughed excessively" on seeing the plant in 1629 saying their colour reminded her of a "cardinal's scarlet stockings".

225 HONESTY; MOON WORT; MONEY PLANT; SATIN FLOWER; SILVER DOLLAR

Lunaria annua (L. biennis):

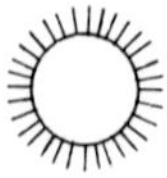

(6)

Family: Cruciferae. From the Latin *luna*, moon, referring to the shape of the seed-pod.
Place of origin: Europe; introduced into Britain in 1595.
Description: a quick growing biennial with branching stems of 2 ft. (60 cm) or more bearing heart-shaped, coarsely toothed leaves and white, lilac, pink or red-purple, 4-petalled, scentless flowers. The silvery scentless partition of the seed pod (shown here) is popular for dried flower arrangements. The cream and green variegated variety is the most attractive and comes true from seed.
Flowering time: spring–early summer.
Use: for odd corners in beds and borders in the spring garden—especially the variegated leaves variety. The seed pods for cutting purposes.
Propagation: by seed; the plant usually perpetuates itself in the garden if the seed is allowed to drop naturally.
Environment and light: sun or partial shade.
Type of soil: ordinary garden soil.
Soil moisture: water regularly, never too much; the soil should always be moist.

---

226 LUPINE or LUPIN

Lupinus polyphyllus (L. Russell hybr.*):*

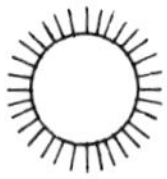

(3)

Family: Leguminosae. Name said to be from Latin *lupus*, wolf; the plants were at one time thought to destroy the fertility of soil.
Place of origin: North-western America; introduced into Europe in 1826.
Description: herbaceous perennial with erect $2\frac{1}{2}$–5 ft. (75 cm–1·5 m) stems, carrying long stalked, digitate, silky leaves and spikes of deep blue, purple, reddish-purple or creamy yellow flowers. Bicolours are common in such cultivars as the George Russell hybrids, but being less hardy than the true species need renewing about every third year. They are however much finer garden plants with larger and heavier flower trusses.
Flowering time: late spring–mid-summer.
Use: to provide masses of colour in early summer.
Propagation: by seed sown in the open immediately after harvesting (in boxes where they are not hardy); by basal cuttings taken with a heel or by careful division in spring. Lupin's transplant badly so move young stock whilst it is still quite small.
Environment and light: full sun.
Type of soil: any good garden soil, preferably lime-free.
Soil moisture: ground should be moist at all times.

227 CAMPION; ROSE CAMPION

Lychnis coronaria (Agrostemma coronaria):

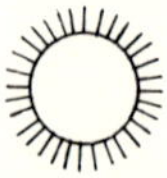

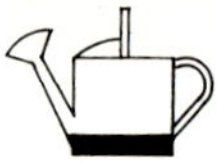

3

Family: Caryophyllaceae. From the Greek *lychnos*, lamp, referring to the brilliant flowers of some species.
Place of origin: S. Europe; introduced into Britain in 1596.
Description: herbaceous, tomentose perennial with $1\frac{1}{2}$–2 ft. (45–60 cm) upright stems, opposite ovate-lanceolate grey-green leaves; flowers on long stems with rounded obovate petals, entire or marginated, with two prickly scales at the base. Colour—vivid cerise in the natural state—varies from white to red, pink, crimson etc.
Flowering time: late spring–mid-summer.
Use: for borders, flowerbeds, rockeries, to provide clumps of colour.
Propagation: by division, also from seed in spring.
Environment and light: full sun; sheltered place.
Type of soil: good garden soil with a little sand added.
Soil moisture: water in dry weather.

---

228 PURPLE LOOSESTRIFE

Lythrum salicaria:

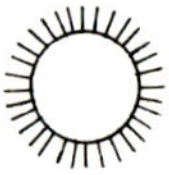

3

Family: Lythraceae. From the Greek *lythrum*, blood, from the colour of the flowers.
Place of origin: northern temperate regions including Britain.
Description: herbaceous perennial of 2–5 ft. (60 cm–1·5 m) with opposite or whorls of lance-shaped leaves, 2–5 in. (5–13 cm) long and axillary clusters to form a terminal spike-like raceme of wary petalled flowers. These are red-purple in the type but vary to deep rose and clear pink in garden varieties.
Flowering time: early summer–early autumn.
Use: to edge damp places by streams, ponds etc., or grouped in bog gardens.
Propagation: by cuttings or division in spring.
Environment and light: full sun to half-shade.
Type of soil: should always be fairly moist, so add a little peat to ordinary garden soil.
Soil moisture: water frequently and generously, unless the ground is naturally moist.

229 FOUR-O-CLOCK PLANT; MARVEL OF PERU

Mirabilis jalapa:

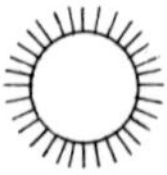

(9)

Family: Nyctaginaceae. From a Latin name meaning wonderful.
Place of origin: Tropical America, Mexico and Peru; introduced into Europe in circa 1525.
Description: herbaceous perennials about 2 ft. (60 cm) in height with tuberous, thickened roots; opposite, entire, smooth, ovate-lanceolate leaves, the lower ones stalked, the upper leaves sessile. Flowers in clusters, with long perianth tubes, fragrant, opening in afternoon and closing next morning. Colours from rosy-purple or red to white and yellow.
Flowering time: mid-summer–mid-autumn.
Use: in tropical gardens for bedding or borders, requiring little attention. Cool climates for summer bedding in containers, pockets in rockeries etc.
Propagation: by seed sown under glass in spring.
Environment and light: full sun.
Type of soil: not fussy, suitable for most soils in tropics. Elsewhere in pots in any good potting compost.
Soil moisture: water frequently in hot weather. Treat as an annual in areas of frost.

---

230 EVENING PRIMROSE

Oenothera biennis:

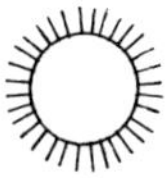

(4)

Family: Onagraceae. Old Greek name of uncertain connection.
Place of origin: Eastern North America; introduced into Europe in 1612.
Description: an extremely variable biennial having erect, 2–4 ft. (60 cm–1·2 m), branched stems and oblong-lanceolate, 6 in. (15 cm), radical leaves and ovate upper leaves. Flowers yellow, funnel-shaped, opening towards evening, closed during day, long tubed with 4 petals and 8 stamens of equal length, richly scented.
Flowering time: summer–early autumn.
Use: as a wild garden plant or between small shrubs, back of flower borders and odd corners; valued for its sweet perfume and evening flowers.
Propagation: by seed—usually establishes itself from self-set seed.
Environment and light: full sun.
Type of soil: light, poor, well-drained.
Soil moisture: water seldom.

231 **FLUTTERMILLS; OZARK SUNDROPS**
Oenothera missouriensis (O. macrocarpa):

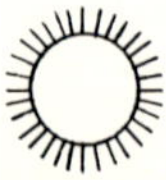

④

Family: Onagraceae.
Place of origin: United States, Nebraska to Oklahoma; introduced into Europe in 1811.
Description: a variable species which may have almost no stem above the ground or may be 20 in. (50 cm) high. Perennial .with narrowly lanceolate to ovate leaves tapering to broad stalks it opens its large, funnel-shaped, lemon-yellow flowers towards evening. These may be 4–6 in. (10–15 cm) across, with drooping flower buds usually mottled with red.
Flowering time: summer.
Use: rock garden pockets, fronts of borders etc.
Propagation: by seed or cuttings.
Environment and light: full sun.
Type of soil: well-drained, sandy loam.
Soil moisture: water seldom.

---

232 **SHOWY EVENING PRIMROSE; WHITE SUNDROP**
Oenothera speciosa (Hartmannia speciosa):

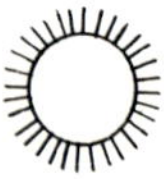

⑤

Family: Onagraceae.
Place of origin: S. Central United States to Mexico; introduced into Europe in 1821.
Description: a perennial with four sepals which are bent back at flowering, four petals and eight stamens. Horizontal leafy stems 4–20 in. (10–50 cm) long (according to conditions), leaves smooth, those on the stem being short stalked, pinnately cleft. Buds pendulous opening white but becoming pink with age. Day-blooming.
Flowering time: summer–mid-autumn.
Use: to edge flowerbeds, for small clumps, and rockeries.
Propagation: by seed or cuttings.
Environment and light: full sun, sheltered hot places.
Type of soil: light, poor, quite dry.
Soil moisture: water seldom, and only in very dry seasons.
Remarks: not reliably hardy in frost-prone countries but maintain stock by keeping rooted cuttings in a frost-free frame or greenhouse over winter.

233 CAPE CHINCHERINCHEE; CHINCHERINCHEE
Ornithogalum thyrsoides:

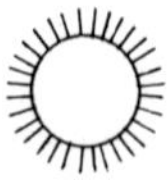

Family: Liliaceae. Name from the Greek *ornis*, bird, *gala*, milk; the flowers are usually white.
Place of origin: Southern Africa, Cape Province; introduced into Europe in 1757.
Description: bulbous plants with showy spikes of long-lasting, cup-shaped, white flowers with yellow stamens and fleshy, strap-shaped leaves 6–12 in. (15–30 cm) long.
Flowering time: early summer.
Use: for edging borders and cut flowers. Not hardy in frost-prone areas but may be planted outside for summer flowering in all but the coldest areas, the bulbs being lifted in autumn. Also for cutting and as pot plants.
Propagation: by small bulbs growing around the parent bulb. These should flower the second or third season.
Environment and light: full sun.
Type of soil: ordinary garden soil with a little sand and peat added.
Soil moisture: water if necessary; pot plants regularly.
Remarks: all parts of the plant are poisonous if eaten.

⑧

---

234 PEONY
Paeonia officinalis "Rubra Plena":

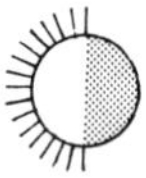

Family: Paeoniaceae. Classical Greek name derived from that of the physician Paeon.
Place of origin: widespread species from France to Albania; introduced into Britain in 1548.
Description: a robust cultivar which has been in cultivation since before biblical times. Flowers large—5 in. (13 cm)—double, crimson, unpleasant smelling, on 2 ft. (60 cm) stems. These bloom before the fragrant Chinese peonies (*P. lactiflora* hybrids). Leaves dark green, deeply cut, slightly hairy beneath.
Flowering time: late spring–early summer.
Use: for borders, flowerbeds, and also for cut flowers.
Propagation: by division in autumn.
Environment and light: semi-shady places; in northern Europe and Scandinavia also in sunny locations.
Type of soil: rich, deep loam with good drainage.
Remarks: plant where not exposed to early morning sun in frost-prone areas or the buds will blacken and fail to open.

④

235 CHINESE PEONY
Paeonia lactiflora: hybr.

Family: Paeoniaceae.
Place of origin: Mongolia, Siberia; introduced into Europe in 1548.
Description: a beautiful, herbaceous perennial with strong $1\frac{1}{2}$–2 ft. (45–60 cm) stems carrying several large—3–4 in. (7–10 cm)—white and fragrant flowers with yellow stamens. Leaves deeply cut, dark green. The species has given rise to many garden varieties, the so-called Chinese peonies, some of which originated in China. These may be pink, red, white, bicoloured or double or $1\frac{1}{2}$–3 ft. (45–90 cm) stems.
Flowering time: towards the end of spring.
Use: to make borders, flowerbeds, for isolated groups, and for cut flowers. Good pot plant.
Propagation: by division in autumn.
Environment and light: in sun or semi-shady places; cooler in sub-tropical climates. Not suitable for tropics.
Type of soil: cool, moist, clayey, soil with good drainage.
Soil moisture: water in dry situations in summer.

---

236 MOUTAN PEONY; TREE PEONY
Paeonia suffruticosa: hybr.

Family: Paeoniaceae.
Place of origin: China, Tibet; introduced in 1787.
Description: the so-called tree peonies are really shrubs of 6–8 ft. (2–2·5 m), weighted at flowering time by the heavy, plate-size—8 in. (20 cm)—blooms. These occur on long slender stems at the tops of the leafy branches and may be single or double, and white, pink, rose, crimson or yellow, usually with maroon basal markings. Leaves large, smooth and 2 pinnate, the terminal leaflets deeply lobed.
Flowering time: early to mid-summer.
Use: as showy specimens in sheltered areas, as at the front of shrubberies, or with roses and others in bloom at the same season. Also for tubs or cutting.
Propagation: named varieties usually grafted on the sturdier rooted *P. lactiflora* or *P. officinalis* in early autumn. Can also be layered.
Environment and light: sheltered spot away from strong spring winds which can snap the brittle slender stems. Full sun or semi-shade in hot areas.
Type of soil: rich, deep, moist. Like lime. Mulch annually.
Soil moisture: water regularly in very dry situations.

237 ORIENTAL POPPY

Papaver orientale:

3

Family: Papaveraceae. Latin name, said to have been suggested by the noise made when chewing poppy seeds.
Place of origin: Armenia; introduced into Europe in 1714.
Description: a brilliant herbaceous perennial with grey-green, hairy, deeply cut leaves up to 1 ft. (30 cm) long and huge scarlet flowers on stout, hairy, 2–3 ft. (60–90 cm) stems. These usually have black blotches at the petal bases. Cultivars exist with deep rose-pink, white, orange, crimson, maroon and orange-red flowers, some of them double.
Flowering time: late-spring–early summer.
Use: to form bright clumps in mixed or herbaceous borders.
Propagation: by seed or root cuttings in winter for named cultivars.
Environment and light: full sun.
Type of soil: any good deep, well-drained soil.
Remarks: the plant becomes untidy after flowering, so plant later blooming perennials in front or use low growing shrubs or annuals for this purpose, to hide the dying leaves.

---

238 BEARD-TONGUE; PENSTEMON

Pentstemon hartwegii (P. gentianoides):

9

Family: Scrophulariaceae. Name from the Greek *penta*, five and *stemon*, stamen; the plants have five stamens one of which is sterile.
Place of origin: Mexico; introduced in 1825.
Description: an erect, branching perennial of 2 ft. (60 cm) or more with opposite, lanceolate, entire leaves; the upper ones stem clasping. Flowers scarlet or blood red, usually in groups of 2 or 3 on long panicles. This is the parent of the florist's penstemon so popular for bedding purposes. Often incorrectly called Pentemon.
Flowering time: early summer for the species; hybrids bloom almost right through to early autumn.
Use: flowerbeds, borders, isolated clumps, and cut flowers.
Propagation: cuttings root easily in a closed propagating case. If these are taken in late summer they can be overwintered in a frost-free place until it is safe to plant them out again in spring; by seed for the species.
Environment and light: full sun. The plant is hardy in mild, practically frost-free climates only.
Type of soil: looose, light, calcareous with a little sand added to make it more porous and for better drainage.
Soil moisture: water so that the ground is always damp.

239 **JERUSALEM SAGE**

Phlomis fruticosa:

(4)

Family: Labiatae. Greek name, possibly not related to this genus.
Place of origin: Mediterranean areas and S. Europe; introduced into Britain in 1596.
Description: a shrubby plant of 2–4 ft. (60 cm–1·2 m) with woolly, hairy branches; oval-oblong, grey wrinkled leaves which are white downy beneath and opposite flowers sage-like, yellow, arranged in whorls of 20 or more flowers along the stems.
Flowering time: early to mid-summer or earlier in warm countries.
Use: grown for its freedom of flower, the foliage associating pleasantly with other and brighter flowers. For beds, borders or the fronts of shrubberies.
Propagation: by seed or cuttings, rooted in sandy compost with bottom heat.
Environment and light: dry sunny places, even arid.
Type of soil: poor well-drained so that the moisture never lies.

---

240 **PHLOX**

Phlox paniculata:

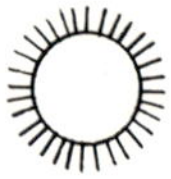

(4)

Family: Polemoniaceae. Name from the Greek *phloks*, flame, because of the colour of flowers of certain species.
Place of origin: E. United States; introduced into Britain in 1732.
Description: unbranched, leafy stems 2–4 ft. (60 cm–1·2 m) tall. Leaves entire, oblong or elliptic; flowers in dense terminal, domed heads, violet-purple in the species, also pink, red, crimson, violet or white in named cultivars.
Flowering time: late-summer–mid-autumn.
Use: as garden plants for mixed or herbaceous borders or grouped in shrubberies; as cut flowers.
Propagation: by soft cuttings rooted in spring with the aid of bottom heat; by division in spring or autumn or root cuttings in early autumn or winter. *Note:* Phlox often contract eelworm which kills the leaves and makes for stunted plants. Stock is re-infected via the foliage so root cuttings are the safest propagation method where the pest is prevalent.
Environment and light: sun or light shade.
Type of soil: deep rich soil which never dries out.
Soil moisture: water in dry weather; mulch the roots.

241 **CAPE GOOSEBERRY; CHINESE LANTERN; GROUND CHERRY**
Physalis alkekengi var. *tranchetii* *(P. tranchetii):*

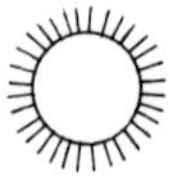

(6)

Family: Solanaceae. Name from Greek *physa*, bladder, referring to the inflated calyx.
Place of origin: Japan; in Europe since 1800.
Description: a persistent perennial with spreading underground, creeping rhizomes; large, long-stalked leaves on $1\frac{1}{2}$ ft. (45 cm) stems and small, white, insignificant flowers followed by decorative, orange-red, inflated calyces. These enclose round, bright red berries which in some species are edible and used in preserves.
Flowering time: summer; fruits late autumn.
Use: grown for the seed pods which can be dried for winter decoration.
Planting: April and early May.
Propagation: by division of the fleshy roots in spring; by seed.
Environment and light: full sun to half-shade. The latter condition is best in hotter climates.
Type of soil: well-drained loam.
Soil moisture: water frequently in dry weather; soil should be damp.
Remarks: under certain conditions the plant can become invasive so plant with care.

---

242 **FALSE DRAGON-HEAD; OBEDIENT PLANT**
Physostegia virginiana (Dracocephalum virginianum):

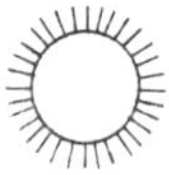

(3)

Family: Labiatae. Name from the Greek *physa*, bladder, *stege*, cover, referring to the inflated calyx.
Place of origin: North America; introduced into Europe in 1683.
Description: an erect perennial plant, herbaceous, with lanceolate, sharply toothed leaves and thick spikes of flesh-pink to purple, sessile tubular flowers. These can be moved around the stems and will stay as placed—hence the English name. "Vivia" is a good bright rose-pink variety and "Alba" white.
Flowering time: mid-summer–early-autumn.
Use: for flowerbeds, borders, isolated groups, and occasionally for balconies as pot plants.
Propagation: by division or seed in spring.
Environment and light: full sun to half-shade.
Type of soil: good ordinary garden soil, with no particular requirements.
Soil moisture: water in dry seasons, aiming to keep soil just moist.

243 BALLOON FLOWER; CHINESE BELL-FLOWER
Platycodon grandiflorum:

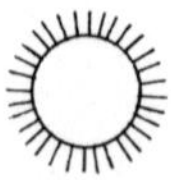

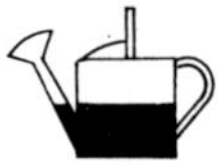

5

Family: Campanulaceae. Name from the Greek *platys*, broad, and *kodon*, bell, referring to the shape of the flower.
Place of origin: China, Manchuria, Japan; introduced into Europe in 1782.
Description: a monotypic genus, the species an erect, smooth, herbaceous perennial of 6–12 in. (15–30 cm) with ovate-lanceolate, toothed, opposite leaves—or whorled at the base of the stem. Flowers campanula-like, resembling swollen balloons when in bud and then popping open to mauve-blue, 5-petalled, saucer-shaped blooms. White and deep blue forms exist.
Flowering time: mid-summer–early autumn.
Use: for rock garden pockets, mixed or herbaceous borders.
Propagation: by division in spring or by seed. Plant out when small as they transplant badly.
Environment and light: full sun.
Type of soil: deep and fertile but well-drained (loam, sand and peat).
Soil moisture: water enough to keep soil fairly moist.

---

244 BLACK-EYED SUSAN; CONE FLOWER; CUT LEAF CONEFLOWER
Rudbeckia laciniata:

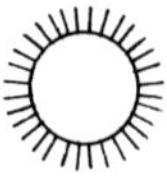

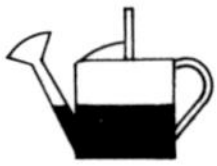

4

Family: Compositae. Named after Olof Rudbeck (1630–1702), founder of the Uppsala botanic garden and his son, also Olof Rudbeck (1660–1740), who befriended Linnaeus when he was a near destitute student.
Place of origin: Canada, United States; introduced into Europe in 1640.
Description: a sturdy branched perennial of 3–7 ft. (1–2 m), according to conditions. Lower leaves dark green, deeply cut, upper leaves entire 3 cleft. Flowers large, golden-yellow with prominent greenish centres which become brownish with age. Petals broad, backward pointing.
Flowering time: mid-summer–mid-autumn.
Use: for backs of borders or grouped in beds or grass.
Propagation: by division in spring or autumn.
Environment and light: best in full sun, but also in light shade.
Type of soil: needs moist soil.
Soil moisture: water frequently in dry weather to keep ground damp.

245 PURPLE CONE-FLOWER; RUDBECKIA

Rudbeckia purpurea (now more correctly *Echinacea purpurea*):

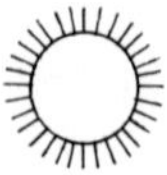

Family: Compositae. Name from Greek *echinos*, hedgehog, referring to prickly ovary scales.
Place of origin: United States; introduced into Europe in 1779.
Description: a strong growing perennial with oval-lanceolate leaves, rough to the touch and slightly toothed and purple-crimson flowers on 3–4 ft. (1–1·2 m) stems. The cone-shaped, prominent centres are deep mahogany red. The variety "The King" has especially fine blooms up to 5 in. (12 cm) across.
Flowering time: late summer–early autumn.
Use: for flowerbeds, borders or small clumps.
Propagation: by division, but do not disturb established plants more than necessary.
Environment and light: full sun.
Type of soil: rich but well-drained, mulch light hungry soils.
Remarks: the black roots are edible.

(5)

---

246 CAUCASIAN SCABIOUS; PINCUSHION FLOWER; SCABIOSA

Scabiosa caucasica:

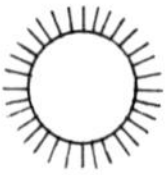

Family: Dipsaceae. Name from the Latin *scabies*, itch. In the olden days it was thought that scabious could heal scabies.
Place of origin: Caucasus; in Europe since 1803.
Description: a good perennial border plant with opposite stem leaves, more or less pinnatifid and basal foliage that is entire, glaucous and lanceolate. The showy flowers come in round, pin-cushion like heads about 3 in. (7 cm) across. These are pale blue but cultivars with white, mauve, misty blue and deep blue flowers are available. Height about 2 ft. (60 cm).
Flowering time: early summer–early autumn.
Use: for borders, flowerbeds and as cut flowers.
Propagation: plant out seed directly in late spring; by division in spring; by cuttings taken with a heel rooted in sandy soil under glass.
Environment and light: full sun; in climates with very cold winters the plants should be sheltered. Plant only in spring.
Type of soil: good well-drained, limy soil.

(3)

247 BIRD OF PARADISE FLOWER; STRELITZIA

Strelitzia reginae:

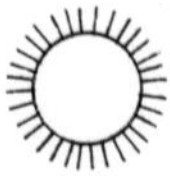

9

Family: Musaceae. Named after Queen Charlotte of Mecklenburg-Strelitz, wife of King George III of England, who died in 1818.
Place of origin: South Africa; in Europe since 1773.
Description: an exotic evergreen perennial, growing to about 5 ft. (1·5 m). Leaves large and oblong with conspicuous mid-ribs and stems approximately the same length. Flowers large and showy bearing some resemblance to the plumaged head of tropical birds. They are purple and orange with free sepals and blue protruding petals.
Flowering time: variable; normally spring but can be forced to bloom at other seasons.
Use: as cut flowers; as accent flowers in tropical garden borders, or in frost-prone climates, in warm greenhouse borders or large containers.
Propagation: by division or by removing offshoots or suckers.
Environment and light: in full sun under glass in cool climates.
Type of soil: rich loam, peat and sand with a little decayed manure for containers. Good garden soil if planted outdoors.
Soil moisture: water liberally in summer but keep reasonably dry in winter.

---

248 AFRICAN MARIGOLD

Tagetes erecta:

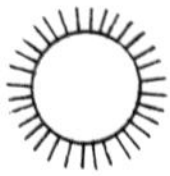

Family: Compositae. Named after an Etruscan deity.
Place of origin: Mexico; in Europe since 1596.
Description: a strongly aromatic, half-hardy annual of branching habit with pinnate, pungent, deeply cut leaves and large single, yellow or orange daisy-like flowers up to 4 in. (10 cm) across on 2 ft. (60 cm) stems. Double flowered cultivars (as in illustration) are available in various colours and different heights (1–3 ft. (30–90 cm)).
Flowering time: summer to early autumn or even later in tropical and subtropical climates.
Use: for bedding, annual borders, containers etc.
Propagation: by seed sown under glass in spring and plants put outside when no more risk of frost. In tropics sow seeds outside where they are to flower.
Environment and light: full sun.
Type of soil: ordinary garden soil; being a sturdy plant it adapts itself to most types of soil.
Soil moisture: water to establish and then only in periods of drought.
Remarks: remove dead flower heads regularly to prevent seeding and to maintain blooming season.

249 GARDEN MONTBRETIIA

Tritonia crocosmiiflora more properly *Crocosmia x crocosmiiflora (Monbretia crocosmiiflora):*

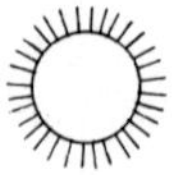

(6)

Family: Iridaceae. Name from Greek, *krokos*, saffron and *osme*, smell; when the dried flowers are placed in water they smell like saffron.
Description: a hybrid derived from *Crocosmia durea* crossed with *C. pottsii*. Herbaceous plant with linear, sword-shaped leaves and many orange-scarlet, tubular flowers with flaring petals, arranged zig-zag fashion on 1½–2 ft. (45–60 cm) stems. The stamens and styles are as long as the petals. Cultivars with yellow, orange or bicoloured flowers exist but are generally less hardy.
Flowering time: late summer.
Use: has become naturalised in parts of England, making wide drifts in open woodland. Suitable for borders, wild gardens, shrub glades. Also as cut flowers.
Propagation: by seed or division.
Environment and light: full sun. In cold climates lift the corms and store them like dahlias for the winter.
Type of soil: light, rich, sandy for sharp drainage.
Soil moisture: water during growing season if ground is dry to prevent a check to development.

---

250 CUT AND COME AGAIN; YOUTH AND OLD AGE; ZINNIA

Zinnia elegans:

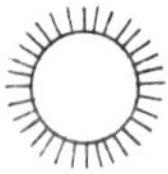

Family: Compositae. Named after Johann Gottfried Zinn (1727–1759), professor of botany, Gottingen.
Place of origin: Mexico; introduced into Europe in 1796.
Description: a variable, erect, 1–3 ft. (30–90 cm) plant, usually treated as a half-hardy annual, especially in cool temperate regions. Leaves opposite, linear to oval-lanceolate, deep green, stem-clasping. Flowers in large heads (2–4½ in. (5–12 cm)), white, red, yellow, violet, orange, crimson, etc., single and doubles. Some dwarf hybrids suitable for window boxes etc.
Flowering time: early summer–late autumn.
Use: as an annual for flowerbeds, borders, cut flowers.
Propagation: by seed in early spring under glass, seedlings put out when all risk of frost is past, or sown outside in early summer where plants are to flower.
Environment and light: definitely a plant for a hot summer. Unsuccessful in cool, cloudy seasons. Full sun.
Type of soil: rich, deep, loamy and moist. Starved plants disappoint.
Soil moisture: water quite generously as necessary.
Remarks: the illustration shows a variety of *Zinnia augustifolia (Z. haageana)* at left and of *Z. elegans* right.

SPRING AND SUMMER PLANTS

251 ALLIUM KARATAVIENSE

Allium karataviense:

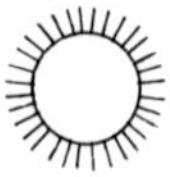

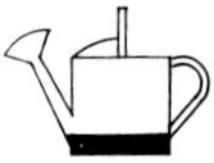

⑤

Family: Alliaceae. The classical name for garlic, a plant much prized by the ancients.
Place of origin: Turkestan; introduced into Europe in 1878.
Description: a striking bulbous plant with very broad flat, blue-green leaves which are occasionally variegated and 6–8 in. (15–20 cm) stems terminating in dense, round, 4 in. (10 cm) umbels of silvery-pink to white flowers.
Flowering time: early summer.
Use: for banks, rocky slopes, rockeries, borders and flowerbeds.
Propagation: by division of the bulbs.
Environment and light: full sun.
Type of soil: ordinary garden soil mixed with sand to ensure good drainage.
Soil moisture: water only in exceptionally dry conditions.
Remarks: flowers often dried and used in decorative arrangements.

---

252 CHIVE

Allium schoenoprasum:

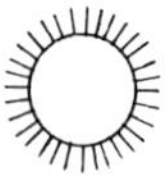

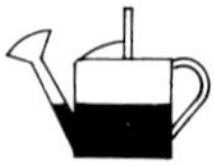

③

Family: Alliaceae.
Place of origin: northern hemisphere, mainly in the Mediterranean area.
Description: a pretty culinary herb with clusters of bulbs, narrow, cylindrical, hollow leaves about 8 in. (20 cm) high and umbels of pink to purplish flowers on 6–9 in. (15–23 cm) stems. A stronger growing form called "Sibiricum" grows 15 in. (37 cm) tall and has rose-pink flowers.
Flowering time: spring–mid-summer.
Use: for herb gardens, edging vegetable plots, growing in containers; grown for its edible foliage which can be used in omelettes and other egg dishes. Also in rockeries for its flowers.
Propagation: by division.
Environment and light: full sun.
Type of soil: good well-drained, but fertile garden soil. If there is poor drainage the bulbs can easily rot.
Soil moisture: water regularly in dry weather.
Remarks: the cutting season (for the foliage) can be prolonged by growing the plant under cloches.

253 **PASQUE FLOWER**

Anemone pulsatilla (now more correctly *Pulsatilla vulgaris*):

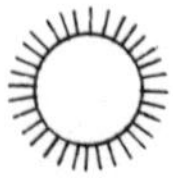

Family: Ranunculaceae. Name from Latin *pulso*, to strike violently; allusion unknown.
Place of origin: Europe (including Britain), usually in limestone districts.
Description: perennial herbaceous plants closely related to *Anemone* with silky, hairy, pinnate and finely cut leaves with linear segments 4–8 in. (10–20 cm) high on hairy stems and solitary, 6-parted, campanulate flowers, sharp pointed, violet to mauve or white (rarely pink) and a central boss of yellow stamens. Seed heads silky, spiky and attractive.
Flowering time: spring.
Use: for rock garden pockets, small beds, pots in alpine house.
Propagation: by seed or by very careful division.
Environment and light: full sun or very light shade.
Type of soil: good fertile soil, well-drained, with a little lime.
Soil moisture: water daily, quite sparingly, to keep the ground moist.
Remarks: if the winter is very severe, protect the plant with leaves and the like.

---

254 **LEATHER BERGENIA; PIG-SQUEAK; SAXIFRAGE**

Bergenia crassifolia (Megasea crassifolia):

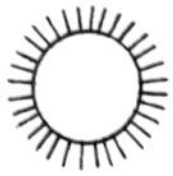

Family: Saxifragaceae. Named after Karl August von Bergen (1704–1760), Professor at Frankfurt.
Place of origin: Siberia; introduced into Europe in 1765.
Description: a coarse perennial with a thick woody rootstock which remains near the surface. Leaves large, tough, fleshy, oval or obovate, toothed; flowers in panicles on stout stems, pinkish-red.
Flowering time: late-winter–spring according to season, climate and zone.
Use: for large rock gardens, beds, borders, edging purposes and open places on banks or even in the wild garden. Leaves much favoured by flower arrangers.
Propagation: by division.
Environment and light: sun or half-shade, in open, cool places; stands up well to low temperatures.
Type of soil: good loamy soil.

255 CALENDULA; COMMON MARIGOLD; POT MARIGOLD; SCOTCH MARIGOLD

Calendula officinalis:

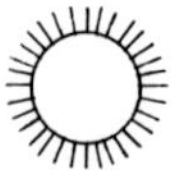

7

Family: Compositae. Name from Latin *calendae*, first of the month, referring to its long flowering season.
Place of origin: Mediterranean; introduced in 1573.
Description: a well-known hardy annual growing 1–2$\frac{1}{2}$ ft. (30–75 cm) tall, according to soil and variety and able to thrive in most gardens. Leaves oblong to oval, simple, thick, pungent, slightly rough to the touch; flowers in large heads (up to 4 in. (10 cm)), with ray and disk florets, orange or yellow. Double varieties are the most popular. Disk florets infertile.
Flowering time: all summer, but often forced for the winter market by florists.
Use: for flowerbeds and borders, window boxes, as cut flowers, container planting, winter pot plants at temperatures of 45°–60°F (7·2°–15·6°C). The petals are used for several culinary purposes.
Propagation: by seed.
Environment and light: full sun.
Type of soil: will grow on poorest soils but naturally do better on good land. Ideal: well-drained, neutral moist soil well-manured from a previous crop. Add a little super-phosphate.
Soil moisture: water if plants show signs of need.
Remarks: flowers are eaten and used to flavour soups.

---

256 LILY OF THE VALLEY

Convallaria majalis:

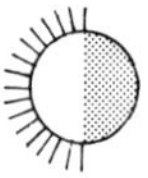

3

Family: Liliaceae. Name from Latin *convallis*, valley, referring to the plant's natural habitat.
Place of origin: throughout Europe (including Britain) except extreme north and south; temperate Asia.
Description: a charming perennial with slender creeping rhizomes, 2 radical leaves which are oval-lanceolate in shape and stemmed and arched racemes of white, drooping, bell-shaped flowers, individually 6-lobed and very fragrant. Varieties exist with lilac-pink flowers, double flowers and gold striped foliage.
Flowering time: late spring–early summer.
Use: for shady or half-shady beds and borders, and for cutting. Can also be forced for winter flowering. Sometimes used as a ground cover in shady areas.
Propagation: by division of the rhizomes in late summer.
Environment and light: shade or half-shade.
Type of soil: moist, acid (pH 4·5–6) with leaf-mould. Mulch in autumn with rotted leaf-mould or compost.
Soil moisture: water regularly during period of growth or in dry weather so that the soil is always moist; then reduce the amount of watering, and stop it altogether, so that the rhizomes can have a normal dormant period.

257 **CORNELIAN CHERRY**
Cornus mas:

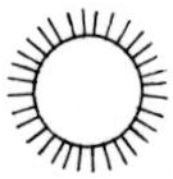

Family: Cornaceae. Latin name for this species.
Place of origin: Europe; cultivated for centuries in Britain.
Description: a deciduous shrub or small tree of open habit, covered in early spring with short-stalked umbels of yellow flowers, backed by yellowish bracts. These come from the joints of the previous year's wood and are about $\frac{3}{4}$ in. (2 cm) across. Leaves ovate, slender pointed, dull green. Fruits bright red, of acid flavour.
Flowering time: late winter–early spring depending on zone.
Use: to make small clumps, or as isolated specimens. Grown for early yellow flowers and edible fruits which, however, are only plentiful following a hot summer.
Propagation: by layering or cuttings.
Environment and light: full sun.
Type of soil: any good garden soil.

④

---

258 **CORYDALIS**
Corydalis solida:

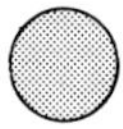

Family: Papaveraceae. Name from Greek *korydalis*, lark, referring to the spurs behind the flowers which resemble the long hind-claws of larks.
Place of origin: Europe including Britain.
Description: a smooth perennial herbaceous plant with a tuberous rootstock and a single erect stem about 12 in. (30 cm) high. Leaves 3 or 4, much incised into wedge-shaped segments; flowers purple-pink, 4-petalled, usually joined at the base with spurs behind.
Flowering time: spring.
Use: for rock gardens, to decorate old walls etc.; for borders.
Propagation: by division of the rhizomes in spring.
Environment and light: half-shade.
Type of soil: moist, well-drained, rather light soil.

⑦

259 **CROCUS**

Crocus neapolitanus (C. vernus):

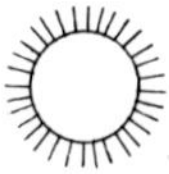

(3)

Family: Iridaceae. Name from Greek *krokos*, saffron; saffron is obtained from *C. sativus*.
Place of origin: Europe.
Description: a variable species from which have come many wild and garden varieties, including the so-called Dutch crocuses. Small corms; leaves long, linear with white lines running down their centres. Flowers white to purple, tubed, flaring to funnel-shaped; self-coloured, solitary flowers on 3–4 in. (7–10 cm) stems or blooms variously feathered with light or dark shades.
Flowering time: spring.
Use: for borders, flowerbeds, rocky spots, and naturalised in grass or light woodland. For forcing in bowls for the home or alpine house.
Propagation: by division of the corms which form at the foot of the plant in late summer.
Environment and light: sun.
Type of soil: good garden soil, with sand and peat added to help drainage.
Remarks: corms do particularly well in zones 7 northwards.

---

260 **BORDER FORSYTHIA; FORSYTHIA; GOLDEN BELL**

Forsythia × intermedia:

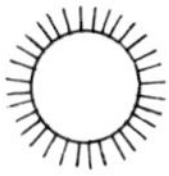

(4)

Family: Oleaceae; named after William Forsyth (1737–1804), Superintendent of the Royal Gardens, Kensington Palace and one of the original founders of the Royal Horticultural Society.
Description: a garden hybrid between *Forsythia suspensa* and *F. viridissima*, a robust shrub with simple or 3-partite leaves which are simple, opposite and dentate. Flowers rich yellow, before the foliage, from lateral buds on previous year's wood; calyx and corolla 4-lobed.
Flowering time: late winter–spring, depending on zone. Cut branches can be forced in winter in gentle heat.
Use: as a garden or park plant for isolated groups and for making hedges.
Propagation: by cuttings of bare wood in autumn, about 9 in. (23 cm) long, rooted in frames or outside (in Britain). Summer cuttings (in leaf) rooted in sand with bottom heat or mist.
Environment and light: full sun, also very light shade.
Type of soil: not fussy but best if rich and well-drained.
Soil moisture: water in summer in dry weather.

261 FREESIA

Freesia refracta:

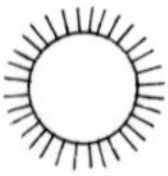

(9)

Family: Iridaceae. Named after a German physician Friedrich Heinrich Theodor Freese (d. 1876).
Place of origin: Southern Africa; in Europe since 1875.
Description: a slender plant of about 18 in. (45 cm) with bright green, linear leaves arising from small corms and one sided spikes of richly scented, tubular flowers with 6 divisions. These are basically yellow but forms exist having white, mauve, purple, pink, red and violet flowers; also full doubles in similar shades. All are delightfully fragrant.
Flowering time: spring, but the season can be prolonged by growing retarded corms.
Use: for greenhouse decoration; as cut flowers; outdoors in warm temperate zones.
Propagation: seed sown in light sandy soil under cover. Seedlings do not transplant well so sow the seed thinly in pots and thin at the earliest opportunity. Sunny situation but sheltered from mid-day sun.
Environment and light: after flowering keep plants cool, but water and feed them until the foliage dies down.
Type of soil: garden soil with peat and sand.
Soil moisture: water regularly in the growing season until flowering. When the leaves are dry, the bulbs should be removed from the ground and kept in a dry, cool place until replanting in the autumn.

---

262 SPRING GENTIAN

Gentiana verna:

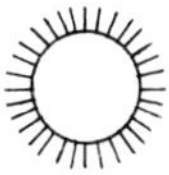

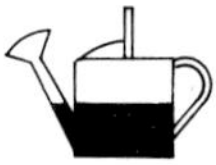

(4)

Family: Gentianaceae. Named after King Gentius of Illyria, circa 500 B.C., who discovered the medicinal properties of *G. lutea* roots.
Place of origin: Europe (including Britain), Asia.
Description: a tufted perennial to 4 in. (10 cm), with erect, unbranched stems. Basal leaves elliptic-lanceolate, half as wide as long; stem leaves smaller and ovate. Flowers solitary, terminal, saucer-shaped, deep blue but variable from white and pale blue to deep purple-blue.
Flowering time: late spring–early summer depending on zone.
Use: not an easy plant to cultivate but worth the effort. Rock gardens, sink gardens, alpine houses.
Propagation: by seed in spring or by division.
Environment and light: sunny to half-shade, but always in damp places.
Type of soil: loose and mainly calcareous.
Soil moisture: water regularly so that the ground is always moist.

263 HYACINTH

Hyacinthus orientalis:

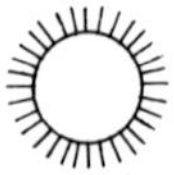

6

Family: Liliaceae. Old Greek name.
Place of origin: Balkans and Asia Minor.
Description: the well-known florist's hyacinths are derived from this species and few plants adapt so well to forcing for winter bloom. The bulbs are large, with white, violet or blue scales. Leaves 4 or 6, linear, fleshy, hooded at tip; flowers of various colours—white, yellow, pink, red, blue to purple in long, closely packed spikes, individually bell-shaped with 6 outward curving divisions, very fragrant.
The slender Roman hyacinth, var. "Albula" from Southern France has white flowers and is more delicate but among the first to bloom after forcing.
Flowering time: spring.
Use: for forcing for indoor bloom or as a greenhouse plant; for formal bedding outdoors or grouped in borders, window boxes and other containers and for cut flowers.
Propagation: by separation of the bulbils, but this is not easy, and flowering occurs only after four years; it is best to buy new bulbs each year from Holland.
Environment and light: half-shade, sunny.
Type of soil: deep loam fertilized, with peat and sand.
Soil moisture: water regularly, sparingly, reduce and stop after flowering; once the leaves are dry, the bulbs should be dug up, left to dry and then stored.

---

264 WINTER JASMINE

Jasminum nudiflorum:

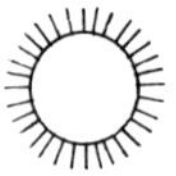

5

Family: Oleaceae. Latinized Arabic name for jasmine.
Place of origin: China; introduced to Europe in 1844.
Description: a deciduous shrub of loose, pendent habit; slender green shoots carrying many solitary, axillary, 6-lobed, bright yellow flowers ($\frac{3}{4}$–1 in. (2–2·5 cm)) before the leaves which are 3-foliate, opposite, smooth.
Flowering time: in southern regions, late winter; elsewhere from early spring.
Use: in cool temperate climates as a wall shrub; in protected positions or warm temperate zones as solitary free-standing specimens; for loose hedging.
Propagation: by layers or cuttings of ripe wood in autumn in sandy soil in a frame, or rooted with mist in mid-summer.
Environment and light: full sun or part shade.
Type of soil: light with plenty of humus and sand.
Soil moisture: water in dry springs or summer.
Remarks: this plant must be boldly pruned after flowering by cutting back flowering shoots almost to the old wood. They then make strong young shoots to carry next season's flowers.

265 GRAPE HYACINTH

Muscari szovitsianum:

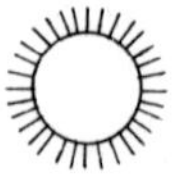

(3)

Family: Liliaceae. Turkish name.
Place of origin: northern Persia, Caucasus.
Description: a slender species, closely allied to *M. armeniacum* but paler in colour. Bulb globose and fleshy; leaves grass-like, linear, beginning to grow in the autumn; flowers flask-shaped, borne in dense racemes, faintly scented.
Flowering time: spring.
Use: for edging flowerbeds, rockeries, paths etc. Naturalize in sunny places as in open woodland or in grass.
Propagation: spreads naturally by division and seed; or by offsets in late summer.
Environment and light: full sun.
Type of soil: rich, open, well-drained soil; do not object to lime. Top-dress with good soil in spring.
Remarks: do not leave bulbs long out of the ground.

---

266 FORGET-ME-NOT

Myosotis sylvatica:

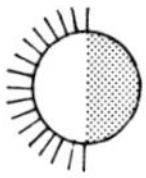

(3)

Family: Boraginaceae. Name from Greek *mus*, mouse and *otos*, eat, referring to shape of the leaves.
Place of origin: Europe including Britain.
Description: charming plants for spring flowering, either in the open or under glass. Bushy perennials, 8–12 in. (20–30 cm) high with narrow, pointed, alternate rough-hairy leaves and axillary sprays of bright blue, gold-eyed, 5-petalled flowers. Pale pink, light blue and white forms occur.
Flowering time: spring.
Use: as a bedding background to tulips and other spring flowers; for deep drifts in the wild garden; for edging borders, as winter pot plants and for cutting.
Propagation: plants usually increase naturally from dropped seed. Shake old plants over spare ground; the seedlings can be planted out in the autumn.
Environment and light: plants do best in partial shade but sun is all right if the ground is very moist.
Type of soil: deep, moist, rich in humus and slightly acid. Must be well-drained or plants will die in winter.
Soil moisture: apart from pot plants which require regular attention water only when absolutely necessary.
Remarks: North of zone 6 treated as annual or biennial.

267 & 268 NARCISSUS; Daffodil

Narcissus: sp.

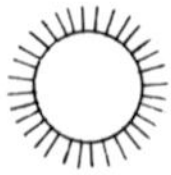

4

Family: Amaryllidaceae. Classical Greek name for a handsome youth who was so entranced with his own beauty that the gods turned him into a flower.
Place of origin: Europe, Mediterranean area and W. Asia.
Description: handsome and well-known bulbous plants with a multiplicity of garden uses. Leaves long and narrow, usually flat but sometimes rush-like. Flowers variable but usually with 6 perianth segments and an inner cup or corona of varying lengths. Ovary inferior. The genus is difficult from a taxonomic point of view and has accordingly been split up (Royal Horticultural Society and American Daffodil Society) into 11 divisions. These are subdivided again according to colour and relative measurements of the perianth and corona.
Bulbocodium group: large funnel shaped coronas; perianth segments small and strap-like. Usually small like hoop-petticoats.
Cyclamineus group: small moisture lovers with reflexed perianth segments and long tubular coronas. Example: *N. cyclamineus Jonquils:* Noted for their rich scent and bunches of short-cupped flowers with rushy stems (See No. 269).
Poeticus group: Showy, sweetly scented, starry, short-cupped flowers with white perianth segments.
Tazettas: Sweetly fragrant, bunch flowered, popular for early forcing. Example: Paper whites.
Triandrus group; small rock garden or alpine house sorts 6–12 in. (15–30 cm). Example: "April Tears".
Larger narcissi are split according to the size of the corona. *Trumpet:* trumpet or corona as long as or longer than the perianth segments. *Large-cupped:* corona more than $\frac{1}{3}$ but less than the length of the perianth segments. (Example No. 268).
Small cupped (less than $\frac{1}{3}$ of the perianth segments. (See No. 267).
Additionally there are doubles and species. Although yellow of various shades are the main colours for narcissi, whites, pinks and reds appear in certain coronas or perianth segments—or both.
The illustration is of a small cupped narcissus of garden origin with medium to large flowers, having flat, pure white perianth segments and a large, flat, cherry-red corona.
Flowering time: spring depending on zone and breed.
Use: for bedding, wild garden naturalising, forcing, pots in greenhouses, containers, rock gardens, growing in grass etc.
Propagation: by offsets.
Environment and light: full sun or light shade.
Type of soil: moist, well-drained, on heavy side.
Soil moisture: water regularly, but do not let water stagnate.

8

Remarks: plants are best north of zone 8, except for the Tazettas (only hardy in 8–10) Bulbocodiums, cyclamineus and jonquils 6–10.

269 JONQUIL

Narcissus jonquilla:

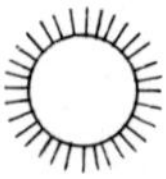

6

Family: Amaryllidaceae.
Place of origin: South Europe and Algeria.
Description: a plant with nearly round, rush-like leaves, grooved and quite long, with bright yellow flowers, in groups of 2–6, orange-scented, with a very flared and slightly puckered corona. There is a double form known as "Queen Anne's Jonquil".
Flowering time: spring.
Use: for parks and gardens, borders and flowerbeds, rockeries and slopes.
Propagation: by offsets of bulbs.
Environment and light: sunny.
Type of soil: no special requirements, but best if the substratum is made up of good garden soil with sand and peat.
Soil moisture: the ground must be fairly moist, but never waterlogged.

---

270 POET'S NARCISSUS

Narcissus poeticus "Actaea":

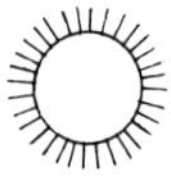

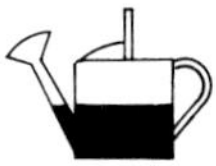

6

Family: Amaryllidaceae.
Place of origin: Southern Europe (Spain to Greece).
Description: the latest flowering narcissi belong to this group, of which "Actaea" is perhaps the best and most popular variety. Flowers very sweet-scented, perianth segments white, cup shallow with canary-yellow eye, edged red. Height 17 in. (42 cm).
Flowering time: spring.
Use: good garden plant and for cutting; can be forced for February bloom.
Propagation: by division of bulbs.
Environment and light: full sun.
Type of soil: good garden soil mixed with sand and peat so that the substratum is light and loose.
Soil moisture: never over-water; but enough to keep the ground fresh, without being too wet.

271 PERSIAN BUTTERCUP; PERSIAN RANUNCULUS

Ranunculus asiaticus:

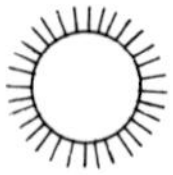

8

Family: Ranunculaceae. Name from Latin, *rana*, frog. Many of the species, like the frog, inhabit damp places.
Place of origin: Asia Minor.
Description: the wild species is no longer cultivated, but hybrids are very colourful with large double or semi-double buttercup-like flowers in shades of yellow, orange, scarlet, crimson, pink and white. Height 12–15 in. (30–45 cm). Leaves deeply cut and divided. Roots tuberous with divisions known as "claws".
Flowering time: summer.
Use: for grassy areas which are cool and damp, to create small clumps near water, streams etc.
Propagation: by division.
Environment and light: full sun, sheltered spot.
Type of soil: light, well-drained; plant tubers "claw" side down, $1\frac{1}{2}$ in. (4 cm) deep and cover with sand and then soil.
Soil moisture: the ground should be moist.

---

272 SPANISH BLUEBELL; SPANISH SQUILL

Scilla hispanica (now more correctly *Endymion hispanicus (S. campanulatus):*

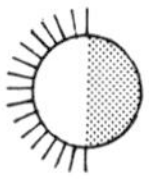

5

Family: Liliaceae. Name from Greek *skilla*, squill, originally applied to *Urginea scilla*.
Place of origin: Spain, Portugal.
Description: a stout bulbous plant of 18 in. (45 cm), with smooth, strap-shaped leaves and sturdy spikes of scentless, bell-shaped flowers varying in colour from pale china-blue to deep blue or indigo. White and lilac-pink forms also occur. The plant is larger than the English bluebell (*Endymion* (*Scilla*) *non-scriptus*).
Flowering time: late spring.
Use: to make small, isolated clumps in shady borders, large rockeries, woodlands, shrubberies or to naturalise.
Propagation: by seed or division. Bulbs fairly large and fleshy so should not be left long out of the ground or disturbed frequently. Plant 3 in. (7 cm) deep.
Environment and light: light shade; do best in moist heavy loam and the dappled shade cast by tall trees, e.g. in light woodland, shrubberies etc.
Type of soil: add sand and peat to ordinary garden soil to make for good drainage, and water retention.
Soil moisture: the bluebell stands up to dryness better than wetness; too much water can damage the bulbs.

273 PERUVIAN SQUILL

Scilla peruviana:

6

Family: Liliaceae.
Place of origin: Mediterranean region; introduced into Britain in 1607.
Description: popularly but erroneously known as Cuban lily or Peruvian squill, this is an interesting European bulb which produces a rosette of 6–9 strap-shaped leaves. The dense conical flowerheads elongate with age and may have up to 100 brilliant blue, reddish-lilac or white (according to variety) florets on one 9 in. (23 cm) stem.
Flowering time: late spring–early summer.
Use: for borders, rockeries, slopes and banks in partial shade.
Propagation: by seed or division.
Environment and light: half-shade. Plant 4 in. (10 cm) deep.
Type of soil: garden soil with sand and peat added for good drainage.

---

274 TULIP

Tulipa gesneriana:

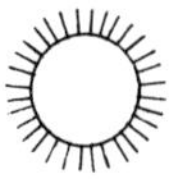

3

Family: Liliaceae. Name from Turkish *tulbend*, a turban.
Place of origin: S.E. Europe and central Asia; introduced into N. Europe from 1554 onwards.
Description: a genus of some 100 species, of varying heights and seasons of flowering. Cultivars are legion. Bulbs large with rich brown skins; leaves broad or linear; flowers borne single (or in twos and threes rarely), erect, large, shapely with 6 perianth segments in various colours or combinations of shades.
Flowering time: late winter–early summer, according to species (earlier by forcing) and depending on zone.
Use: for formal bedding, grouped in mixed borders, window boxes etc., and as cut flowers.
Propagation: by offsets of bulbs.
Environment and light: full sun to half-shade.
Type of soil: tulips enjoy heavier soil than most bulbs, the ideal being heavy well-drained loam. Plant bulbs in early winter if tulip fire disease is feared. For pot work use equal parts of loam, peat and sand.
Soil moisture: water regularly, sparingly but seldom.
Remarks: most varieties do not do well south of zone 7 or 8 except some large flowered types.

275 BAND-PLANT; CUT-FINGER

Vinca major:

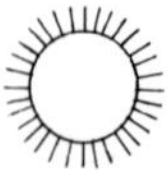

Family: Apocynaceae. Name from Latin *vincio*, to bind; the long shoots have been used as a styptic to stop bleeding.
Place of origin: Europe (including Britain).
Description: a hardy perennial with long trailing stems, often rooting at their tips. Leaves ovate or with heart-shaped bases; flowers salver-shaped, 5-lobed, blue-purple. The variegated leaved variety "Variegata" is a particularly desirable plant.
Flowering time: spring–early summer.
Use: for shady banks, under trees in woodland, shrubberies or the wild garden.
Propagation: by cuttings in spring or autumn; by division.
Environment and light: any soil type in sun or light shade. Inclined to spread but easy to keep in check.
Soil moisture: damp soil is the ideal.

⑤

---

276 LESSER PERIWINKLE; MYRTLE

Vinca minor:

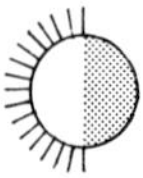

Family: Apocynaceae.
Place of origin: Europe, including Britain.
Description: perennial herbaceous plant with 8 in.–2 ft. (20–60 cm) prostrate stems. Leaves elliptic-ovate, 1–1½ in. (2·5–4 cm) long, smooth, entire, opposite and somewhat shiny. Flowers blue-purple with 5 lobes, 1 in. (2·5 cm) across. Varieties are available with variegated leaves; white, lavender and deep purple flowers; also double, in purple, reddish-purple and rich blue.
Flowering time: spring.
Use: as ground cover in shady flowerbeds or rockeries, shrubberies or shady places. Also makes a good pot plant.
Propagation: by cuttings or division.
Environment and light: half-shade to total shade.
Type of soil: leaf-mould with peat and wood-loam.
Soil moisture: keep soil damp.

⑤

277 SWEET VIOLET; VIOLET

Viola odorata:

Family: Violaceae. Latin name for a variety of fragrant flowers.
Place of origin: Europe, including Britain.
Description: perennial plants of low stature with short rhizomes producing long rooting runners. Leaves, broadly ovate to heart-shaped, crenate, long-stalked; flowers deep violet, lilac, white or pink, about $\frac{3}{4}$ in. (2 cm) long, sweetly scented with 5 irregular segments. Garden forms larger, often double and in various shades.
Flowering time: spring.
Use: for hedgerow planting, warm banks, light woodland, amongst shrubs etc. Larger named sorts for pot or frame culture and as cut flowers.
Propagation: by division after flowering or seed.
Environment and light: total or partial shade.
Type of soil: any good moist garden soil, preferably on the heavy side. Add decayed compost to maintain fertility.

---

278 GARDEN PANSY

Viola × wittrokiana (V. tricolor hortensis):

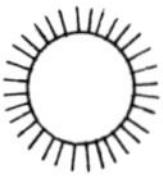

Family: Violaceae.
Description: a popular annual or short-lived perennial, obtained by hybridising and selecting forms derived from *V. tricolor* crossed with various other species. Height 4–9 in. (10–23 cm), stems leafy, terminating in large rounded flowers about 2 in. (5 cm) across with prominent basal markings on the 5 irregular petals. Leaves rounded or oblong, dentate, long-stalked. Flower colours and patterns vary.
Flowering time: spring–mid-summer.
Use: for edging borders, underplanting, container planting, rock garden pockets, slopes and for cutting.
Propagation: by cuttings rooted in sandy soil in spring in a propagating frame or in summer in cold frames. Shade until rooted; also by seed.
Environment and light: sunny to very light.
Type of soil: cool, moist; add compost to light soils.
Soil moisture: water in summer to keep ground moist.
Remarks: old flowers must be regularly removed or plants stop blooming. Pansies do best in cool climates, treated as annuals further north and south.

LILIES, AMARYLLIS AND THEIR LIKE

279 ALOE FEROX

Aloe ferox:

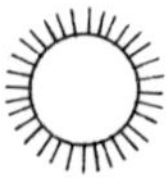

Family: Liliaceae. Arabic name for these succulents.
Place of origin: Natal; introduced to Europe in circa mid-eighteenth century.

Description: a succulent perennial with rosettes of striking leaves on 10–12 ft. (3–3·6 m) trunks. Leaves long and tapering from wide bases, glaucous-green, fleshy, spiny thorned (with reddish teeth) along the edges and on the upper surface. Flowers in long conical spikes, individually tubular, orange.
Flowering time: late spring.

Use: chiefly grown for its spectacular foliage; flowers only produced in warm or hot climates, where it is suitable for banks, key positions and rocky slopes. Frost-prone areas; grow in containers, outside in summer but wintered under glass.
Propagation: by offsets from the base of adult plants.
Environment and light: full sun.
Type of soil: well-drained, loam and peat or leaf-mould with plenty of sand and a little bonemeal.

Soil moisture: water as required during the growing period, little or none in the resting period.
Remarks: repot every two or three years. Plant is used medicinally in veterinary medication.

---

280 PERUVIAN LILY

Alstroemeria pelegrina:

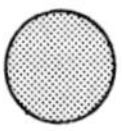

Family: Alstroemeriaceae. Named after Baron Claus Alstroemer (1736–1794), friend of Linnaeus.
Place of origin: Chile; in Europe since 1754.
Description: herbaceous plant with thick fibrous roots, leafy stems and terminal umbels of showy flowers. Height 2 ft. (60 cm). Leaves variable, lanceolate, to 2 in. (5 cm); flowers lilac, spotted red-purple, 2 in. (5 cm). Other colours appear under cultivation like "Alba" which has white flowers.

Flowering time: summer but can be earlier or later.
Use: for cut flowers or border decoration. Not hardy in cool temperate regions but may be planted out in spring, lifted after flowering and stored in damp soil for winter. Also for pot plants for greenhouses, but repot annually.

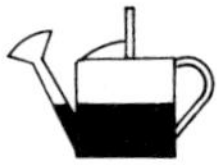

Propagation: by division or by seed.
Environment and light: shade or full sun.
Type of soil: deep, loose, rich and moist do not let it become waterlooged.

Soil moisture: water to keep soil moist.
Remarks: the roots are a source of starch which have provided Amerindians with food.

281 BELLADONNA LILY
Amaryllis belladonna:

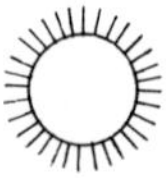

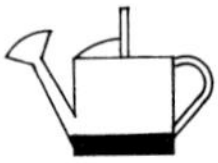

9

Family: Amaryllidaceae. Named after the shepherd, Amaryllis, in classical poetry.
Place of origin: South Africa.
Description: a monotypic genus, the species a showy, late-flowering bulb. Leaves strap-shaped, channelled, appearing in winter or early spring. Flowers large, funnel-shaped, 6 parted, rose-red or paler, sweet-scented, on stout 18–30 in. (45–75 cm) stems, before the foliage in autumn.
Flowering time: early autumn.
Use: in temperate climates, against sunny walls or as pot plants; in climates with mild winters, in small flower beds or borders.
Propagation: by division of the bulbs at the base of the mother plant.
Environment and light: full sun.
Type of soil: plant bulbs 6–9 in. (15–23 cm) deep. Equal parts good fibrous loam, leaf-mould and sand.
Soil moisture: water quite sparingly, only as required.
Remarks: hardy. Cover with 1–2 in. (2–5 cm) soil. Reasonably hardy zones 5–8. Cover 9 in. (22 cm) of soil and give plenty of sun and shelter.

---

282 BRODIAEA; GRASSNUT; ITHURIEL'S SPEAR
Brodiaea laxa (syn. *Tritelia laxa*):

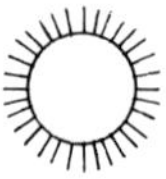

6

Family: Alliaceae. Named after James Brodie of Brodie (1744–1824), Scottish botanist.
Place of origin: western America, in particular California.
Description: closely related to *allium* and bearing its flowers similarly in umbels at the tops of smooth naked stems. Bulbs corm-like and leaves narrow and grassy. *B. laxa* is one of the finest with 30 or more pale violet-mauve, funnel-shaped flowers.
Flowering time: late spring–early summer.
Use: for rock garden pockets, borders, pots etc., and for cut flowers.
Propagation: by seed sown as soon as ripe or by separation of the bulblets.
Environment and light: warm sunny situation such as clearings in woodland, warm borders close to walls and similar. Deep rooting and hardy over most of Britain and Europe except in severe winters.
Type of soil: well-drained, warm for preference, sandy and light but enriched with some humus.
Soil moisture: water only if necessary; water pot plants whilst growing.

283 KAFFIR LILY; NATAL LILY
Clivia miniata:

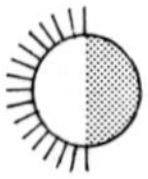

9

Family: Amaryllidaceae. Named after Charlotte, Duchess of Northumberland, née Clive, (d. 1866) (descendant of Clive of India) who first flowered the plant.
Place of origin: South Africa.
Description: a fine bulbous plant with evergreen, leathery, strap-shaped foliage arranged in double rows. Flowers funnel-shaped, with 6 perianth segments and 6 stamens, orange-red with yellow throats. Also yellow and deep red in cultivars.
Flowering time: winter–spring and sometimes early summer.
Use: in tubs or large pots in greenhouses or sun lounges; also as a house plant. Minimum winter temperature 50°F (10°C). In frost-free climates in beds in light shade of trees.
Propagation: by division.
Environment and light: well-lit but never in direct sun.
Type of soil: equal parts of fibrous loam, decayed manure, leaf-mould or peat and coarse sand. Top dress pots after flowering.
Soil moisture: water plentifully in growing period, very little after flowering.
Remarks: plants dislike disturbance and flower most freely when crowded.

---

284 CAPE LILY; JAMAICA CRINUM
*Crinum bulbispermum (*syn. *C. longifolium):*

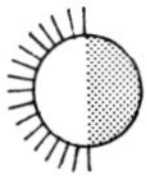

8

Family: Amaryllidaceae. Name from Greek *krinon*, lily, referring to its appearance.
Place of origin: Natal, Transvaal; introduced in 1750.
Description: evergreen, long-necked, ovoid bulbs, long strap-shaped, grey-green, fleshy, floppy leaves 3 ft. (1 m) long. Stalks 12 in. (30 cm), fleshy, carrying 6–12 fragrant white flowers which are pink flushed outside. The species is one parent of the popular *C. × powellii.*
Flowering time: early summer.
Use: pot plants, greenhouse borders and flowerbeds.
Propagation: by division of the offshoots.
Environment and light: cool and frost-prone areas; warm and sunny, fairly dry borders against walls and protected in winter with leaves etc. Cold climates; greenhouse borders or large pots. Sub-tropics and warm areas as border plants.
Type of soil: rich with humus mixed with sand.
Soil moisture: needs plenty of moisture during the growing season but keep almost dry in winter.
Remarks: Crinums resent disturbance so leave pot plants alone for five years or so. Plant with necks above soil level. If planted out of doors in zones 6–7, mulch with wood chips or leaves in winter.

285 GIANT SUMMER HYACINTH; SPIRE LILY

Galtonia candicans (Hyacinthus candicans):

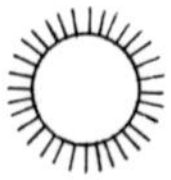

8

Family: Liliaceae. Named after Sir Francis Galton (1822–1911), anthropologist and South African explorer.
Place of origin: Natal, South Africa; introduced into Europe in 1870.
Description: a useful summer-blooming herbaceous plant with a large round, tunicated bulb; long strap-shaped basal leaves up to $2\frac{1}{2}$ ft. (75 cm.) long and long slender stems of up to 4 ft. (1·2 m) or more, carrying loose racemes of white, scented, pendent, funnel-shaped flowers each about $1\frac{1}{2}$ in. (4 cm) in length.
Flowering time: summer.
Use: for grouping in borders, flowerbeds and on lawns, forcing in conservatories etc.
Propagation: by offsets or seed. Self-set plants often arise and can be carefully transplanted. They flower in 3 years from seed.
Environment and light: sunny, well-drained, light but rich soil. Plant bulbs 6–7 in. (15–18 cm) deep.
Type of soil: light, loose, permeable.
Remarks: hardy in all but most exposed parts of the temperate zones in colder parts protect with leaves as a precautionary measure in winter. In zones 5–7 give mulch of leaves, salt hay or wood chips in winter.

---

286 BLOOD FLOWER; BLOOD LILY

Haemanthus puniceus:

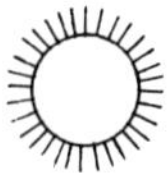

9

Family: Amaryllidaceae. Name from Greek *haima*, blood and *anthos*, flower.
Place of origin: South Africa.
Description: handsome plants with round, thick bulbs about 2 in. (5 cm) across by 2–4 in. (5–10 cm) long; wavy-edged and nerved, brilliant green leaves about 9 in. (23 cm), long and dense round heads of bright scarlet flowers with long anthers on 1 ft. (30 cm) stems.
Flowering time: early summer.
Use: walls, areas not subject to severe frost: at base of warm walls, 4 in. (10 cm) deep. In small beds in tropics. Cold areas: in pots in greenhouses or tubs taken under cover in winter.
Propagation: by offsets.
Environment and light: full sun in warm climates; potted plants need warmth and light.
Type of soil: equal parts of rich fibrous loam, peat or leaf-mould, decayed compost or cow-manure with enough sand to ensure quick drainage.
Soil moisture: water as required during growing season. When leaves turn yellow and die stop watering; rest bulbs until spring. Restart with warmth and moisture.
Remarks: Does better when roots are confined.

287 DAY LILY; EARLY DAY LILY

Hemerocallis dumortieri:

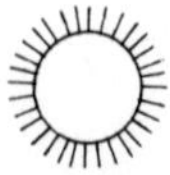

Family: Liliaceae. Name from Greek *hemera*, day and *kallos*, beauty; the flowers only last a day.
Place of origin: Japan; introduced into Europe in 1832.
Description: strong growing herbaceous perennial of $1\frac{1}{2}$–2 ft. (45–60 cm) with thick fleshy roots and tufts of stiffly ascending, strap-shaped leaves about 18 in. (45 cm) long and 1 in. (5 cm) wide. Flowers funnel-shaped, in stalked clusters near tops of stems, soft apricot-orange, brownish externally, perianth segments pointed.

Flowering time: mid spring–late summer.
Use: for mixed borders, flowerbeds, light woodland, isolated clumps.

Propagation: by division after dormant period, namely in spring in northern regions and late autumn in southern ones.
Environment and light: full sun or partial shade.
Type of soil: any good garden soil, preferably fairly moist with added humus.
Soil moisture: water only under dry arid conditions.

2

---

288 LEMON DAY LILY

Hemerocallis lilio-asphodelus (syn. *H. flava*):

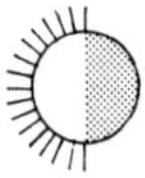

Family: Liliaceae.
Place of origin: temperate zones of E. Asia, China, Japan. Also now naturalised in Central Europe; introduced into Britain in 1570.
Description: a widely distributed species found in nature in damp, low-lying meadows and one of the earliest to bloom. Fibrous fleshy roots and short underground rhizomes. Leaves linear, radical, in 2 ranks, ascending, spreading and recurving, 30–36 in. (75–90 cm) long. Flowers on slender scapes just above foliage; few branched, lemon-chrome, pleasantly scented. The species is the parent of many garden hybrids.

Flowering time: late spring–mid-summer.
Use: for mixed borders, flowerbeds, isolated clumps and undergrowth.

Propagation: by division after the dormant period, in spring in northern regions and late autumn in southern regions.
Environment and light: half-shade or full sun.
Type of soil: ordinary garden soil with humus.
Soil moisture: water regularly in dry weather, so that the ground is always moist.

2

289 AMARYLLIS

Hippeastrum: hybr.

Family: Amaryllidaceae.
Description: of hybrid origin, the first cultivar was raised by Arthur Johnson in 1799 by crossing *H. reginae* with *H. vittatum*. Today's cultivars include scarlet, pink, crimson, deep red and white forms, often striped, mottled or blended with other shades. The flowers are trumpet-shaped, with 6 perianth segments, huge, about 4 per stem and on stout, smooth stems. Leaves broadly strap-shaped.
Use: for indoor culture use "prepared" bulbs of good size. In temperate climates grow in warm sheltered situations, take under cover in winter. Good cut flowers for florists.
Propagation: by offsets, bulbs or seeds for new varieties.
Environment and light: give pot plants bottom heat to start them (e.g. by standing them in a box of peat placed over a radiator or warm pipes). Temperature 55°–65°F (13°–18°C) to start; 60°F (15·6°C) when flower spikes appear.
Type of soil: rich, well-drained. For pot plants, use fibrous loam, mushroom compost and gritty sand.
Soil moisture: water throughout the growing season but stop when the foliage yellows and dies. Withhold all water from then until bulbs are restarted the following spring. Evergreen but do best when forced to rest.

---

290 AMARYLLIS; BARBADOS LILY; EQUESTRIAN STAR-FLOWER

Hippeastrum equestre:

Family: Amaryllidaceae. Name from Greek *hippeus*, equestrian knight and *astron*, star.
Place of origin: West Indies; introduced in 1725.
Description: a handsome species with globose and stoloniferous bulbs. Leaves radical, strap-shaped, glaucous green; flowers funnel-shaped, vivid scarlet, green at base, 4–5 in. (10–13 cm) across. There is a double form.
Flowering time: grows prolifically in warm countries, but summer flowering in Europe and most of the United States. "Prepared" bulbs can be forced to earlier bloom.
Use: as indoor plant or for cut flowers.
Propagation: division of bulbs in dormant period.
Environment and light: full sun to half-shade, and draught-free. Sunny outdoors, protected with bracken, wood chips etc. or a light frame in winter. Shade pot plants from direct sun.
Type of soil: rich, deep but porous and well-drained. For pot plants use equal parts of grit, fibrous loam and decayed cow-manure or mushroom compost.
Soil moisture: water occasionally at start of growing season; increase until flowering time, then reduce and stop when leaves begin to yellow. Never over-water.

291 AMARYLLIS

Hippeastrum vittatum:

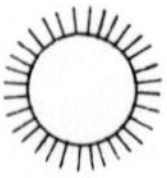

9

Family: Amaryllidaceae.
Place of origin: central Andes; introduced into Britain in 1769.
Description: a vigorous species with 6–8, 2 ft. (60 cm) long, bright green, strap-shaped leaves. Flowers creamy-white with red stripes, 4–5 in. (10–13 cm) across. Each 2 ft. (60 cm) flowering stem carries about 3 or 4 blooms.
Flowering time: spring.
Use: as greenhouse or indoor plants; grown in pots or sheltered beds in suitable, mild areas.
Propagation: by division of bulbs during dormant period.
Environment and light: sun outdoors, light shade in tropics. Indoors full sun to half-shade, and draught-free.
Type of soil: equal parts of fibrous loam, leaf-mould, well-rotted organic material and sand or grit.
Soil moisture: as for No 290.

---

292 FRAGRANT PLANTAIN LILY; PLANTAIN LILY

Hosta plantaginea (H. subcordata):

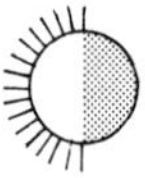

5

Family: Liliaceae. Name commemorates Nicholaus Tomas Host (1761–1834), Austrian physician.
Place of origin: China; introduced into Britain in 1789.
Description: fine foliaged herbaceous perennials related to *Hermerocallis*. Leaves large, radical, ovate-cordate, yellowish-green with prominent longitudinal veins. Flowers fragrant, in short racemes, individually tubular with 6 spreading lobes, white.
Flowering time: mid-summer to early autumn.
Use: in key positions where fine foliage effects can be appreciated—as in containers, shady borders, near a gate or garden pool etc.
Propagation: by division in spring as new growth is starting.
Environment and light: light to full shade, according to locality—sun burns the foliage.
Type of soil: light, moist, sandy, well-fertilized.
Soil moisture: water so that the soil is moist to the touch, never sodden.
Remarks: clumps improve with age so don't disturb more than necessary. Often known as *Funkia*.

293 CHALICE-CROWNED SEA DAFFODIL; PERUVIAN DAFFODIL; SPIDER LILY

Hymenocallis narcissiflora (syn. *H. calathina*):

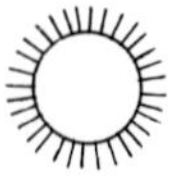

8

Family: Amaryllidaceae. Name from Greek *hymen*, membrane and *kallos*, beautiful, referring to the corona.
Place of origin: Peruvian Andes; in Europe since 1794.
Description: a globose bulb with an elongated, cylindrical neck. Leaves strap-shaped, in double rows, up to 2 ft. (60 cm) long. Flowers about 3 in. (8 cm) across, carried in umbels of 2–8, white fragrant, with wide corona with wavy margin and linked by stamens, the whole set off by 6 narrow, spidery segments. Tube at back of flowers greenish.
Flowering time: spring.
Use: outdoors only in open, sunny situations and reasonably frost-free areas. Elsewhere in the greenhouse. Tropics; grow in shade in moist woodland or island beds in grass.
Propagation: by offsets or seed (the latter blooms in 3–4 years).
Environment and light: well-lit, draught-free.
Type of soil: loam, leaf-mould or peat, mushroom compost or decayed cow-manure in equal parts with a liberal helping of coarse sand or grit.
Soil moisture: keep fairly dry until growth starts, give plenty of water in the growing season. Dry in winter.
Remarks: if grown further north winter under cover.

---

294 RED HOT POKER; TORCH LILY

Kniphofia (Tritoma) uvaria:

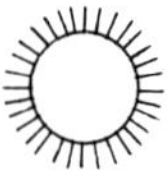

7

Family: Liliaceae. Named after Johann Hieronymous Kniphof (1704–1763), author of a work devoted to nature-printed illustrations of plants (1747).
Place of origin: South Africa; in Europe since 1707.
Description: noble grassy-leaved plants with conspicuous spikes of brilliant coral-red, tubular, drooping tubular flowers with long stamens. These are borne in dense oval-oblong racemes and become orange and yellow with age. Leaves evergreen, widely strap-shaped, $1\frac{1}{2}$–3 ft. (45–90 cm) long, arching. This is the parent of many cultivars of 6 to 9 ft. (1·8–2·7 m), variously coloured in reds, oranges, creams and scarlet-reds.
Flowering time: summer–mid-autumn.
Use: grow in bold clumps for maximum effect, alone in borders or with other plants.
Propagation: by careful spring division or seed.
Environment and light: full sun.
Type of soil: rich, deep, fertile loam, well-drained.
Soil moisture: water only under drought conditions.
Remarks: to protect crowns of plants in winter, gather leaves together and tie them over like a top knot. Leave established plants undisturbed as long as possible.

295 GOLDBAND LILY; GOLDEN-RAYED LILY OF JAPAN

Lilium auratum:

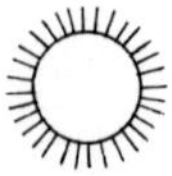

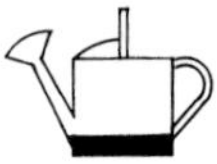

3

Family: Liliaceae.
Place of origin: Japan; introduced in 1862.
Description: one of the finest garden lilies but unfortunately subject to virus infection, so purchase disease-free stock and keep away from doubtful bulbs. Bulbs 3–4 in. (7–10 cm) across; stems purplish-green, 3–6 ft. (1–3 m) high and leafy. Foliage dark green, stalked, ovate, up to 9 in. (45 cm) in length. Flowers very fragrant, bowl-shaped with reflexed petals, 20–30 on each stem, waxy-white with gold streaks and crimson spots.
Flowering time: late summer–mid-autumn.
Use: for borders, flowerbeds, to make isolated groups and for cut flowers.
Propagation: seed is best to ensure clean stock.
Environment and light: in full sun; leave alone when happy.
Type of soil: sharp drainage is essential. They seem to do best when deeply planted at 8–10 in. (20–25 cm) in poor soil on gravel, amongst shrubs which protect the lower parts of the stems from hot sun. In heavy soils work in plenty of sand or grit.
Soil moisture: water sparingly in summer; the ground should always be moist but never waterlogged.

---

296 ORANGE LILY

Lilium bulbiferum (syn. *L. croceum*)*:*

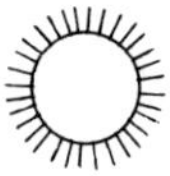

4

Family: Liliaceae.
Place of origin: S. Europe, alpine regions; introduced into Britain in 1878.
Description: bulb rounded, flattened above; stems rigid, woolly above and leafy, $1\frac{1}{2}$–5 ft. (45–150 cm) according to soil and conditions. Leaves sparse, linear-lanceolate, to 6 in. (15 cm). Flowers wide, cup-shaped, erect, light orange with deeper orange at tips of perianth segments.
Flowering time: late spring–mid-summer.
Use: for isolated groups, borders, flowerbeds and cut flowers.
Propagation: by division every 3–4 years. Bulbils often occur—but not invariably. These can be grown.
Environment and light: full sun to half-shade, but in the latter case the flowers will be less brightly coloured. Long lasting, hardy. Plant 4–6 in. (10–15 cm) deep as it is a stem rooter.
Type of soil: any good fertile, garden soil.
Soil moisture: water sparingly; the ground should be moist.
Remarks: grows plentifully in gardens in Northern Ireland where it is the emblem of the Orange Order.

297 BOURBON LILY; MADONNA LILY; WHITE LILY

Lilium candidum:

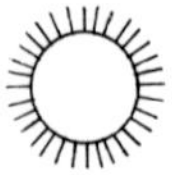

4

Family: Liliaceae.
Place of origin: not positively known.
Description: oldest lily in cultivation in the world, stretching back thousands of years. Bulbs ovoid, yellowish; foliage: basal leaves oblanceolate, ground hugging, remaining all winter; stem leaves verticillate, lanceolate. Height 4–6 ft. (1·2–1·8 m). Flowers pure white, fragrant, broadly bell-shaped, perianth segments glossy, conspicuous yellow anthers on white filaments.
Flowering time: summer.
Use: for small isolated clumps, border, flowerbeds, and as cut flowers.
Propagation: by division of the small bulbs taken from around parent bulbs.
Environment and light: one of the hardiest for British and American gardens, but temperamental and subject to virus infection. Half-shade or sunny but protected from prevailing winds which loosen the bulb-stems. Plant shallowly (just covered) when dormant (which is normally in mid-summer). Head in sun, feet in shade is the aim.
Type of soil: moist garden soil. Likes lime.
Soil moisture: water only if necessary.
Remarks: the fragrant oil used in perfumery.

---

298 EASTER LILY

Lilium longiflorum:

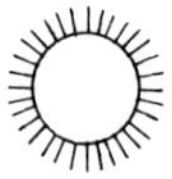

8

Family: Liliaceae.
Place of origin: endemic to Japan but grown and naturalised in China; introduced in 1819.
Description: a popular lily for weddings and funerals and much cultivated commercially. Long leafy stems of up to 3 ft. (1 m) with sessile, lanceolate, alternate leaves and several fragrant, pure white, funnel-shaped flowers which are recurved at their tips and 5–6 in. (12–15 cm) long.
Flowering time: summer; forced for spring blooms.
Use: for isolated groups, borders, flowerbeds, and for cut flowers. Not really hardy in frost-prone and exposed areas although some of its cultivars will succeed outside in warm sheltered places if protected with leaves in winter. Pre-cooled bulbs grown for early work in pots need a night temperature around 40°–50°F (4·4°–10°C) and day temperatures of 65°F (18·4°C). These can be tried outdoors in subsequent seasons.
Propagation: grow from seed.
Environment and light: warm, fairly sunny. This is a stem rooter so plant 8 in. (20 cm) deep.
Type of soil: fertile well-drained loam. Likes lime.

299 MARTAGON LILY; TURK'S CAP LILY

Lilium martagon:

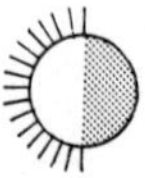

(3)

Family: Liliaceae.
Place of origin: widespread in Europe including Britain where it is probably an escape or naturalised.
Description: upright grower of 3–6 ft. (1–2 m) (according to conditions) with leafy stems, latter dark green, arranged in whorls or scattered, oblanceolate, sometimes hairy. Flowers: many, pendulous, unpleasantly scented; reflexed perianth segments, purplish-black, wine-coloured, pinkish or white, usually spotted with darker shades.
Flowering time: summer.
Use: can be naturalised in rough grass, open woodland, in shady borders.
Propagation: by seed or bulbils taken from around parent bulbs.
Environment and light: part shade.
Type of soil: any good garden soil; will grow on calcareous soils.
Soil moisture: water sparingly, so that the earth is just moist.
Remarks: a very variable species. The bulbs are dried in the sun and eaten with reindeer milk in some parts of Russia.

---

300 REGAL LILY

Lilium regale:

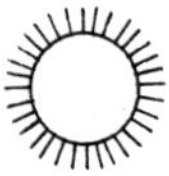

(3)

Family: Liliaceae.
Place of origin: western China; introduced to cultivation by G. F. Wilson in 1905.
Description: a stem-rooting lily of great beauty and one of the most satisfactory for gardens. Sweetly scented with strong stems of 4–6 ft. (1·2–1·8 m). Bulbs up to 6 in. (15 cm); leaves scattered, dark green, one veined, linear, along the stems. Flowers funnel-shaped, in umbels of 10–30, creamy-yellow, rose-purple shaded outside, up to 6 in. (15 cm) long.
Flowering time: summer.
Use: for borders, flowerbeds, and cut flowers.
Propagation: seed is the best method. Seedlings bloom second or third year after sowing. Also from bulbils around parent bulb.
Environment and light: plant bulbs 8–10 in. (20–25 cm) deep, or less if the ground is mulched high.
Type of soil: most types if drainage is good.
Soil moisture: water to keep soil moist in growing season but never waterlogged; all species of lily dislike excessive watering which rots the bulbs; avoid over-aridity, the ground should always be quite moist.

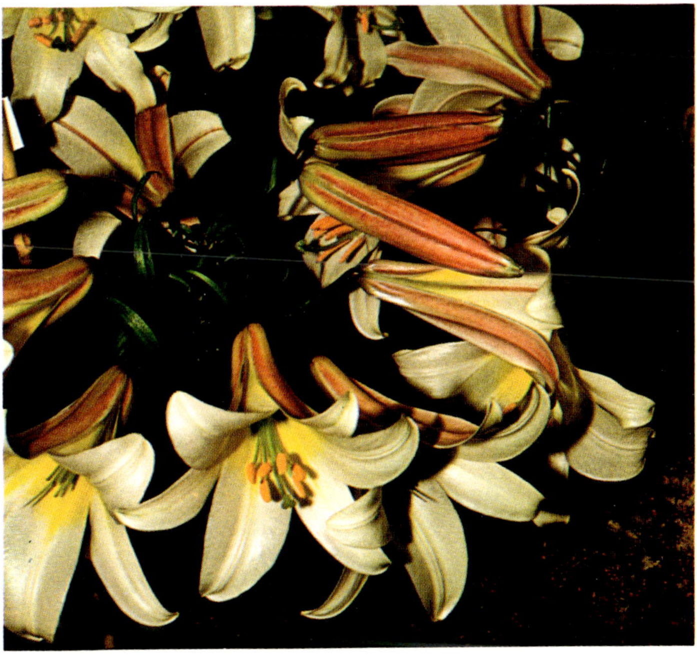

301 SPECIOSUM LILY

Lilium speciosum (L. lancifolium):

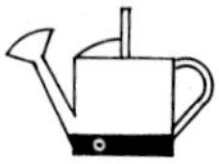

4

Family: Liliaceae.
Place of origin: South Japan; introduced into Europe in 1830.
Description: a highly variable plant with a globose, yellowish to purple-brown bulb; stems 3–6 ft. (1–1·8 m), with short-stemmed, ovate-lanceolate, slightly leathery leaves up to 7 in. (17 cm) and bunches of large, pendent, fragrant flowers. These may be 4–6 in. (10–15 cm) across, pinkish-white heavily suffused with crimson spots and suffusions. Perianth segments reflexed with wavy margins.
Flowering time: late summer–early autumn.
Use: amongst shrubs, in borders, as cut flowers for a cool greenhouse.
Propagation: by seed (flowers in 4 years), bulbils or scales.
Environment and light: the bulbs hate to be wet when dormant and are stem rooters so plant them 6–9 in. (15–23 cm) deep in humus and sand type soil. Full sun.
Soil moisture: water generously until flowering; reduce when the flowers begin to wither and stop altogether when the leaves turn yellow.
Remarks: in Japan the bulbs are cultivated as food.

---

302 LILY

Lilium szovitsianum (L. monadelphum var. *szovitsianum):*

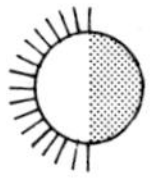

4

Family: Liliaceae. Latin name derived from Greek *leirion*, lily.
Place of origin: Caucasus.
Description: a bulbous plant of 4–6 ft. (1·2–1·8 m) with 20–30, nodding, Turk's cap, pendulous, campanulate flowers with reflexed perianth segments on each stem. These are golden-yellow spotted with brown. Pollen orange.
Flowering time: summer–early autumn.
Use: for isolated clumps, borders, shady flowerbeds, for cut flowers; also for edges of woodland and similar shaded areas.
Propagation: by division of the small bulbs or from scales.
Environment and light: half-shade.
Type of soil: fairly stiff garden loam; mulch occasionally with leaf-mould.
Soil moisture: keep soil always moist.
Remarks: takes time to establish, then generally hardy and reliable. If grown in frost-free zones should be lifted and refrigerated for 8 weeks to give a rest period.

303 OGRE LILY; TIGER LILY
Lilium tigrinum:

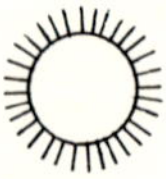

(5)

Family: Liliaceae.
Place of origin: China, Japan, Korea; introduced in 1804.
Description: a plant which has been cultivated in the Orient for over a thousand years, originally for food and still sold in the markets. Bulb white, broadly ovoid, about 3 in. (7 cm); stems purplish to 4 ft. (1·2 m), covered with white downy hairs. Leaves dark green, linear-lanceolate with one to three bulbils in the axils of most. Flowers in racemes of 12–20, scentless, nodding, reflexed, orange-red plentifully dotted with purple-brown spots.
Flowering time: mid-summer–early autumn.
Use: for open woodland, amongst shrubs, grouping in borders and for cut flowers.
Propagation: the flowers are self-sterile but can be reproduced from the bulbils in the leaf-axils. It is possible to pollinate the flowers artificially for seed.
Environment and light: full sun. These are stem rooting so plant bulbs 7–9 in. (18–23 cm) deep.
Type of soil: suitable for most types of lime-free soils. Plenty of humus maintains moisture and helps drainage.
Soil moisture: water to keep soil moist in growing season.
Remarks: bulbs are valued as a food in the Orient.

---

304 CORSICAN LILY; SPIRIT LILY
Pancratium illyricum:

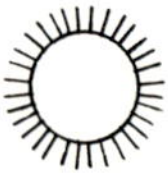

(8)

Family: Amaryllidaceae.
Place of origin: Mediterranean region, in particular Corsica; introduced into Britain in 1615.
Description: a bulbous plant native to the warm sand dunes of the Mediterranean coastline. Produces large, pear-shaped bulbs with glaucous, strap-like leaves and umbels of white, sweetly scented, 3 in. (8 cm) flowers on 18 in. (45 cm) stems.
Flowering time: early summer (in greenhouses).
Use: will not flower unless the bulbs are well ripened so in cool climates is only suitable for growing outdoors at the base of a warm wall. Protect in winter with glass or leaves. Frost-prone areas or those with wet winters is best grown in frames or greenhouses; outside in tropics and sub-tropics.
Propagation: by division in autumn.
Environment and light: full sun.
Type of soil: light, loose, made up of heath-mould, sand and leaf-mould.
Soil moisture: water regularly until flowering, then reduce and stop almost completely in dormant period in winter.

305 SEA DAFFODIL; SEA LILY
Pancratium maritimum:

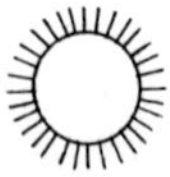

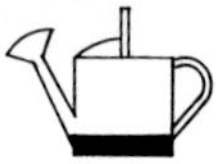

(8)

Family: Amaryllidaceae. Greek name for the plant.
Place of origin: S. Europe, Mediterranean region; introduced into Britain in 1759.
Description: a hardier bulb than the preceding but found in the wild under similar conditions. Leaves slightly glaucous, lance-shaped, persistent; flowers in loose umbels, fragrant, white with a well-defined narcissus-like corona and a green stripe on the outside of each perianth segment.
Flowering time: summer–early autumn.
Use: as for *P. illyricum* (No 304).
Propagation: by division in autumn.
Environment and light: full sun.
Type of soil: light, loose, made up of heath-mould, sand and leaf-mould; can also live in sand alone, as in its natural habitat.
Soil moisture: water regularly until flowering, then reduce and stop almost completely during dormant period.

---

306 AZTEC LILY; JACOBEAN LILY; ST. JAMES' LILY
Sprekelia formosissima:

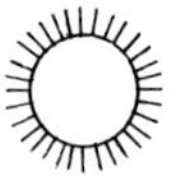

(9)

Family: Amaryllidaceae. Named after a Hamburg lawyer Johann Heinrich von Sprekelsen (1691–1764).
Place of origin: Mexico; introduced in 1658.
Description: a monotypic genus, the species having small, 2 in. (5 cm) bulbs. Leaves after the flowers, thick, narrow, strap-shaped; flowers one or occasionally two, on a 1 ft. (30 cm) stem, large, deep crimson, up to 5 in. (13 cm) long and across. The illustration shows their shape clearly, the irregular petals, and bright red filaments supporting the stamens. Hollow stems.
Flowering time: spring indoors or late summer outdoors.
Use: as an unusual plant for the cool greenhouse, or outside in warm beds, protected in winter in fairly mild climates. In tropics and sub-tropics in open beds.
Propagation: by division during dormant period.
Environment and light: full sun. Plant with top of bulb and neck exposed in pots and very lightly covered outdoors. Temperature 55°F (12·8°C) ideal.
Type of soil: when grown in pots use good loam, leaf-mould, decayed mushroom compost in equal parts with sand for good drainage; use fairly small pots.
Soil moisture: water plentifully during growing season.

307 ADAM'S NEEDLE; MOUND LILY; SPANISH BAYONET

Yucca gloriosa:

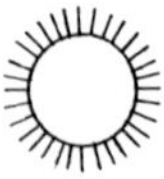

Family: Agaraceae. Carib name for cassava, erroneously applied to these plants.
Place of origin: South Eastern U.S.A.; introduced into Britain in 1550.

Description: an evergreen shrub-like plant with a short, thick stem, occasionally branched. Leaves up to 2 ft. (60 cm) long, 2–3 in. (5–8 cm) wide, leathery, glaucous-green, spined at tips, growing in a rosette. Flowers impressive, in large panicles of 3–6 ft. (1–2 m) or more, closely packed, creamy-white, hooded, tinged with red outside.

Flowering time: summer–early autumn.
Use: as an accent plant in key situations, also for deep containers, beds, isolated on lawns and similar. Hardy over most of British Isles and similar climates.
Propagation: by division of offsets in spring.

Environment and light: full sun; in mild climates will stand up well to winter in normal conditions; should be protected in winter in colder climates.
Type of soil: rich, permeable, sandy.
Soil moisture: water seldom and sparingly.

---

308 FAIRY LILY; FLOWER OF THE WEST WIND; RAIN LILY; ZEPHYR LILY

Zephyranthes carinata (Z. grandiflora):

Family: Amaryllidaceae. Name from Greek *zephyros*, west wind and *authos*, flower, referring to their New World (i.e. western) habitat.
Place of origin: West Indies; introduced in 1824.

Description: a pretty little bulbous plant of 5–10 in. (12·5–25 cm). Leaves narrowly strap-shaped, with the blooms. Flowers solitary, 4 in. (10 cm) across, bell-shaped, pink with golden anthers, on a hollow stem.
Flowering time: late spring–early summer.
Use: in cool temperate climates use as a pot plant for sun-lounges, cool greenhouses or sunny rooms indoors. In tropics used as edging for borders.

Propagation: by division in winter, when plant is dormant.
Environment and light: full sun. Plant bulbs 1–2 in. (2·5–5 cm) deep outdoors.
Type of soil: outdoors: garden soil mixed with leaf-mould and sand to make substratum more permeable. Pot plants grow in a compost of equal parts fibrous loam, leaf-mould and decayed manure plus sand.

Soil moisture: pot plants: keep moist and feed monthly during growing season. Withhold water for 10 weeks when leaves wither and then start the cycle again.
Remarks: the plants flower best when pot bound.

ROSES AND THE ROSE FAMILY

309 JAPANESE QUINCE

Chaenomeles speciosa (C. lagenaria; Cydonia japonica):

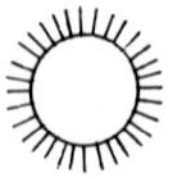

4

Family: Rosaceae. Name from Greek *chaino*, to gape, and *melon*, apple; the fruit was once believed to be split.
Place of origin: Japan (uncertain); introduced into Europe in 1796.
Description: a shrub to $6\frac{1}{2}$ ft. (2 m) in height, with spiny branches. Leaves oblong, serrated, shiny above; flowers 2–4 together in a cluster, $1\frac{1}{4}$–2 in. (3·5–5 cm) across and crimson with yellow stamens, opening before the leaves appear. Also pink, white and scarlet cultivars. Fruit rounded, yellow or yellowish-green, fragrant. (Used for a marmalade.)
Flowering time: spring.
Use: for shrubberies, the backs of mixed borders, as a hedging plant, to train up walls.
Propagation: by seed after the fruits have been stratified; named forms grafted on seedlings of the type species, also by cuttings or layers.
Environment and light: full sun or very light shade.
Type of soil: any good moist garden soil, preferably on the heavy side.
Soil moisture: water in periods of drought.
Remarks: in the U.S. this variety is susceptible to San Jose scale.

---

310 WILLOWLEAF COTONEASTER

Cotoneaster salicifolia:

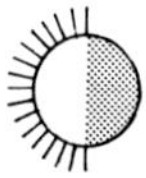

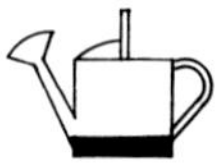

6

Family: Rosaceae. Name from Latin *cotonea* (cydonia), quince and *aster*, "kind of".
Place of origin: China, introduced into Europe in 1908.
Description: a graceful evergreen (or partly evergreen) shrub or small tree to 15 ft. (4·5 m) with spreading branches, turning reddish with age. Leaves narrow, shiny above, pale and woolly below, prominently veined. Flowers small, pinkish in compact, woolly corymbs. These are succeeded by attractive bright red berries in late autumn.
Flowering time: summer.
Use: at the back of mixed borders, in shrubberies, as boundary trees of low height and similar.
Propagation: by cuttings at the end of summer, or by seed in spring.
Environment and light: full sun to half-shade.
Type of soil: any good garden soil.
Soil moisture: water in dry weather, so that the ground is moist, but never sodden.

311 GEUM; SCARLET AVENS

Geum chiloense (G. coccineum):

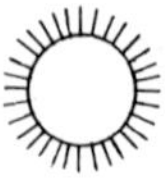

Family: Rosaceae. Name from Chiloe, an island and province on the northern borders of Patagonia.
Place of origin: Chile, introduced into Europe in 1826.
Description: herbaceous perennial, 16 in.–2 ft. (40–60 cm) high with chalice-shaped flowers of vivid scarlet. Leaves deeply divided and irregularly lobed. This is the parent of the well-known garden cultivar "Mrs Bradshaw" with semi-double flowers in character practically all summer. Double gold ("Lady Stratheden"), yellow and copper and orange forms exist. The blooms are carried on branching panicles.
Flowering time: summer.
Use: for herbaceous and mixed borders, slopes and banks.
Propagation: by division after flowering or seed.
Environment and light: full sun.
Type of soil: no special requirements, but fertile and well-drained.
Remarks: in zones further north treat as an annual.

⑥

---

312 KERRIA

Kerria japonica "Plena"*:*

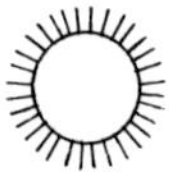

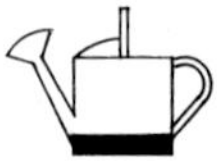

Family: Rosaceae. Named after William Kerr who introduced the single form in 1804. Its double form "Plena" had been known in Europe since 1700.
Place of origin: China.
Description: erect, slender branched, deciduous shrub of 4–6 ft. (1·2–1·8 m). Leaves alternate, ovate-lanceolate, double serrated—much larger on the flowerless shoots than the flowering twigs. Flowers small, yellow, 5-petalled—but less grown than the larger and more showy double kind. There is also a variegated leaved form.
Flowering time: spring–early summer.
Use: as a wall or fence shrub, for its early flowers. The green shoots are also attractive in winter. In isolated clumps or fronts of shrubberies.
Propagation: by soft cuttings rooted with bottom heat; by division or layering.
Environment and light: full sun to half-shade; in harsher climates must be well sheltered, especially the variegated kind.
Type of soil: any good loamy soil.
Soil moisture: water if necessary.
Remarks: thin out old shoots occasionally.

④

313 **JAPANESE FLOWERING CRAB APPLE**
Malus floribunda (Pyrus floribunda):

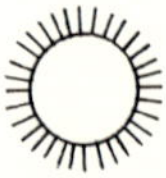

4

Family: Rosaceae. *Malus* is the Latin name for apple tree.
Place of origin: introduced into Europe in 1862 from Japan.
Description: a small rounded, wide-spreading tree, ultimately 20–25 ft. (6–7·6 m) high. Leaves dense, ovate, coarsely toothed, dull green above, pale and downy beneath. Flowers densely clustered, rosy-red in bud, opening to pink finally almost white. One of the earliest crabs to flower and very popular in English gardens. Fruits round, yellow.
Flowering time: late spring.
Use: a most beautiful tree when in bloom; it is ideal for isolated positions in grass; also at the back of borders, edging roads, etc.
Propagation: mostly increased by grafting on various crab and apple stocks.
Environment and light: full sun in cooler climates, elsewhere in half-shade.
Type of soil: any good fertile soil, preferably on the heavy side.

---

314 **RED FLOWERING CRAB APPLE**
Malus × purpurea:

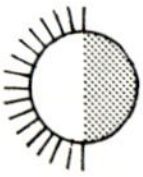

4

Family: Rosaceae.
Place of origin: of garden origin, obtained for Royal Botanic Gardens, Kew in 1912 from the raisers Messrs Barbier of Orleans. Hybrid between *M. niedzwetzkyana* and × *atrosanguinea*.
Description: a beautiful crab, 19½–23 ft. (6–7 m) high, fairly open in growth, the branches festooned with clusters of rosy-crimson flowers with purplish-red leaves which are particularly attractive when young. Red fruits about the size and shape of cherries.
Flowering time: late spring.
Use: as isolated specimens or to line avenues and pathways in parks and gardens.
Propagation: by grafting on crab stock.
Environment and light: full sun in colder climates, elsewhere in half-shade.
Type of soil: fertile, deep loam.

315 HIMALAYAN CINQUEFOIL
Potentilla atrosanguinea:

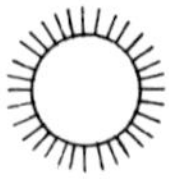

⑥

Family: Rosaceae. Name from Latin *potens*, powerful, referring to the medicinal properties of some species.
Place of origin: Himalayas; introduced into Europe in 1824.
Description: the parent of many good herbaceous perennials. The type species has dark reddish-purple flowers but is rarely grown in gardens. Instead there is a host of hybrids whose flowers vary from rich scarlet and orange to yellow. The one portrayed is "Gibson's Scarlet". Leaves strawberry-like, palmately lobed and coarsely toothed, velvety greyish underneath. Flowers: saucer-shaped, 5-petalled. Height 2 ft. (60 cm).
Flowering time: summer–early autumn.
Use: as edging for beds, grouping in herbaceous borders and the like.
Propagation: by division in spring or autumn or seed sown outside in late spring.
Environment and light: full sun to half-shade.
Type of soil: ordinary garden soil.
Soil moisture: water regularly.
Remarks: in more northerly areas treat as an annual.

---

316 BUSH CINQUEFOIL; SHRUBBY CINQUEFOIL
Potentilla fruticosa:

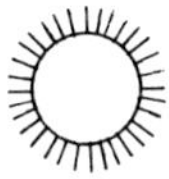

②

Family: Rosaceae.
Place of origin: temperate regions of Europe (including Britain), Asia and America.
Description: a deciduous, low-growing shrub of variable habit and height, but averaging 3–5 ft. (1–1·5 m) high. Leaves small, pinnate, usually with 5 leaflets (occasionally 3 or 7), narrow and pointed, downy beneath. Flowers solitary or a few together; like strawberry flowers, pale to bright yellow in the varieties, also white.
Flowering time: summer–early autumn.
Use: valued for its compact habit and long flowering season. Fronts of shrub borders, rock gardens, as container plants on roof gardens, balconies etc.
Propagation: by seed or cuttings of late summer wood, rooted with mist or in a frame of sandy soil.
Environment and light: full sun, well exposed, but damp.
Type of soil: ordinary garden soil with a little peat to keep it moist.
Soil moisture: water in dry weather.

317 GEAN; MAZZARD; WILD CHERRY

Prunus avium "Plena":

3

Family: Rosaceae.
Place of origin: of garden origin; cultivated since 1700.
Description: this is the largest of the double white flowering cherries and one of the latest. It makes a pyramidal tree, up to 79 ft. (24 m) in height with smooth shining bark, somewhat reddish. Leaves oblong-ovate, serrated, with a drawn-out point, serrate. Flowers abundant, crowded, full double, white in long-stalked clusters. Fruits rarely or never.
Flowering time: late spring.
Use: as a solitary tree in a key situation. In parks, large gardens to make avenues.
Propagation: by cuttings of young wood taken with a heel and rooted with bottom heat or grafted or budded on type species *P. avium*.
Environment and light: full sun.
Type of soil: any good, fertile, loamy soil.
Soil moisture: the soil should always be slightly moist.

---

318 ALMOND

Prunus dulcis (P. communis; P. amygdalus):

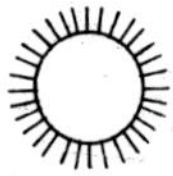

6

Family: Rosaceae. The Latin name.
Place of origin: W. Asia and N. Africa, but cultivated since very early times so complete habitat not really known.
Description: a very early small flowering tree, common in suburban gardens but inclined to be short-lived. Grey-black bark with open centre and ascending branches. Leaves ovate-lanceolate, finely serrulate, prone to curl in spring due to the disease "Peach-leaf curl". Flowers ahead of the leaves, wreathed along the young shoots, pink, borne singly or in pairs. Fruits yellowish-green. The edible almonds of commerce mainly come from southern Europe.
Flowering time: late winter–early spring.
Use: valued for its early flowering; in borders and shrubberies for lining streets.
Propagation: named sorts by grafting on type species, or by seed of the latter.
Environment and light: full sun but sheltered.
Type of soil: deep and fertile. Tolerates a little chalk.
Remarks: white forms occur, also doubles.

319 PEACH

Prunus persica "Alboplena":

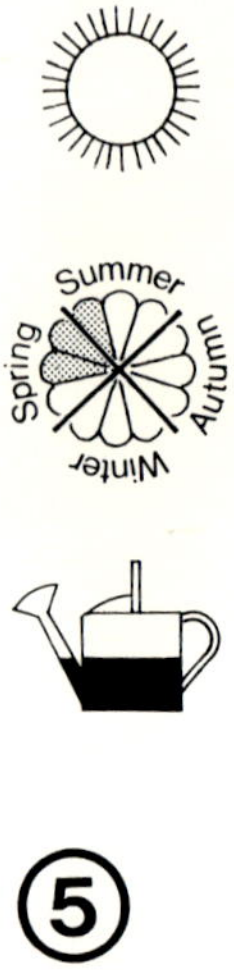

Family: Rosaceae.
Place of origin: a garden form of a species believed to be a native of China, i.e. the edible peach (which has been cultivated for thousands of years in that country).
Description: one of the numerous forms of the peach tree derived for ornamental use. Height to 26 ft. (8 m); many branched with pointed, serrated leaves; flowers, short-stalked, double white. Other notable varieties are "Windle Weeping" a pendent, semi-double purplish-pink and "Foliis Rubis", single, deep pink flowers and rich red foliage which becomes bronze-green with age.
Flowering time: spring.
Use: for parks, gardens and avenues.
Propagation: by grafting or budding scions on plum stock or by half-ripe heel cuttings rooted with gentle bottom heat.
Environment and light: full sun.
Type of soil: any good, deep, loamy soil.
Soil moisture: soil should be moist.
Remarks: this tree does not do well in the tropics.

---

320 FLOWERING ALMOND

Prunus triloba (P. triloba "Plena"*):*

Family: Rosaceae.
Place of origin: of garden origin but native to China from whence Fortune introduced it to England in 1855. The name was founded by Lindley on this double form. The wild form *simplex* (from China) with single pink flowers was not introduced to Europe until 1884.
Description: a deciduous shrub or small tree up to 12 or 15 ft. (3·5 or 4·5 m) high. Leaves small, often 3-lobed obovate, coarsely serrated. Flowers large, double, in pinkish-white rosettes, appearing singly or in pairs all along the slender branches.
Flowering time: spring.
Use: as a wall shrub (cutting the blossoming twigs hard back after flowering), in the open ground in mild climates; can be forced in the greenhouse as an early pot plant.
Propagation: by layers or cuttings of ripe wood.
Environment and light: full sun, somewhat sheltered.
Type of soil: light but fertile and deep.
Soil moisture: soil always moist to the touch.

321 FIRETHORN

Pyracantha coccinea (Crataegus pyracantha; Cotoneaster pyracantha):

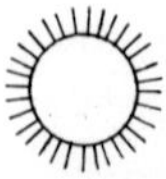

Family: Rosaceae. Name from Greek *pyr*, fire and *akantha*, thorn, referring to the bright fruits and spiny branches.
Place of origin: southern Europe and Asia Minor; introduced into Britain in 1629.
Description: a large evergreen shrub or small tree with thorny branches. Leaves narrowly obovate or oval, finely toothed, dark glossy green above, paler beneath, short-stalked. Flowers white, in many flowered corymbs, followed by dense bunches of rich red fruits all along the branches. These hang all autumn and winter except when attacked by birds. "Lalandei" is a stronger growing, larger fruited cultivar raised in France since 1874.
Flowering time: early summer.
Use: as a free-standing tree or a wall shrub (trained) or for hedging.
Propagation: by stratified seeds or half-ripe cuttings rooted in gentle warmth.
Environment and light: full sun to half-shade.
Type of soil: fairly heavy loam, fertile. Succeeds in clay soils.
Remarks: plant stands quite hard pruning but transplants badly, retain a ball of soil around the roots.

(6)

---

322 RHAPHIOLEPIS

Rhaphiolepis sp. probably *R. umbellata:*

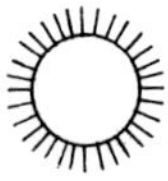

Family: Rosaceae. Name from Greek *rhaphe*, needle and *lepis*, scale, referring to narrow bracts on inflorescence.
Place of origin: Japan and Korea; introduced into Europe in 1862 (into the U.S. 1859).
Description: a slow-growing evergreen shrub with stout leathery leaves, broadly oval or obovate, tapering at the base and lightly toothed. Flowers in stiff, terminal panicles of 3–4 in. (7–10 cm), scented, pure white with 5 narrow pointed lobes.
Flowering time: summer.
Use: handsome shrub for a sheltered spot in cool temperate climates. Also as a container plant wintered under cover.
Propagation: by seed or half-ripe summer cuttings rooted with bottom heat.
Environment and light: sunny sheltered place except in hot climates when it should be grown in partial shade. Will not tolerate much frost.
Type of soil: good well-drained, loamy soil.
Soil moisture: water pot plants regularly, more in summer.

(8)

323 ROSE

Rosa "Fragrant Cloud":

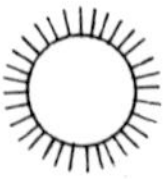

④

Family: Rosaceae.
Place of origin: introduced by Duftwolke in 1964 (parentage, seedling × "Prima Ballerina".
Description: a splendid hybrid tea rose, with large and substantial orange-red flowers with a delicious fragrance. Free-flowering with large, glossy, dark green foliage. Good for cutting.
Flowering time: summer.
Use: mainly as a cut flower.
Propagation: by budding on such rose stocks as *canina*.
Environment and light: full sun.
Type of soil: good heavy loam, well manured the previous autumn. Mulch in spring in later years.
Soil moisture: water only in very dry weather.
Remarks: prune in early spring, removing old, diseased or weak shoots and cutting back the rest fairly hard to an outward-pointing bud.

---

324 FLORIBUNDA ROSE

Rosa "Sarabande":

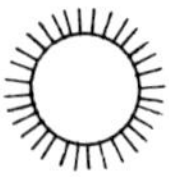

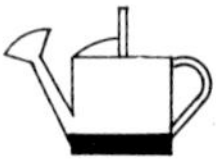

④

Family: Rosaceae.
Place of origin: introduced in 1957 by the French grower Meilland (parentage "Cocorico" × "Moulin Rouge").
Description: a short but excellent bedding rose, hardy and brilliant in colour. The single, clear scarlet flowers come in medium-sized but prolific clusters throughout the season and do not fade in sun or rain. Height 2 ft. (60 cm).
Flowering time: summer–early autumn.
Use: for bold displays in formal beds in parks and gardens.
Propagation: by half-ripe or ripe cuttings in late summer or early autumn or often grafted on rose stocks.
Environment and light: full sun.
Type of soil: see R. "Fragrant Cloud".
Soil moisture: water only if required.
Remarks: prune in spring, cutting out very old, weak or diseased branches and reducing other branches by about one third.

325

Rosa multiflora:

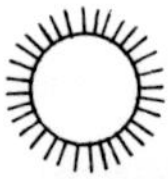

5

Family: Rosaceae. The Latin name for this flower.
Place of origin: Japan, Korea; introduced into Britain before 1886.
Description: a vigorous climbing species growing to 20 ft. (6 m) with slender prickles, pinnate leaves divided into 7 or 9 ovate-lanceolate leaflets and rambler-like trusses of small, fragrant, white or pink flowers. Fruits (hips), small, round bright scarlet, lasting into winter.
Flowering time: summer.
Use: for backs of rose shrub borders; to climb over trees, arbours, summer houses and the like. Also makes a good hedge to 10 ft. (3 m). In the U.S.A. often used as a windbreak and against erosion; also as a crash barrier on some trunk roads. Can be employed to contain sheep and deer and as a stock plant for budding other kinds of roses.
Propagation: by late summer or autumn cuttings; these usually flower in one year.
Environment and light: sunny to half-shade.
Type of soil: any good garden soil, preferably on the heavy side.
Remarks: prune to shape or to suit individual requirements only.

326

MOUNTAIN ASH; ROWAN

Sorbus aucuparia:

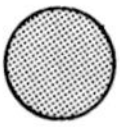

2

Family: Rosaceae. Name from Latin *sorbus*, old name for the fruit of the Service-tree. (*S. domestica*).
Place of origin: Europe (including Britain), Asia.
Description: a deciduous tree of 30–50 ft. (9–15 m) with downy winter buds; leaves variously pinnate with from 9–19 leaflets, individually narrowly ovate-oblong, sessile. These colour to fine autumnal tints of red and crimson before falling. Flowers in dense inflorescences, white followed by abundant hanging bunches of bright red berries (see photograph), much loved by birds.
Flowering time: spring–early summer.
Use: for parks, streets and gardens, edge of woodlands.
Propagation: by seed, which is quick and easy. Also, various cultivars can be grafted on this species.
Environment and light: moist, cool situation—leaves scorch if too hot and dry.
Type of soil: moist, cool, well-drained.

327 **GOAT'S BEARD**

Spiraea aruncus, now *Aruncus dioicus (A. sylvester):*

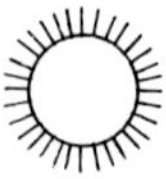

Family: Rosaceae. Classical name for these plants.
Place of origin: Northern Hemisphere; introduced into Britain in 1633.
Description: a handsome moisture-loving herbaceous perennial 3–4 ft. (about 1 m) high which forms an imposing clump. Leaves pinnate with several lanceolate leaflets. Flowers: in crowded, compound panicles, creamy-white and slightly fragrant. Although once known as *Spiraea* this name now only applies to shrubs; all herbaceous spiraeas now referred to other genera.

Flowering time: summer.
Use: as a specimen plant for key situations, especially in a moist situation, for island beds, backs of herbaceous borders, near water gardens.
Propagation: by seed or division.
Environment and light: sun or light shade.
Type of soil: deep rich, moist soil which does not dry out in summer.

②

---

328 **JAPANESE SPIRAEA**

Spiraea japonica:

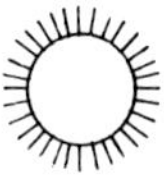

Family: Rosaceae. Name from Greek *speiraira*, a word used for garland plants.
Place of origin: Japan; introduced into Europe in 1870.
Description: a small upright deciduous shrub, which is the parent of many summer flowering forms of various types and colours. The species grows to 5 ft. (1·5 m), with pointed, coarsely toothed, lanceolate to ovate leaves and flat, compound corymbs of rich rosy-red flowers. Forms and cultivars have white, crimson and rose-red flowers and there are others of dwarf habit.

Flowering time: summer.
Use: for shrubberies, banks, isolated groups and near water gardens.

Propagation: by sucker growths from the base or summer cuttings rooted with the aid of mist or bottom heat.
Environment and light: full sun.
Type of soil: good moist loam with abundant moisture.
Remarks: prune in spring by thinning out the older and weak wood and cut back the rest to a convenient length. Does not do well in tropics.

⑤

BALCONY AND TERRACE PLANTS

329 TUBEROUS BEGONIA
Begonia tuberosa: hyb.

3

Family: Begoniaceae. Named for Michel Bégon.
Place of origin: South America.
Description: are highly popular, long flowering plants with many uses. Tubers are small, rounded and flattened. Leaves alternate, stemmed, dark green and irregularly lobate, usually rough to the touch. Stems more or less branching, succulent. Flowers fully double, hiding the central stamens; wide range of colours—orange, yellow, white, pink, red and crimson often edged in other shades, or fimbriated or frilled at the petal edges.
Flowering time: summer–mid-autumn.
Use: for bedding in temperate to warm climates, as show plants and for windowboxes and containers.
Propagation: seed from good strains come almost true to colour. Sow in temperatures of 65°F (18°C).
Environment and light: cool conditions, protected from direct sunlight in both gardens and greenhouse.
Type of soil: light but rich with peat or leaf-mould.
Soil moisture: water often, but sparingly, in hottest months; towards the end of flowering reduce watering and stop when the leaves yellow; dig up the tubers, dry in the open and store in a cool dry place.
Remarks: dry tubers are started in warmth in early spring and planted outside when risk of frost is past.

---

330 ITALIAN BELLFLOWER
Campanula isophylla:

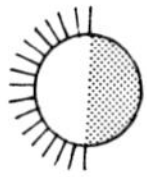

7

Family: Campanulaceae. Name from Latin *campana*, bell, referring to the shape of some of the flowers.
Place of origin: Italy; introduced into Britain in 1868.
Description: a trailing plant, free flowering and of great beauty in summer. Rootstock thickened; leaves oval to heart-shaped, on long stems from the base and similar foliage scattered along the much branched, trailing stems. Flowers salver-shaped, 1 in. (2·5 cm) or more across, numerous, sky-blue. Also one with white flowers "Alba" and another having green and white leaf variegations called "Mayii".
Flowering time: summer–autumn.
Use: for hanging baskets, sides of containers, dry walls in good climates.
Propagation: by cuttings of young shoots in spring rooted under glass with slight bottom heat.
Environment and light: light shade from hot or mid-day sun. Not dependably hardy in Britain or northern Europe so overwinter stock under cover.
Type of soil: any good light potting compost.
Soil moisture: water copiously, when required.
Remarks: does not do well in frost or in tropical areas.

331 CANTERBURY BELL

Campanula medium:

②

Family: Campanulaceae. See No 330.
Place of origin: Southern Europe; introduced into Britain in 1597.
Description: a popular biennial, growing 2–3 ft. (60 cm–1 m) high (taller in rich soil), forming a large, leafy rosette of roughish, ovate-lanceolate, crenate leaves with petioles the first year. In second season develops erect, branched, tough, leafy stems and large, 2 in. (5 cm) axillary and terminal, bell-shaped flowers of white, pink, blue or mauve. In var. *calycanthema*, or "cup and saucer" varieties there is an additional, flat, lobed corolla surrounding the base of the bell.
Flowering time: summer.
Use: for borders, isolated clumps, flowerbeds, balconies and terraces.
Propagation: by seed.
Environment and light: full sun.
Type of soil: good garden soil; calcareous. Found in nature amongst rocks.
Soil moisture: water so that the ground is moist, to encourage robust growth and good flower spikes.

---

332 WALLFLOWER

Cheiranthus cheiri:

⑤

Family: Cruciferae. Origin of name obscure but possibly from Arabic, *keiri*, a hand bouquet.
Place of origin: Europe; naturalised in Britain.
Description: an erect showy plant, usually treated as biennial for garden purposes and much esteemed for its early, very fragrant blooms. Height variable according to the strain but from 9 in.–2 ft. (23–60 cm); leaves narrow, lance-shaped, pointed, smooth. Flowers in close spikes, very variable—from creamy-white, through shades of yellow, brown, red, pink and purplish.
Flowering time: spring, or forced under glass in winter.
Use: for balconies, terraces, mixed borders, flowerbeds, banks, rockeries, slopes. Windowboxes, containers, in crevices in old walls (usually as perennials).
Propagation: by seed sown soon after harvesting.
Environment and light: full sun.
Type of soil: ordinary garden soil with lime.
Remarks: when transplanting seedlings, break off point of tap root to encourage fibrous root formation. These plants are very fond of climates with a good annual rainfall.

333 SWEET WILLIAM

Dianthus barbatus:

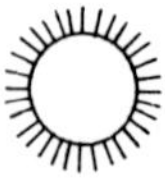

4

Family: Caryophyllaceae. Name from Greek *dios*, divine, and *anthos*, flower, referring to its fragrance.
Place of origin: S. and E. Europe; introduced into Britain in 1573.
Description: strictly speaking a perennial but invariably grown as a biennial, otherwise it deteriorates. Forms dense basal clusters of broad lanceolate leaves and the following year strong, leafy stems terminating in large, bracted heads of fragrant, vividly coloured flowers. These may be basically white, pink, scarlet or crimson, often ringed and dotted in contrasting colours.
Flowering time: late spring–summer.
Use: as cut flowers, for balconies and terraces, borders, rockeries, small flowerbeds.
Propagation: by seed. Once established will replace itself with self-sown plants.
Environment and light: full sun.
Type of soil: any good garden soil, manured if possible for a previous crop.
Soil moisture: water if necessary.

---

334 CARNATION

Dianthus caryophyllus:

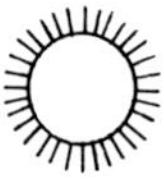

7

Family: Caryophyllaceae.
Place of origin: Southern Europe.
Description: a plant with a long history of cultivation. Illustrated is a border carnation, hardy in areas with mild frost, with woody base, evergreen, narrow, linear, grey-green leaves, often in tufts and large, double, fragrant flowers with curled petal margins. Colours vary from white and yellow through shades of pinks and red.
Flowering time: summer, if grown outdoors. Glass-house carnations grown will flower all year round.
Use: for borders, flowerbeds, pot plants, but mainly as cut flowers.
Propagation: by layers preferably, taken in mid-summer. Also by pipings, i.e. tops of leafy shoots, pulled out by hand and rooted in sand under glass.
Environment and light: full sun.
Type of soil: sharp drainage and rather dry conditions. Most soils but particularly those of a calcareous nature.
Remarks: in zones north of 9 these need winter protection. Carnation flowers are the source of an essential oil used for high grade perfumery.

335 BLEEDING HEART

Dicentra spectabilis (Dielytra spectabilis):

(2)

Family: Fumariceae. Name from Greek *dis*, twice, *kentron*, a spur; the blooms have 2 spurs.
Place of origin: Japan; introduced into Europe in 1816.
Description: an elegant, slender-stemmed plant with soft green, much-divided leaves. Flowering sprays up to 3 ft. (90 cm) long, crowded with rosy-pink, heart-shaped, hanging flowers with whitish tips.
Flowering time: spring–mid-summer.
Use: for deep containers on balconies and terraces, for small flowerbeds, borders or isolated clumps. Can also be forced under glass for early blooms. Temperatures of 50°–55°F (10°–13°C).
Propagation: by division in spring or root cuttings.
Environment and light: full sun or light shade.
Type of soil: good sandy loam, rich, light, well-drained. Plenty of humus.
Soil moisture: water plentifully when plants are in full flower.

---

336 FUCHSIA

Fuchsia triphylla var. "Mantilla":

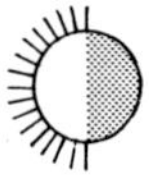

(7)

Family: Onagraceae. Named after Leonhart Fuchs (1501–1566), German physician and herbalist.
Place of origin: species from Haiti and Santo Domingo; introduced into Britain in 1872.
Description: a garden hybrid from *F. triphylla*, much-esteemed for hanging basket work. Height 1–2 ft. (30–60 cm), stems few branched. Leaves bronzed, stemmed, opposite or verticillate, entire, oval lanceolate. Flowers deep carmine, borne in pendulous terminal racemes.
Flowering time: summer.
Use: in window boxes, baskets, containers or bedding.
Propagation: by soft cuttings rooted in spring.
Environment and light: shade or half-shade.
Type of soil: three parts leaf-mould to one of well-rotted manure and one of sand.
Soil moisture: water frequently; soil should always be damp.
Remarks: outdoors if in a protected area in a nearly frost-free climate, otherwise best grown in pots.

337 BALSAM

Impatiens balsamina:

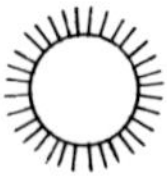

4

Family: Balsaminaceae. Name from Latin, impatient; the seeds are ejected at the slightest touch.
Place of origin: India, Malaya, China; introduced into Europe in 1596.
Description: herbaceous annual up to about 20 in. (50 cm) in height, with brittle, succulent stem. Leaves toothed. Flowers irregular, double or single, red, pink or white. Numerous cultivars vary in form of leaf and size and colour of flower.
Flowering time: summer–mid-autumn.
Use: for balconies and terraces, but in quite large pots, and in greenhouses and homes.
Propagation: by seed in early spring.
Environment and light: sunny to half-shade.
Type of soil: proprietary peat or lime-free, loam compost.
Soil moisture: water regularly so that the ground is always moist, but not wet.
Remarks: cultivated in India as a perennial; the flowers are used in parts of Asia instead of henna for dyeing finger-nails.

---

338 BUSY-LIZZY; IMPATIENCE; PATIENCE; SNAPWEED

Impatiens wallerana sultanii:

10

Family: Balsaminaceae.
Place of origin: Zanzibar; introduced into Europe in 1896.
Description: a confused genus; the forms of several species—*I. holstii*, *I. sultanii* and *I. petersiana* now included under the collective name *I. wallerana.* Those normally listed as *I. sultanii* are usually pink with 5 petals, a spur behind the flower, watery stems, alternate, smooth, toothed leaves on branching 1–2 ft. (30–60 cm) stems. Busy Lizzies belong to the *I. holstii* group and are variously coloured.
Flowering time: late spring–mid-autumn.
Use: as house and greenhouse plants; in flowerbeds in sub-tropical areas only.
Propagation: by seed in spring or soft cuttings.
Environment and light: dark to shady in outdoor places; well-lit and out of the sun when indoors.
Type of soil: proprietary peat compost or lime-free loam compost.
Soil moisture: water frequently so that the soil is always moist.

339 LANTANA

Lantana camara:

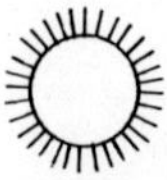

8

Family: Verbenaceae. *Lantana* is the Latin name for Viburnum, transferred to this genus.
Place of origin: tropical South America; introduced into Britain in 1692.
Description: evergreen shrub with somewhat prickly stems, 6½–10 ft. (2–3 m) high. Leaves rough, pointed, toothed and scented. Flowers axillary, borne in dense umbels usually changing with age from white, through yellow to red.
Flowering time: late spring–mid autumn.
Use: in containers, greenhouses or as a summer bedding plant in frost-prone countries. In tropics and sub-tropics, in mixed beds and borders.
Propagation: by cuttings towards late summer, or seed.
Environment and light: sunny to half-shade.
Type of soil: good garden soil, fertile, mixed with peat and sand.
Remarks: care should be exercised when planting the shrub outdoors in tropical countries as it seeds itself about and can become a bad weed. Grow as an annual in areas north of zone 8. Infusion from leaves used in native America as a tonic and stimulant.

---

340 MALLOW

Lavatera trimestris (L. rosea):

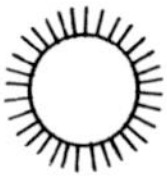

7

Family: Malvaceae. Named after J. R. Lavater, sixteenth-century Swiss naturalist.
Place of origin: Mediterranean region, Portugal; introduced into Britain in 1633.
Description: a beautiful annual, making an erect bushy plant with branching stems, 3–4 ft. (about 1 m) high. Leaves rounded, smooth, pale green, coarsely toothed. Flowers large, up to 4 in. (10 cm) across, solitary, from white to deep rose-pink and red with deeper veining. Var. *splendens* is a particularly good, deep rose-pink form.
Flowering time: summer–early autumn.
Use: in flowerbeds, borders, isolated groups, as well as for cut flowers.
Propagation: by seed.
Environment and light: sunny, rather sheltered positions in cool, temperate climates; in the open, in warmer areas.
Type of soil: most soils are suitable but not too rich or they flower badly.

341 STOCK
Matthiola incana:

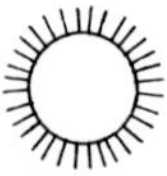

7

Family: Cruciferae. Named after Andrea Mattioli.
Place of origin: Southern Europe; introduced in 1731.
Description: upright biennial with stems 1–2 ft. (30–60 cm) high and slightly woody at base. Leaves downy, lanceolate. Flowers richly scented, usually purple in wild state, in compact terminal clusters. In cultivation, purple, mauve, red, pink, lilac and white varieties occur, single and double. Only the latter are considered of merit. Many races have been derived from this species, including Brompton or Queen Stocks, Intermediate and Ten Week Stocks.
Flowering time: early summer outdoors, but by forcing or pre-cooling from spring until autumn. Winter blooms are induced by giving plants additional illumination.
Use: for greenhouses, decoration, sun-lounges etc.; for cutting; outdoors, in containers or flower beds. Esteemed for their rich scent and charming flower colours.
Propagation: by seed. Double varieties can be detected in the seedling stage, as they are usually more vigorous and have long, pale green concave leaves whereas singles have convex, shorter leaves.
Environment and light: sunny.
Type of soil: well fertilized, soft and light with ash.
Soil moist e: water regularly.
Remarks: most frequently treated as an annual in U.S.

---

342 LADY WASHINGTON PELARGONIUM; MARTHA WASHINGTON PELARGONIUM; REGAL PELARGONIUM
Pelargonium × domesticum form:

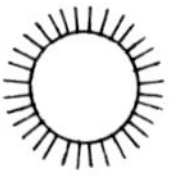

9

Family: Geraniaceae. Name from Greek *pelargos*, stork, referring to the long beak-like fruits.
Place of origin: South Africa; introduced in 1794.
Description: hybrid derived from *P. × domesticum* with rounded clusters of stalked flowers in the leaf axils at the ends of branches. These are in various shades from white to pink to red and purple, variously marked with central petal blotches or spottings. Leaves heart-shaped, toothed at edges.
Flowering time: late-spring–mid-summer (one flowering).
Use: for balconies, terraces, window boxes etc.
Propagation: by cuttings.
Environment and light: sunny or light shade.
Type of soil: three parts good fibrous loam to one of decayed mushroom compost or manure, peat and sand.
Soil moisture: water often, daily in summer.
Remarks: after flowering, prune shoots back in mid-summer to within 1 in. (15 cm) of base. When new shoots form, turn from pots, remove soil and repot.

343 **IVY GERANIUM; IVY-LEAVED GERANIUM**
Pelargonium peltatum:

Family: Geraniaceae.
Place of origin: South Africa; introduced into Europe in 1701.
Description: perennial with weak, trailing stem up to 3 ft. (1 m) long. Leaves ivy-like, glossy, 5-angled and often reddish-zoned. It flowers freely; most cultivars are double, shades ranging from whitish to carmine-rose and reddish-mauve.
Flowering time: spring–autumn.
Use: for hanging baskets, urns and similar containers on balconies, terraces and windows in places which allow the branches to be pendent. Also in cool greenhouses, sun lounges and the like.
Propagation: by cuttings in spring or late summer.
Environment and light: sunny.
Type of soil: loamy soil with sharp drainage.
Soil moisture: water often, daily in summer.
Remarks: in areas north of zone 9 treated as a pot and house plant.

344

Pelargonium radula (P. radens):

Family: Geraniaceae.
Place of origin: South Africa, Cape Province; introduced into Europe in 1774.
Description: shrubby, many-branched, to about 2–3 feet (1 m) in height. Leaves rough, angular, heart-shaped, much-divided, grey-green, with a fragrance of balsam. Flowers rose with purple streaks and dark central markings; flowers freely.
Flowering time: summer.
Use: as a pot or container plant for indoors, for balconies, terraces, entrance-halls and flowerbeds.
Propagation: by cuttings.
Environment and light: sunny.
Type of soil: loam compost, free drainage.
Soil moisture: keep just moist in winter but give plenty of water in summer.
Remarks: repot annually. This pelargonium is the source of an oil, Geranium Oil, used in perfumery.

345 HORSESHOE GERANIUM; ZONAL GERANIUM
Pelargonium zonale form:

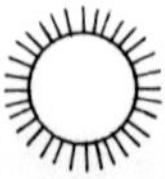

Family: Geraniaceae.
Place of origin: South Africa; introduced into Europe in 1710.
Description: a favourite bedding plant and parent of many forms of popular "Scarlet Geraniums". Perennial, with upright stems, usually about 1½ ft. (45 cm) high. Leaves rounded, irregularly lobed, pungent when bruised, typically with a dark horseshoe-shaped mark near centre. Flowers single or double, white, pink and various shades from light to deep red.
Flowering time: spring–autumn without interruption.
Use: for balconies, terraces, entrance-halls; also for borders and flowerbeds, windowboxes and pots. In the tropics, leave outside against a wall and it will grow to 6–10 ft. (2–3 m).
Propagation: by cuttings in spring or late summer.
Environment and light: sunny.
Type of soil: good, well-drained, loamy soil.
Soil moisture: water frequently in summer. Keep on the dry side in winter.
Remarks: will not tolerate frost, so must be wintered (as rooted cuttings preferably) under cover.

⑨

---

346 PETUNIA
Petunia hybriden:

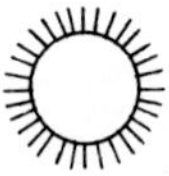

Family: Solanaceae. Name from native Brazilian word, *petún*, for the closely-related tobacco. Hybrid of *P. axillaris* (*P. nyctaginiflora*) and *P. violacea.*
Place of origin: tropical America, Argentine.
Description: showy-flowered plants, perennial but best treated under cultivation as annuals. Trailing forms most suitable for balconies and hanging baskets; height otherwise to about 1½ ft. (45 cm). Leaves entire, rather small. Flowers trumpet-shaped, 4 in. (10 cm) or more across, in variety of colours—white, pink, purple, mauve, yellow, often speckled, striped or veined in contrasting shades; single or double, petals with simple, wavy or fringed edges.
Flowering time: summer–early autumn.
Use: for all types of containers; balconies, terraces, windows, flowerbeds, banks, rockeries etc.
Propagation: by seed in spring.
Environment and light: sunny.
Type of soil: any good rich but well-drained soil.
Soil moisture: water often, as required.

347 CORAL PLANT; FOUNTAIN PLANT

Russelia equisetiformis (R. juncea):

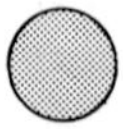

Family: Scrophulariaceae. Named after Dr. Alexander Russell (1715–1768), author of *The Natural History of Aleppo* (1756).
Place of origin: Mexico; introduced into Europe in 1873.
Description: a drought-resistant, shrubby plant of 3–4 ft. (90–120 cm) with green, slender, rush-like branches; flowers, very small and narrow, tubular, $1\frac{1}{4}$ in. (3 cm) long, bright scarlet, in loose drooping clusters.
Flowering time: late summer.
Use: for balconies and terraces, hanging baskets, pots etc. In flowerbeds and borders in tropics and frost-free climates.
Propagation: by cuttings or division.
Environment and light: shaded from hot sun.
Type of soil: loam-based compost.
Soil moisture: water only if necessary.

(10)

---

348 SPEEDY JENNY; WANDERING JEW

Tradescantia fluminensis "Variegata"*:*

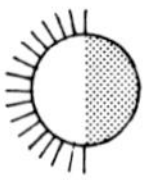

Family: Commelinaceae. Named after John Tradescant of England. He visited Virginia in 1654.
Place of origin: South America.
Description: perennial herb of trailing habit. Leaves oval, pointed, deep green but striped in this form with creamy-white variegations. Flowers small, 3-petalled, white.
Use: as a pot plant, for hanging baskets etc. in homes and greenhouses, also as a garden plant for borders or banks in sub-tropical frost-free climates.
Propagation: by cuttings throughout the year.
Environment and light: shade or half-shade.
Type of soil: adapts to any kind of soil, but loose and fertile, with sand and peat.
Soil moisture: water often, but sparingly.

(8)

349 SPIDERWORT
Tradescantia virginiana "Isis":

(7)

Family: Commelinaceae.
Place of origin: Eastern N. America; introduced into Europe in 1629.
Description: erect, branching, herbaceous perennial. Leaves narrow, strap-like, 6–14 in. (15–35 cm) long, dull green. Flowers deep blue, 2 in. (5 cm) across, 3-petalled with fluffy stamens. Many varieties have been derived from the species.
Flowering time: late spring–mid-autumn.
Use: hardy in areas with only mild frost and can be used for borders, balconies, terraces, verandas etc. Occasionally used in containers.
Propagation: by division in spring.
Environment and light: shade–half-shade or sun.
Type of soil: any good garden soil or compost.
Soil moisture: water if necessary to keep ground moist.
Remarks: in more northerly zones treat as a house or pot plant.

---

350 NASTURTIUM
Tropaeolum majus:

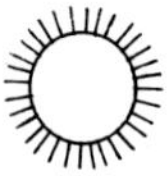

Family: Tropaeolaceae. Name from Greek *tropaion*, trophy; the leaves reminded Linnaeus of the shields used by soldiers in battle, the red and yellow flowers of their blood-stained helmets.
Place of origin: Peru; introduced into Europe around 1686.
Description: strong-growing climbing or trailing annual. Leaves rounded or shield-shaped with a central stem, rather fleshy. Flowers simple or double, large, long-stalked, irregular, yellow, orange or red in colour (orange in the wild state).
Flowering time: summer–late autumn.
Use: for borders, balconies, terraces, window boxes etc.
Propagation: by seed in spring.
Environment and light: sunny or half-shade.
Type of soil: any garden soil.
Soil moisture: water if required to keep ground moist.
Remarks: the leaves can be used in salads and the green fruits pickled as a substitute for capers.

BORDER PLANTS

351 **AGERATUM; FLOSS FLOWER**
Ageratum houstonianum:

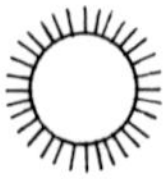

Family: Compositae. Name from Greek *ageratum*, long-lasting, referring to the flowers; specific name in honour of Dr William Houstoun, Scottish surgeon and plant collector who visited Central America early in the eighteenth century.
Place of origin: Mexico; introduced in 1822.
Description: an annual, reaching a height of some 1 ft. 8 in. (50 cm). Leaves ovate to heart-shaped. Flowers clustered, tassel-like, bright blue varying to pink and white. Many varieties, varying in height and colour.

Flowering time: summer.
Use: for edging borders, for flowerbeds, window boxes etc.
Propagation: by seed sown under frost-free conditions in spring and planted out later.
Environment and light: full to half-shade in particularly hot places.

Type of soil: ordinary garden soil.
Soil moisture: water as required.
Remarks: seedlings are not always satisfactory because they dislike being transplanted so do not disturb the root ball at such times, or else plant them out from pots.

---

352 **ROCK CRESS**
Arabis albida; recently referred to as *A. caucasia:*

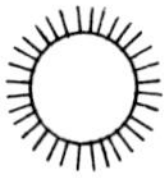

Family: Cruciferae. Name possibly derived from "Arabia".
Place of origin: S.E. Europe and Middle East; introduced into Britain in 1798.

Description: low, mat-forming perennial, 4–16 in. (10–40 cm) high. Leaves radical, hairy, ovate-oblong. Flowers white, fragrant, in loose clusters. Cultivated varieties include a fine double and another having variegated foliage; these are the best kinds for gardens.
Flowering time: spring.
Use: although rather invasive it is suitable for large rock gardens and dry walls, also for slopes and borders.

Propagation: by division or by cuttings.
Environment and light: sunny.
Type of soil: ordinary garden soil.
Soil moisture: water in very dry weather.
Remarks: prune back long shoots almost to source after flowering.

3

353 THRIFT
Armeria caespitosa:

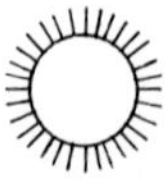

3

Family: Plumbaginaceae. Name from old French *armoires*, referring to flowers of a species of *Dianthus*.
Place of origin: Spain; introduced into Britain in 1885.
Description: herbaceous perennial forming dense cushions of narrow-pointed, needle-like leaves about 2 in. (5 cm) high and masses of flower-heads, globular, pinkish-lilac, or red (illustration shows var. "rubra"), on short stems.
Flowering time: spring–early summer.
Use: for flowerbeds and borders, small grassy banks and slopes, for pockets in rockeries and in dry walls.
Propagation: by division in autumn.
Environment and light: full sun in very cold regions, where in winter the plant should be protected with foliage; sunny elsewhere.
Type of soil: light, well-drained.
Soil moisture: water to keep the ground constantly moist.

---

354 BEGONIA
Begonia semperflorens:

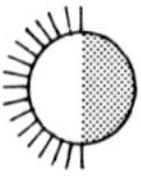

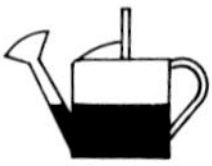

9

Family: Begoniaceae. Named after M. Michel Bégon, seventeenth-century French naturalist.
Place of origin: Brazil; introduced into Britain in 1829.
Description: herbaceous perennial with succulent stems, to $1\frac{1}{2}$ ft. (45 cm) high. Leaves roundish, smooth, somewhat toothed, shiny green. Flowers pink, red or white, in axillary cymes. Variable in height and coloration of the leaves: from green to bronze-purple; also doubles.
Flowering time: summer–autumn; or spring if forced under glass.
Use: for massing as bedding plants in flowerbeds, borders. In pots etc. for greenhouse and sun lounge.
Propagation: by seed or by cuttings from double-bloomed specimens.
Environment and light: half-shade or sun outdoors. Not frost tolerant so winter young struck cuttings under glass or sow afresh from seed.
Type of soil: soft compost, peat and sand in equal parts.
Soil moisture: water regularly; the ground should be moist, never wet.
Remarks: does not winter over in zones north of 9.

355 **DAISY; ENGLISH DAISY**
Bellis perennis "Flore Pleno":

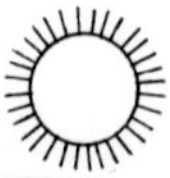

Family: Compositae. Name from Latin, *bellus*, pretty.
Place of origin: Europe (including Britain), Asia Minor.
Description: rosette-forming perennial with leafless flowering stem to about 4 in. (10 cm) high. Leaves basal, numerous, obovate, sparsely hairy. Flowers $\frac{3}{4}$–1 in. (1·5–2·5 cm) across, yellow disk with white or pinkish ray-florets; flower stems 1–6 in. (3–15 cm) long. Longer-flowered and variously coloured forms are derived from this so-called "English daisy", a common weed of lawns. Illustration shows a double red.
Flowering time: spring.
Use: for edging borders, for slopes and banks, grassy areas, and as potted plants.
Propagation: by division in autumn, or by seed.
Environment and light: sunny, half-shade.
Type of soil: any good garden soil.
Soil moisture: the soil must always be moist in the growing season.
Remarks: in areas north of zone 6 treat as an annual.

(4)

---

356 **CANNA; CANNA LILY; INDIAN SHOT**
Canna indica:

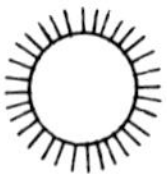

Family: Cannaceae. Name from Greek *kanna*, reed.
Place of origin: Tropical America; introduced in 1570.
Description: perennial with tuberous roots; stems glabrous, to 5 ft. (1.5 m) high. Leaves large, green or crimson, markedly veined, ovate-oblong, slender-pointed, to $1\frac{1}{2}$ ft. (45 cm) long. Flowers showy in loose racemes, petals and petaloid stamens red, pink, orange or yellow; often spotted with other colours.
Flowering time: summer to late autumn.
Use: for summer bedding, greenhouse decoration and containers; in tropics, in borders and flowerbeds.
Propagation: by division of tubers in spring, or by seed which is round and hard, like gun-shot.
Environment and light: sunny to half-shade.
Type of soil: rich and moist.
Soil moisture: water often and generously in summer.
Remarks: rhizomes of various *Canna* species were collected and widely used as food in pre-Columbian times. Plants not frost tolerant, so after foliage is cut by first cold spell, lift and clean tubers and store for winter in just damp soil or sand. Restart in spring in temperature of 60°F (15·5°C), plant out early summer.

(7)

357 BACHELOR BUTTON; KNAPWEED; PERSIAN CENTAUREA

Centaurea dealbata:

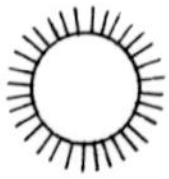

6

Family: Compositae. Name from Greek *kentauros*, centaur, referring to the healing properties attributed to *C. umbellatum* and used by the centaur Chiron to treat an arrow-wound in his foot.
Place of origin: Caucasus, Persia; introduced into Britain in 1804.
Description: upright perennial, 1½–2 ft. (45–60 cm) high. Leaves pinnate, deeply cut and pointed, coarsely toothed, the lower whitish beneath. Buds and flowers thistle-like, flowers rose-pink with paler or whitish central disk. White, deep magenta-pink and rose-purple cultivars exist.
Flowering time: summer.
Use: for borders and flowerbeds.
Propagation: by division in spring or autumn or by seed in spring.
Environment and light: full sun or fairly sunny spots.
Type of soil: ordinary garden soil.
Remarks: treat as an annual north of zone 6. Does not flourish in tropical or semi-tropical climates.

---

358 SHASTA DAISY

Chrysanthemum maximum:

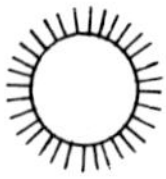

3

Family: Compositae.
Place of origin: Pyrenees.
Description: a coarse but robust perennial, 2½–3 ft. (75–90 cm) high. Leaves toothed, narrow, lanceolate; the lower stalked. Flowers large and single on solitary heads, daisy-like, white with golden centre, 2½–3¼ in. (6–8 cm) across. The type has been superseded by numerous cultivars with double and semi-double inflorescences.
Flowering time: summer.
Use: for cut flowers, borders, small flowerbeds.
Environment and light: sunny, rarely half-shade.
Type of soil: ordinary garden soil on the heavy side, fertile.
Soil moisture: water in dry weather.

359 GODETIA; SATIN FLOWER

Godetia grandiflora (G. amoena whitneyi):

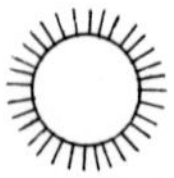

Family: Onagraceae. Named after Charles Godet (1797–1879), Swiss botanist.
Place of origin: California; introduced into Britain in 1867.
Description: compact, bushy annual, normally 12–15 in. (30–37 cm) high. Leaves oblong and pointed. Flowers satin-textured, funnel-shaped, 2 in. (5 cm) across, in clusters, white ranging to pink, red and carmine, often suffused or blotched with darker shade; singles and doubles.
Flowering time: summer to early autumn.
Use: for borders and flowerbeds, small isolated clumps; may be cultivated in boxes or pots; as cut flowers.
Propagation: by seed.
Environment and light: usually in full sun; in particularly hot places the plant does better in half-shade.
Type of soil: light and moist.
Soil moisture: water as required; ground should always be moist.

---

360 DWARF SUNFLOWER

Helianthus annuus var. "Nanus"*:*

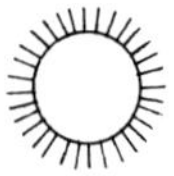

Family: Compositae. Name from Greek *helios*, sun and *anthos*, flower.
Place of origin: Western United States; introduced into Europe in 1596.
Description: a dwarf form of a robust annual, the type growing to 6 ft. (1·8 m) high. Leaves broad, toothed, more or less heart-shaped and rough to touch. Flowers yellow 1–$1\frac{1}{2}$ ft. (30–45 cm) across; the double dwarf much smaller.
Flowering time: summer–early autumn.
Use: for backs of borders, flowerbeds, and wild garden areas.
Propagation: by seed.
Environment and light: full sun.
Type of soil: ordinary garden soil, rich and well fertilized.

361 AARON'S BEARD; HYPERICUM; ROSE OF SHARON (U.K.); ST JOHN'S WORT

Hypericum calycinum:

Family: Guttiferae. Name from Greek *hypereikon—hyper*, above and *eikon*, picture, where the plant was often placed to ward off evil spirits.
Place of origin: S.E. Asia, Asia Minor; introduced into Britain in 1676.
Description: evergreen, or sometimes semi-evergreen shrub which forms a dense, weed-smothering mat, height 1–1½ ft. (30–45 cm) with 4-angled stems. Leaves oval-oblong, entire, leathery, bright green, glaucous beneath. Flowers terminal, usually solitary, about 3 in. (7–8 cm) across, yellow with prominent clustered stamens—like round pincushions.
Flowering time: summer–early autumn.
Use: for shady slopes, banks, flowerbeds, borders etc. Useful ground cover plant.
Propagation: normally by division.
Environment and light: shade or half-shade.
Type of soil: ordinary garden soil, better if fertile and acid.

⑥

---

362 CANDYTUFT

Iberis sempervirens:

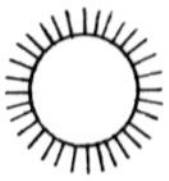

Family: Cruciferae. Generic name from Iberia, where several species occur.
Place of origin: mountains of southern Europe; introduced into Britain in 1820.
Description: spreading, evergreen (except in areas of deep frost) perennial, 9 in. (22 cm) high. Leaves narrow, flat, blunt. Flowers pure white, in dense flat-topped heads, 1½–2 in. (4–5 cm) across. Variegated and double varieties are known.
Flowering time: spring–early summer.
Use: fine border edging plant, also for decorating corners of rock gardens, slopes and banks.
Environment and light: full sun to half-shade.
Type of soil: ordinary garden soil, light and fertile.

③

363 SEA LAVENDER; STATICE
Limonium sinuatum:

Family: Plumbaginaceae. Name from Greek *leimon*, meadow (plant).
Place of origin: eastern and southern Mediterranean regions; introduced into Britain in 1629.
Description: erect perennial, 16 in.–2 ft. (40–60 cm) high, usually grown as a half-hardy annual; stems winged. Leaves ovate-lanceolate, with deeply lobed and waved margins. Flowers white, yellow, blue or red, papery-textured, in comb-like clusters; individual flowers tubular and tiny.
Flowering time: summer–early autumn.
Use: for flowerbeds, borders, small clumps, rockeries and cut flowers dried for winter arrangements.
Propagation: by seed.
Environment and light: full sun.
Type of soil: any rich garden soil.
Soil moisture: water in dry weather.

②

---

364 CREEPING JENNY; MONEYWORT
Lysimachia nummularia:

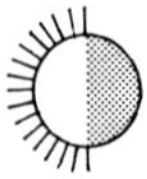

Family: Primulaceae. Named after Lysimachus, king of Thrace.
Place of origin: Western Europe, including Britain.
Description: creeping perennial, rooting at nodes, trailing to about 2 ft. (60 cm). Leaves oval, opposite, short-stalked. Flowers erect, yellow, cup-shaped, $\frac{3}{4}$–1 in. (1·5–2·5 cm) across. "Aurea", a form with golden leaves, is the most garden-worthy.
Flowering time: summer–autumn.
Use: to cover shaded slopes and banks, for walls, also for hanging baskets, in the bog garden and as an aquarium plant (submerged).
Propagation: by cuttings or division.
Environment and light: Sun, half-shade to total shade; the Creeping Jenny also lives in the shade of thickets in quite damp places.
Type of soil: ordinary garden soil with a little sand and leaf-mould.
Soil moisture: likes moist conditions.

③

365 GERMAN CAMOMILE; SCENTLESS MAYWEED

Matricaria inodora (M. maritimum) (Tripleorospermum inodorum):

Family: Compositae.
Place of origin: Europe (including Britain).
Description: erect, branched, bushy annual or biennial, 1–2 ft. (30–60 cm) high. Leaves smooth, deeply cut. Flowers white with yellow disk-florets, in terminal heads up to $1\frac{1}{2}$ in. (4 cm) across. The double garden variety as illustrated (probably a cultivar of *Chrysanthemum parthenum* (*Matricaria eximia*)) is the only one worth growing.
Flowering time: summer–early autumn.
Use: for edging flowerbeds, small clumps.
Propagation: by seed.
Environment and light: full sun.
Type of soil: ordinary garden soil.

---

366 LIVINGSTONE DAISY

Mesembryanthemum criniflorum (now *Dorotheanthus bellidiflorus,* sometimes spelt *D. bellidiformis*):

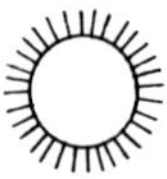

Family: Aizoaceae. Name from Greek *mesos*, middle, *embryon*, embryo and *anthemon*, flower, referring to the position of the ovary.
Place of origin: South Africa; introduced from the Cape Province into Britain circa 1880.
Description: annual, forming a low mat an inch or so high (about 3 cm) with thick, almost cylindrical, succulent leaves. Flowers bright, daisy-like, about $1\frac{1}{2}$ in. (3–4 cm) across, white tipped with pink; also crimson, orange, yellow, apricot, buff and pale mauve.
Flowering time: summer.
Use: suited for borders or small flowerbeds, in warm areas.
Propagation: by seed sown in warmth in spring.
Environment and light: sunny and dry. Must be very bright; the flowers close in dull weather, cannot tolerate frost.
Type of soil: quite poor and sandy.
Soil moisture: not too wet as this can cause rotting.

367 BERMUDA BUTTERCUP; BUTTERCUP OXALIS; CAPE SORREL

Oxalis pes-caprae (O. cernua):

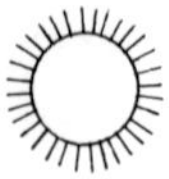

9

Family: Oxalidaceae. Name from Greek *oxys*, acid, referring to the sap which is sour and sharp to the taste.
Place of origin: South Africa; introduced into Britain in 1757.
Description: low-growing herbaceous perennial, forming bulbils at surface of soil. Leaves trefoil-like, slightly succulent, on long stalks. Flowers 5-petalled, yellow, about 1 in. (2–3 cm) long, grouped together in loose umbels.
Flowering time: summer.
Use: for borders, small clumps of colour on rockeries or as shrubbery species, but exercise caution (*see* Remarks). Makes a pretty pot plant for the greenhouse, sun lounges etc.
Propagation: by seed in spring or division.
Environment and light: full sun to light shade; not frost tolerant.
Type of soil: light, mixed with sand.
Soil moisture: water generously until flowering; then reduce and stop altogether for 20–30 days.
Remarks: the plant spreads rapidly and has become a serious weed in parts of the Mediterranean region.

---

368 OXALIS

Oxalis rosea:

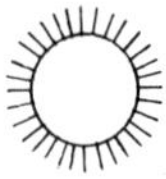

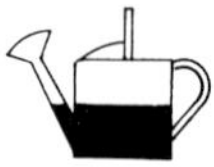

8

Family: Oxalidaceae.
Place of origin: Chile; introduced into Europe in 1823.
Description: erect annual, to 1 ft. (30 cm) high. Leaves divided, with heart-shaped leaflets, bright green, often reddish below. Flowers rose-coloured, dark-veined, in dense clusters.
Flowering time: summer–early autumn.
Use: for small beds, pots or rock garden pockets.
Propagation: by seed in spring, usually sown where plants are to flower.
Environment and light: full sun to half-shade. Flowers close in dull weather.
Type of soil: any moist soil.
Soil moisture: water quite generously.

369 POLYANTHUS; ENGLISH PRIMROSE (U.S.)

Primula vulgaris: hyb.

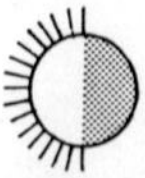

Family: Primulaceae. Name from Latin *primus*, first (early flowering).
Place of origin: S. and W. Europe, including Britain.
Description: perennial plants, leaves in basal rosette, 3–16 in. (8–15 cm) long, obovate, puckered, downy beneath. Flowers about 1 in. (2–3 cm) across, pale yellow, on long thin stalks. Pink and red flowered forms are plentiful in N. Turkey and some have been selected for naming. The British forms are all yellow.

Flowering time: early spring.
Use: for borders, flowerbeds, rock gardens, grassy areas, and as pot plants.

Propagation: by division towards the end of summer; by seed in spring in soft light soil (loam, peat and sand).
Environment and light: half-shade or full sun whilst flowering; remove to deep shade for summer.
Type of soil: moist, fertile, on the heavy side but well-drained.

(5)

Soil moisture: water regularly so that the soil is moist, but not wet; reduce watering temporarily for two months after flowering.
Remarks: polyanthus are derived from crossing primroses (*P. vulgaris*) with cowslips (*P. veris*): *see* illustration. The flowers come in umbels and are variously coloured.

---

370 RED SALVIA; SCARLET SAGE

Salvia splendens:

Family: Labiatae.
Place of origin: Brazil; introduced into Britain in 1822.
Description: erect, bushy annual mostly about 1 ft. (30 cm) high but can be up to 3 ft. (90 cm). Leaves oval, long-pointed, smooth with rounded teeth. Flowers in long spikes, floral parts bright scarlet. Varieties include white and dwarf forms.
Flowering time: summer.

Use: for annual borders, windowboxes, mixed bedding to create fine splashes of colour.
Propagation: by seed sown in spring under glass, planting out seedlings when all risk of frost is over.
Environment and light: full sun.
Type of soil: fertile, well-drained.
Soil moisture: water occasionally, so that the soil is moist, but never wet.

371 LAVENDER COTTON

Santolina chamaecyparissus:

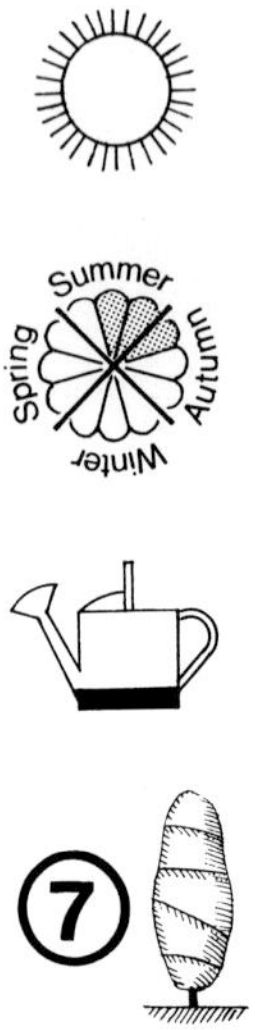

Family: Compositae. Name from Latin *sanctum linum*, holy flax which refers to *S. virens*.
Place of origin: southern Europe; introduced into Britain in 1596.
Description: a bushy, aromatic, evergreen, much-branched shrub, up to $2\frac{1}{2}$ ft. (15 cm). Leaves crowded, narrow, indented with comb-like teeth, grey-green or silvery. Flower-heads globular, long-stalked, yellow, about $\frac{1}{2}$ in. (1–1·5 cm) across, without ray-florets.
Flowering time: mid-summer–early autumn.
Use: normally grown for its aromatic foliage. Suitable for sunny banks, borders, flowerbeds, to make small hedges.
Propagation: by half-ripe cuttings in summer.
Environment and light: full sun.
Type of soil: with gravel or stony.
Soil moisture: water if necessary; in cold winter climates the base of the plant should be protected.
Remarks: used as an insecticide and vermifuge. Also as an ingredient of pot-pourri.

---

372 MOTHER OF THOUSANDS; STRAWBERRY GERANIUM

Saxifraga stolonifera (S. sarmentosa):

Family: Saxifragaceae. From Latin *Saxum*, rock and *frango*, to break, referring to the ability of the roots to penetrate crevices thereby assisting in the fracture of rocks; derived from this was the supposed medicinal attribute of removing stones from the bladder.
Place of origin: China, Japan; introduced into Europe in 1815.
Description: tufted perennial with many, thin trailing, strawberry-like runners carrying countless new plants. Leaves round, marbled. Flowers in pyramidal panicles, 5-petalled, the paired upper of which are small with yellow markings, central petal with two red spots at base, and two outer petals long and drooping. "Tricolor", with green, cream and pink leaves, is the best.
Flowering time: summer.
Use: for hanging baskets, greenhouse or container decoration. Not frost tolerant. Grown for its foliage.
Propagation: by detaching the young plants from the runners and potting separately.
Environment and light: half-shade in cool frost-free places.
Type of soil: loam, sand and leaf-mould or peat compost.
Soil moisture: water regularly, more often in summer.

373 **SEDUM; STONECROP**

Sedum ellacombianum (related to and now considered a variety of No 374):

Family: Crassulaceae. Name from Latin *sedere*, to sit, referring to the manner in which some species grow on rocks.
Place of origin: a garden hybrid.
Description: perennial, some 10 in. (25 cm) high, with unbranched stems. Leaves spathulate, broadly indented. Flowering inflorescence dense, above leaves; flowers yellow.
Flowering time: summer.
Use: for edging rock gardens.
Propagation: by division.
Environment and light: full sun.
Type of soil: ordinary garden soil on the dry side.

④

374

Sedum kamtschaticum:

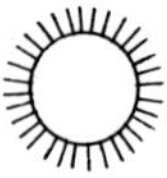

Family: Crassulaceae.
Place of origin: N. China, Kamchatka, E. Siberia; introduced into Europe in 1829.
Description: an easily grown, mat-forming plant with dark green, fleshy, spoon-shaped leaves with toothed edges and clusters of small 5-petalled yellow flowers. A form with white leaf margins ("Variegatum") is the one most frequently grown.
Flowering time: summer–early autumn.
Use: for rock gardens, edging, slopes and banks.
Propagation: by seed or self-layering.
Environment and light: full sun.
Type of soil: ordinary garden soil.
Soil moisture: water seldom; this plant, like all succulents, dislikes too much moisture.

③

375 **SPRING BELL**
Sisyrinchium striatum:

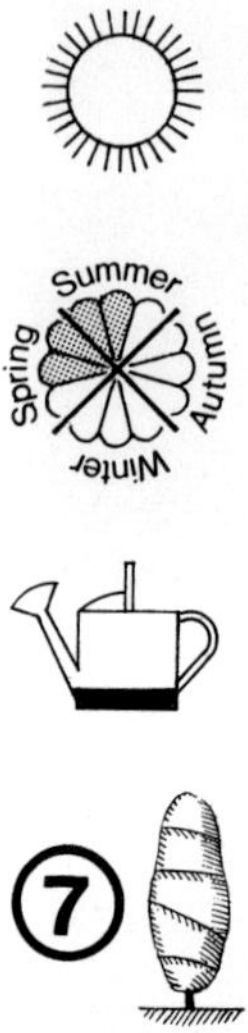

Family: Indaceae. Ancient Greek name used by Theophrastus.
Place of origin: Chile; introduced into Europe 1788.
Description: an erect growing plant to 1 ft. (30 cm), with the habit and similar sword-shaped foliage to iris. The creamy yellow flowers, however, are quite deep-set, being smaller and arranged in closely placed spikes of 9 to 12 blooms. There is a variegated foliage form.
Flowering time: early summer.
Use: grouping in borders for flower and foliage effect.
Propagation: by seed or division.
Environment and light: full sun.
Type of soil: light and well-drained.
Soil moisture: water if necessary.
Remarks: the plants resent wet, cold conditions in winter and so should be sheltered.

---

376 **FRENCH MARIGOLD**
Tagetes patula:

Family: Compositae. Named after Tages, an Etruscan deity.
Place of origin: Mexico; introduced into Europe in 1573.
Description: bushy annual with erect stems 6–12 in. (15–30 cm) high. Leaves dark green, deeply divided and toothed, unpleasant smelling in type but less so in cultivars. Flowers red or yellow, solitary. Varieties with red, gold, striped and mottled flowers; also dwarf and higher-growing forms.
Flowering time: summer–early autumn.
Use: for borders, flowerbeds, bedding out and containers.
Propagation: by seed sown under glass in spring; put the young plants out in early summer.
Environment and light: full sun. Not frost tolerant.
Type of soil: ordinary garden soil.
Soil moisture: water in periods of drought or very dry conditions.
Remarks: remove spent flowers regularly to encourage continuity of flowering.

377 MOSS VERBENA
Verbena laciniata (V. erinoides):

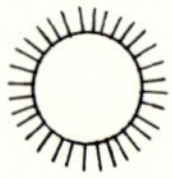

Family Verbenaceae. Name from the ancient Latin name for the vervain, *V. officinalis*.
Place of origin: S. America; introduced into Britain in 1818.
Description: herbaceous annual with sprawling stems about 6 in. (15 cm) long. Leaves finely divided. Flowers small, 5-petalled, pinkish-lilac, also red, blue and violet, in dense heads.

Flowering time: summer.
Use: for borders and rockeries.
Propagation: by seed in seedboxes in spring, or in the open ground in milder climates.
Environment and light: full sun in places protected from the wind.
Type of soil: ordinary garden soil.
Soil moisture: water in the hottest months.

---

378 SPEEDWELL; VERONICA
Veronica gentianoides:

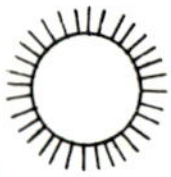

Family: Scrophulariaceae. Plants named in honour of St Veronica.
Place of origin: Caucasus; introduced into Europe in 1784.
Description: tufted perennial with simple erect stem, 6–12 in. (15–30 cm) high. Leaves glossy, oblong, lower ones forming a rosette. Flowers white to pale blue, in loose terminal racemes, 10 in. (25 cm) long.

Flowering time: early summer.
Use: for borders, or rock gardens.
Propagation: by division in spring.
Environment and light: full sun to half-shade.
Type of soil: good but well-drained.
Soil moisture: water in the hottest months; the soil should always be moist.

4

MEDICINAL AND AROMATIC PLANTS

379 **MONKSHOOD**
Aconitum napellus:

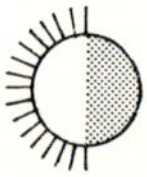

3

Family: Ranunculaceae. The name *Aconitum* was used by Theophrastus for a poisonous plant.
Place of origin: widely distributed in Europe and Asia.
Description: a very variable, leafy, herbaceous perennial, 3–4 ft. (about 1 m) high, with very poisonous rootstocks. Leaves palmately cut into 5 lobes, each of which is divided into narrow segments. Flowers dark blue with 5 petaloid sepals, one of which forms a hood, borne in simple or branched spikes; pale blue, reddish-purple and white forms occur.
Flowering time: summer.
Use: for herbaceous borders and shaded flowerbeds. Medicinally applied externally in neuralgia; internally as sedative, but rarely used today owing to powerful cardiac effects. Used in past as an arrow poison.
Propagation: by seed sown as soon as ripe or by division of the roots in spring or autumn.
Environment and light: half-shade.
Type of soil: most soils.
Soil moisture: soil should be moist.
Remarks: poisonous constituents are alkaloids, which remain effective after drying. Death can follow consumption of the leaves or roots.

---

380 **HOLLYHOCK**
Althaea rosa (now more correctly *Alcea rosea*):

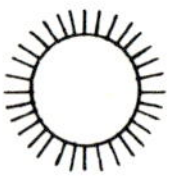

4

Family: Malvaceae. Name from Greek *altheo*, to cure; some species have been used medicinally.
Place of origin: probably Eastern Mediterranean region and not China as is frequently stated.
Description: perennial plants of stately habit, up to 6 ft. (1·8 m) tall; stems, strong, leafy, the last 5–7 angled, heart-shaped and rough to the touch. Flowers many, along the tops of the spike, short-stalked, saucer-shaped with prominent yellow centre; white, cream, pink, red and purplish; also doubles.
Flowering time: summer.
Use: for key positions, as by a front door, garden gate etc., or backs of borders.
Properties: the leaves were formerly used as pot herbs; and the petals employed to colour wine and cure coughs.
Propagation: by seed.
Environment and light: full sun.
Type of soil: well worked ordinary garden soil.
Remarks: although perennial, hollyhocks are usually treated as biennial, and in certain areas as an annual because of a rust disease which attacks the plants.

381 STRAWBERRY TREE

Arbutus unedo:

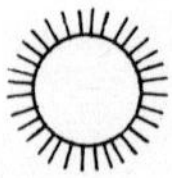

(8)

Family: Ericaceae. Name from Latin, but of unknown definition.
Place of origin: Mediterranean region and S.W. Ireland.
Description: shrub or small evergreen tree, occasionally reaching a height of 39 ft. (12 m); bark rough and shreddy. Leaves glossy, dark green, toothed. Flowers white or pinkish, urn-shaped, in drooping clusters, usually appearing at same time as the older fruits. Fruit round, strawberry-like, about $\frac{3}{4}$ in. (1·5–2 cm), orange-red, rough-surfaced.
Flowering time: late autumn–winter.
Use: as an evergreen, shade or boundary tree for gardens and parks.
Propagation: by seed in winter.
Environment and light: full sun to half-shade, but only in climates where the winter is not too cold.
Type of soil: loose, slightly sandy soil; non-calcerous.
Soil moisture: water quite sparingly; this plant, especially after the first few years, adapts well to long dry spells.
Remarks: Fruits are edible (but unpalatable), being used in wine-making and for liqueurs and preserves; leaves and branches of other species are used for tanning.

---

382 BIRTHWORT

Aristolochia clematitis:

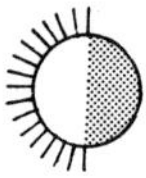

(4)

Family: Aristolochiaceae. Name from Greek *aristos*, best and *lochia*, childbirth, referring to its medical uses.
Place of origin: Europe (including Britain).
Description: upright, herbaceous perennial, up to about 3 ft. (1 m) in height, with strong, unpleasant smell. Leaves cordate. Flowers pale yellow, curved and trumpet-shaped, in clusters in leaf-axils.
Flowering time: late spring–mid-summer.
Use: the source of an astringent bitter in modern pharmacy. An infusion from the roots used medicinally in the past in childbirth, and as a cure for snake-bite. Poisonous.
Propagation: by cuttings rooted with bottom heat.
Environment and light: well-lit, but not in direct sun.
Type of soil: any good loam with rotted manure and sand to assist drainage.
Soil moisture: this species usually grows in damp places.

383 ARNICA
Arnica montana:

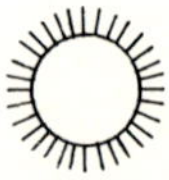

Family: Compositae. Classical name of unknown derivation.
Place of origin: mountains of Central Europe.
Description: upright, perennial herb, flowering stem to 2 ft. (60 cm) in height. Leaves downy, lance-shaped, aromatic, larger basal ones arranged in a rosette. Flowering capitulum usually solitary, orange-yellow, $1\frac{1}{2}$–3 in. (4–8 cm) across, the outer florets wide-spreading.
Flowering time: late spring–mid-summer.
Use: for decorating grassy banks.
Properties: used as a stimulant, febrifuge and for treatment of bruises and sprains; diuretic; reputed to make the hair grow if applied to the scalp, and a tincture of same said to prevent sea-sickness.
Propagation: by division in spring or autumn.
Environment and light: full sun.
Type of soil: light, loose and calcerous.
Soil moisture: water regularly.

⑥

---

384 ABSINTHE; WORMWOOD
Artemisia absinthium:

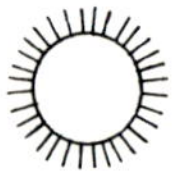

Family: Compositae. Named in honour of Artemis, Greek goddess of chastity; in earlier days the plant was associated with calamity and sorrow.
Place of origin: Europe; also widespread in Britain.
Description: many-branched, aromatic, silvery perennial, 20–40 in. (50–100 cm) high. Leaves 2- or 3-pinnate, with silky hairs. Flower-heads rounded, pendent, borne in axillary spikes forming a slender, pyramidal inflorescence 6–18 in. (15–45 cm) long; flowers yellow.
Flowering time: mid-summer–early autumn.
Harvesting time: late spring–early autumn.
Use: the leaves and flowering tops are used for infusions and to flavour liqueurs.
Properties: digestive, gastric, cholagogic etc.
Propagation: by seed in spring or by division.
Environment and light: full sun.
Type of soil: dry, but best if clayey.
Remarks: of considerable medicinal value; the liqueur absinthe (which is illegal in several countries) is flavoured with this and other herbs. Much cultivated for making the liqueur and in the preparation of liniments.

③

385 ITALIAN ARUM
Arum italicum:

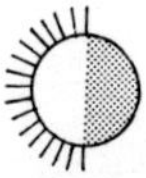

Family: Araceae. Name from Greek *aron*, name for these plants.
Place of origin: S.E. Europe to Canary Islands.
Description: herbaceous perennial 1–2 ft. (30–60 cm) high. Leaves glossy, long-stalked, arrow-shaped; in the best forms the leaves are heavily cream-splashed; these appear in late autumn. Flowering spadix yellow, surrounded by yellowish-green, purple-edged spathe up to 16 in. (40 cm) long.
Flowering time: spring.
Use: the rhizome, when fresh, has expectorant and purgative properties, but it is very poisonous. The variegated forms are highly desirable garden plants, especially for shady areas. Much esteemed by flower-arrangers.
Propagation: by seed or division after flowering.
Environment and light: sun (in cool climates) or half-shade.
Type of soil: any moist but well-drained soil.
Remarks: Starch from the tubers once used for stiffening linen, but abandoned because of the irritation caused to the hands of laundresses.

7

---

386 DEADLY NIGHTSHADE
Atropa belladonna:

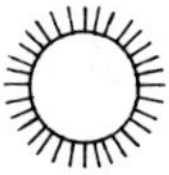

Family: Solanaceae. Named after Atropos who, in Greek mythology, was concerned with curtailing life.
Place of origin: Central and Southern Europe (including Britain) and Western Asia.
Description: erect, vigorously-growing, perennial herb, 3–4 ft. (90–120 cm) high, with more or less hollow stems and large ovate leaves; flowers bell-shaped, about 1 in. (2·5–3 cm) long, greenish-yellow or brownish-purple, followed by large, round, glossy berries the size of cherries.
Flowering time: summer–early autumn.
Use: despite being highly poisonous, has important medicinal uses as anti-spasmodic, sedative and narcotic; as a cosmetic, used formerly by women to dilate the pupils of the eyes.
Propagation: by seed.
Environment and light: sun or light shade in cool places.
Type of soil: fresh, light, well fertilized.
Soil moisture: likes most soil.
Remarks: often confused with Woody Nightshade (*A. dulcamara*).

9

387 POT MARIGOLD
Calendula officinalis:

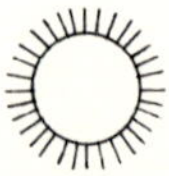

Family: Compositae.
Place of origin: Southern Europe.
Description: annual, 1 ft.–1 ft. 8 in. (30–50 cm) high, with lower leaves spathulate, narrowing towards stem, upper leaves lance-shaped. Flowers $1\frac{1}{2}$–2 in. (4–5 cm) across, orange to yellow, variable in shade.
Flowering time: summer–late autumn.
Use: grown mainly as a decorative plant, especially the double forms (*see* No 255).
Properties: as a pot-herb, only the outer florets so used to flavour soup, broths, stews and cakes—also to give a yellow colour to butter and cheese; can also be made into marigold wine, marigold puddings.
Propagation: by seed.
Environment and light: full sun.
Type of soil: ordinary garden soil.
Remarks: culinary uses in flavouring and colouring, also as a tonic and in herbal remedies for sprains.

⑥

---

388 CASSIA
Cassia: sp.

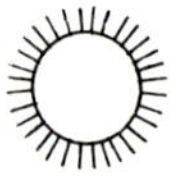

Family: Leguminosae. Name from Greek *kasia*, from a Hebrew word *gatsa*, cut off bark.
Place of origin: a large genus of some 500–600 trees, shrubs and herbs from tropical and warm temperate parts of the world, excluding Europe.
Description: flowers mostly yellow (occasionally pink or red), uneven but with petals of equal size and up to 10 stamens. Leaves alternate, pinnate. Pods: flattened.
Flowering time: summer–mid-autumn.
Harvesting time: summer.
Use: infusions, liquid extracts, dyes and syrups are made from the pinnules. In places with mild winters Cassia can be grown as a small tree or bush.
Properties: purgative.
Propagation: half-ripe cuttings rooted with bottom heat.
Environment and light: full sun. Not hardy outdoors in frost-prone climates.
Type of soil: sandy loam, mixed with sand.
Remarks: many species are cultivated for their leaves, which provide senna when dried; *C. acutifolia* provides Alexandrian senna, *C. obovata* Italian senna and *C. fistula* has a laxative pulp.

③

389 FEVERFEW

Chrysanthemum (Matricaria) parthenium:

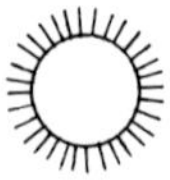

4

Family: Compositae. From Greek *chryos*, gold and *anthos*, flower.
Place of origin: Asia Minor, Europe (including Britain); widely introduced.
Description: upright, herbaceous perennial to about 2 ft. (60 m) high, strongly aromatic with a chamomile-like scent. Leaves much-divided, with fairly short stalks. Flower-heads up to 1 in. (1–2·5 cm) across, a yellow disk surrounded by white florets. The double variety is an attractive garden plant.
Flowering time: summer.
Harvesting time: flowers early summer; leaves any time.
Use: dried flowers have been used medicinally to allay fevers (anti-spasmodic) and in a tincture as an insect repellant; also used for a tea and in wine. At one time sold in the streets of London as a plague preventative.
Propagation: by seed in spring.
Environment and light: full sun.
Type of soil: ordinary garden soil.

---

390 FOXGLOVE

Digitalis purpurea:

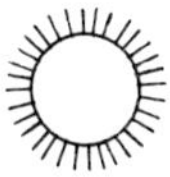

4

Family: Scrophulariaceae. Name from *digitus*, flower, referring to the finger-like shape of the flowers.
Place of origin: Western Europe (including Britain).
Description: a stately biennial of 2–5 ft. (60–150 cm) (according to condition). Leaves form a radical rosette the first year, large, dentate, broad, oblong, coarse and hairy-surfaced. Flowers on erect, leafy spike, purple varying to white, with darker spots on lower inside of the corolla tube.
Flowering time: late spring–early summer.
Use: a handsome garden plant, especially for light shade. Source of the drug digitalin, a heart stimulant, but poisonous if taken too liberally. In N. Wales a dye from the leaves is used to colour stonework.
Properties: diuretic, cardiotonic.
Propagation: by seed sown after harvesting to flower following year.
Environment and light: full sun to half-shade.
Type of soil: woodland type—leaf-mould, loam and sand.
Soil moisture: likes moist soil.

391 GOAT'S RUE
Galega officinalis:

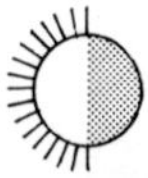

3

Family: Leguminosae. Name from Greek, *gala*, milk, as it was supposed to increase the flow of milk in livestock; *officinalis*, from the Latin, plants with supposed medicinal properties sold in shops.
Place of origin: Southern Europe, Asia Minor; introduced into Britain in 1568.
Description: herbaceous perennial, 3–4 ft. (90–120 cm) tall. Leaves pinnate, with 11–17 leaflets, finely-pointed. Flowers pea-shaped, in dense axillary clusters, white or pale blue.
Flowering time: summer.
Harvesting time: from late spring to August.
Use: the whole above-ground parts are used for infusions, liquid extracts and tinctures (dyes). Cultivated as animal food plant; used medicinally as mild astringent, tonic.
Propagation: by seed or division.
Environment and light: half-shade to sunny, unsuited to very dry places.
Type of soil: ordinary garden soil, but fresh and moist.

---

392 GREAT YELLOW GENTIAN; YELLOW GENTIAN
Gentiana lutea:

6

Family: Gentianaceae. Named after Gentius, King of the Illyrians, said to have discovered the medicinal value of the root.
Place of origin: wet pastures in mountainous parts of Central and Southern Europe, and Asia Minor.
Description: upright, glabrous perennial, $1\frac{1}{2}$–$6\frac{1}{2}$ ft. (0·5–2 m) high. Leaves 8–12 in. (20–30 cm), rounded, strongly-nerved, the upper ones clasping the stem. Flowers tubular, 1 in. (2·5 cm) long, petals divided, golden yellow, in dense whorls (*see* illustration).
Flowering time: summer.
Harvesting time: Sept–Oct.
Use: used in home-remedies as a tonic and antiseptic. The roots are also collected in late summer and autumn, allowed to ferment and then employed in tonics and bitters and to make a liqueur.
Properties: aperient, gastric, febrifuge, digestive.
Propagation: by seed or by division in autumn.
Environment and light: quite sunny.
Type of soil: deep and quite moist.
Soil moisture: water if necessary so that the ground is always moist whilst plants are growing.

393 LAVENDER

Lavandula spica:

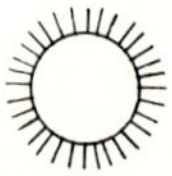

5

Family: Labiatae. Name from Latin *lavare*, wash, referring to the plant's use in toilet preparations.
Place of origin: native of the Mediterranean region; cultivated since the mid-sixteenth century.
Description: fragrant shrub up to 3 ft. (1 m) in height with square (when young), greyish-white stems. Leaves slender, downy, pale grey. Flowers blue-grey, borne on long-stemmed, slender spikes.
Flowering time: mid-summer–early autumn.
Harvesting time: just before the flowers are fully open.
Use: a good garden plant for hedges and flowerbeds. In cold climates grow in containers. Widely used for perfumery, soap industry, scenting linen, lavender water and other concoctions.
Properties: anti-tussive, antiseptic, antispasmodic etc.
Propagation: by heel cuttings in mid-summer.
Environment and light: full sun. Plant not too hardy in cold climates.
Type of soil: stony, and poor.

---

394 LEMON VERBENA

Lippia citriodora (now more correctly *Aloysia citriodora*)*:*

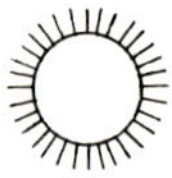

8

Family: Verbenaceae. Named after Augustin Lippi, seventeenth-century Italian naturalist.
Place of origin: Southern S. America; introduced in 1784.
Description: deciduous shrub, usually to about $6\frac{1}{2}$ ft. (2 m) in height. Leaves lance-shaped, lemon-scented. Flowers insignificant and small, pale purple, borne in terminal spikes.
Flowering time: summer.
Use: Grown as a cool greenhouse plant and for warm corners in cool temperate climates, for its aromatic foliage.
Properties: aromatic oil from leaves, known as verbena oil, used in perfumery and for scenting linen, pot pourri etc. A tea is made from the leaves in parts of South America, which is good for the digestion.
Propagation: cuttings in summer.
Environment and light: sunny and warm.
Type of soil: ordinary garden soil with sand. Well-drained.

395 **COMMON MALLOW**
Malva sylvestris:

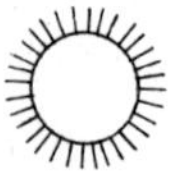

Family: Malvaceae. Old name of obscure origin.
Place of origin: Europe (including Britain), Asia and introduced into N. and S. America and Australia.
Description: a robust, herbaceous plant $1\frac{1}{2}$–4 ft. (45–120 cm), biennial or perennial, little-branched. Leaves with toothed margins, broad, rounded, with 5–7 lobes. Flowers large, rosy-purple with darker veins, 5-petalled.
Flowering time: spring–late summer.
Harvesting time: summer/early autumn.
Use: leaves used as a substitute for tea and as a vegetable, flowers for gargling and mouth-washes (Flores Malvae).
Properties: emmolient, antitussive, laxative, sedative etc. This plant shares to a lesser degree the same properties as the Marsh Mallow. In Devonshire called "Chucky Cheese" because of the appearance of its fruits which children nibble.
Propagation: by seed.
Environment and light: full sun. A weedy plant in cultivated land or at roadsides.
Type of soil: ordinary garden soil.

(6)

---

396 **WILD CAMOMILE (also spelt CHAMOMILE)**
Matricaria chamomilla:

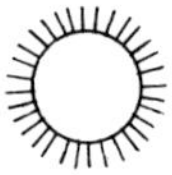

Family: Compositae. Name possibly from *matrix*, womb, from its earlier use in affections of the uterus.
Place of origin: Europe.
Description: an aromatic annual, 12–20 in. (30–50 cm) high. Leaves bipinnate, deeply cut into segments, rather downy. Flowers solitary, yellow disk, white rays which have a tendency to curl back.
Flowering time: spring–summer.
Harvesting time: late spring to Aug.
Use: an infusion is made of the unopened flowers.
Properties: this is not the true chamomile (*Anthemis nobilis*, now *Chamaemelum nobile*), although it possesses many of the properties of that plant and is often used as a substitute. The flowers are less bitter and nauseating than those of the true chamomile.
Used for an aromatic tea and medicinally; it has mild sedative properties acting on the nervous system, antispasmodic, digestive, emmenagogic.
Propagation: by seed.
Environment and light: sunny.
Type of soil: widespread in cultivated and recently disturbed ground.

(5)

397 **MYRTLE**

Myrtus communis:

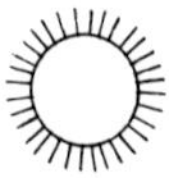

⑧

Family: Myrtaceae. *Myrtus*, held sacred by the Greeks.
Place of origin: S. Europe to W. Asia; cultivated in Britain since 1597.
Description: aromatic, dense, evergreen shrub, 9–14 ft. (3–4·5 m). Leaves lance-shaped, dark shiny green. Flowers white, about 1 in. (2–3 cm) across, fragrant, with long stamens, followed by blue-black berries.
Flowering time: summer–mid-autumn.
Harvesting time: summer.
Use: for hedges or shrubberies and for its ornamental features. A fragrant oil, "Eau d'Anges", is used in perfumery; the fruit is used as a condiment and fermented as an acid drink; the bark and roots are employed in tanning. The wood is hard and close-grained.
Properties: astringent, aromatic, balsamic.
Propagation: by seed or cuttings.
Environment and light: full sunlight. In frost-prone areas as a greenhouse plant, wintered under cover.
Type of soil: well-drained but fertile.
Soil moisture: water during growing season.
Remarks: famous since classical times; wreaths of myrtle were worn by victors in the Olympic Games. It is still used with orange blossom as a traditional bridal flower.

---

398 **SWEET BASIL**

Ocimum basilicum:

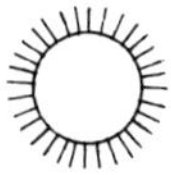

Family: Labiatae. Name in Greek, an aromatic herb; the plant is sacred in the Hindu religion.
Place of origin: Old World tropics, Pacific Islands; introduced into Britain in 1548.
Description: erect, herbaceous annual, about $1\frac{1}{2}$ ft. (45 cm) high, aromatic. Leaves bright green, lanceolate, short-stemmed. Flowers white, pink or lilac, in terminal spikes.
Flowering time: summer–early autumn.
Harvesting time: late summer–early autumn.
Use: use is made of the leaves and terminal part of the scape. The plant is cultivated outdoors and in pots. Source of oil used for condiments and in salads (use sparingly); also in cosmetics and perfumery. Seeds are source of a beverage used in Mediterranean countries.
Properties: gastric, antitussive, carminative.
Propagation: by seed raised in gentle warmth in spring and planted out when no further risk of frost.
Environment and light: full sun.
Type of soil: fresh, light and fertile.
Soil moisture: water generously.

399 RHUBARB

Rheum officinale:

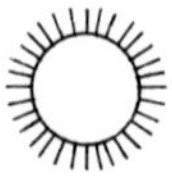

5

Family: Polygonaceae. *Rheum* is the ancient Greek name for rhubarb. Closely allied to the Common (vegetable) Rhubarb (*R. rhaponticum*).
Place of origin: Central Asia; introduced into Britain in 1871.
Description: herbaceous plant 6–10 ft. (2–3 m) high, with thick rhizomes, leafy and much-branched. Leaves rounded with 5 shallow lobes. Flowers dense, greenish-white, on large spikes.
Flowering time: summer.
Harvesting time: autumn.
Use: occasionally grown in gardens, but more important pharmaceutically, because the rhizomes produce tinctures, syrups, liquid extracts etc. Rhizomes used in fourth and fifth years.
Properties: used for stomach disorders and as a laxative. Bitter-tonic, aperient etc.
Propagation: usually by seed or division in spring.
Environment and light: sunny or half-shade in particularly hot places.
Type of soil; any good garden soil.
Soil moisture: water if necessary.

---

400 CASTOR BEAN; CASTOR-OIL PLANT

Ricinus communis:

Family: Euphorbiaceae. Euphorbus was physician to the King of Mauretania. Name from *ricinis*, tick, which the seeds resemble.
Place of origin: tropical Asia and Africa; widely introduced into tropical and temperate countries (in 1590 into Britain).
Description: herbaceous annual or biennial, 3–5 ft. (90–150 cm) high. Leaves large, long-stemmed, deeply lobed, often purplish- or bronzy-green. Flowers greenish, clustered, male and female separate. Fruit capsules containing oily seeds.
Flowering time: summer.
Harvesting time: Sept.
Use: ornamentally for sub-tropical bedding or backs of borders (for its foliage) but mainly for medicinal purposes.
Properties: the seeds yield castor-oil, used in medicine, as a lubricant and in the paint and dye industries.
Propagation: by seed; young plants are put outside in early summer.
Environment and light: sunny and warm. Will not tolerate frost so dies in early autumn.
Type of soil: well fertilized.
Remarks: parts of the plant, but most especially the beans, are poisonous.

401 BLACK LOCUST; FALSE ACACIA; LOCUST TREE

Robinia:

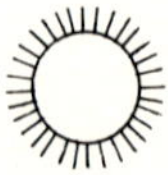

(3)

Family: Leguminosae. Named after Jean Robin, gardener to Henri IV and Louis XIII of France.
Place of origin: Eastern America; introduced into Britain in 1601.
Description: a large tree 82 ft. (25 m) high, with rugged, furrowed bark. Leaves pinnate, divided into 7–19 rounded leaflets. Flowers white, blotched yellow at base of standard petal, fragrant, in long, hanging clusters.
Flowering time: late spring.
Use: ornamentally to make hedges or as isolated specimens in small tree form.
Pharmaceutically speaking the bark of the roots, leaves and flowers are used separately for an infusion which, when not in excessive doses has a mild purgative action. Hard, durable wood. Flowers source of Acacia perfume of commerce. Infusion, acting as a tonic and mild purgative, prepared from the plant. Seeds were eaten by the native Amerindians. Good bee plant.
Propagation: by seed, which should be left in water for a while before sowing.
Environment and light: sun or light shade.
Type of soil: no special requirements.
Soil moisture: water to establish only.

---

402 ROSEMARY

Rosmarinus officinalis:

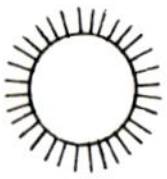

(6)

Family: Labiatae. Name from Latin *ros*, dew and *marinus*, coastal, referring to its habitat.
Place of origin: Asia Minor, Southern Europe.
Description: aromatic, evergreen shrub to $6\frac{1}{2}$ ft. (2 m) high. Leaves narrow, linear, sessile, lustrous, green above and greyish, downy below. Flowers axillary, corolla 2-lipped, pale violet to deep blue (rarely white).
Flowering time: spring–mid-summer.
Use: good for making low hedges and for large specimens in key situations. Used in cheap perfumes, hair washes and the like; also for flavouring stews and in making tea and wine.
Propagation: by seed or half-ripe cuttings in midsummer.
Environment and light: sunny.
Type of soil: any good garden soil.
Remarks: not reliably hardy in cold climates, so protect in winter, or keep small rooted cuttings as stock plants.

403 RUE

Ruta graveolens:

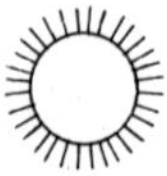

Family: Rutaceae. Name from Latin *ruta*, bitter and *graveolens*, strongly-scented.
Place of origin: Southern Europe; introduced into Britain circa 1652.
Description: aromatic, evergreen, shrub-like perennial, to about 3 ft. (90 cm) high. Leaves pinnately-compound, bluish- or yellowish-green in colour. Flowers $\frac{3}{4}$ in. (about 2 cm) across, in branched terminal clusters, petals widely spaced, dull yellow. The best form is "Jackman's Blue", with blue-green foliage; there is also a variegated variety.
Flowering time: late spring–mid-summer.
Harvesting time: May–Aug.
Use: widely used medicinally in the past to aid digestion, also for flavourings, but many people find the perfume unpleasant.
Propagation: by seed in spring or from slips.
Environment and light: sunny to half-shade.
Type of soil: poor clayey loam, with a little lime.
Remarks: the plant is known in Europe as "Herb of Grace" and still worn clandestinely by some peasants to "avert the evil eye".

4

---

404 GARDEN SAGE

Salvia officinalis:

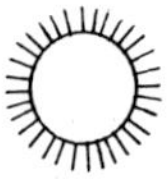

Family: Labiatae. Name from Latin *salvare*, to save or heal, referring to its supposed medicinal properties.
Place of origin: Mediterranean; introduced in 1597.
Description: perennial, strongly aromatic, 8–28 in. (20–70 cm) high, with whitish, woolly stem. Leaves thick, velvety, greyish. Flowers tubular, 2-lipped, violet-blue, in whorls.
Flowering time: summer.
Harvesting time: spring–early summer.
Use: the leaves are used before flowering; for tea, sage cheese, sage and onion stuffing, sage cream etc. and also as infusions, liquid extracts and tinctures. The leaves when rubbed on the teeth have a whitening action.
Propagation: by seed in spring or half-ripe cuttings.
Environment and light: full sun; in harsh climates plant in a sunny spot in the shelter of a wall.
Type of soil: any garden soil except the most acid.
Soil moisture: water if necessary.
Remarks: held in such repute for health-giving properties in the past that Chinese exchanged 3 lbs of tea to the Dutch for 1 lb of dried sage leaves.

3

405 COMMON ELDER; EUROPEAN ELDER
Sambucus nigra:

Family: Caprifoliaceae. *Sambuca*, a kind of harp but significance obscure. (Caprifoliaceae—from the Latin *caper*, goat and *folium*, leaf.)
Place of origin: Europe (including Britain), N. Africa, Western Asia.
Description: small, deciduous tree to 32 ft. (10 m) high, with deeply furrowed bark and white pith. Leaves divided into pointed and toothed leaflets, heavy odour when bruised. Flowers creamy-white, fragrant, in broad flattened heads, 5–8 in. (12–20 cm) across.
Flowering time: summer.
Harvesting time: the bark in spring or autumn; the flowers in late spring, the fruit at the end of summer.
Use: grown ornamentally to make loose hedges and thickets. Both flowers and shining black fruit are used for wine-making; formerly had wide uses medicinally. The soft pith is employed for botanical section cutting in microscopy.
Properties diuretic (bark), diuretic and laxative (flowers) and laxative (fruit).
Propagation: by seed or half-ripe shoots with a heel in summer (with bottom heat).
Environment and light: sunny to half-shade.
Type of soil: no special features.

5

---

406 BOUNCING BET; SOAPWORT
Saponaria officinalis:

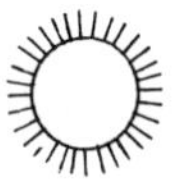

Family: Caprifoliaceae. Name from Latin *sapo*, soap; the chopped roots were used as a substitute for soap.
Place of origin: Europe, temperate Asia; naturalised in Britain.
Description: perennial herb with creeping rhizome, 1–3 ft. (30–90 cm) high. Leaves broadly elliptical-oval, three-veined. Flowers pink, about 1 in. (2·5–3 cm) across, profuse, on erect flowering stems. There is a very handsome double variety for garden adornment.
Flowering time: summer–early autumn.
Harvesting time: leaves in June–July, roots in Sept–Oct.
Use: for wild gardens and rough corners.
Properties: formerly used medicinally and in herbal remedies for gout, rheumatism.
Propagation: by seed or division.
Environment and light: sun or partial shade.
Type of soil: any moist soil.
Remarks: The plant contains saponins which lather with water; currently used for cleaning precious fabrics and wall tapestries.

7

407 **BUTTONS; COMMON TANSY; TANSY**

Tanacetum vulgare (now more correctly *Chrysanthemum vulgare*):

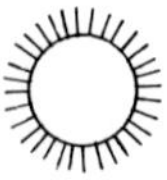

3

Family: Compositae. Name from Greek *athanasia*, immortality; the plant was once rubbed on corpses to preserve them from corruption.
Place of origin: Europe, including Britain.
Description: aromatic, perennial herb with many erect, angular stems, 2–3 ft. (60–90 cm) high. Leaves evenly subdivided, feathery. Flowers rounded, without ray-florets, bright golden yellow, in compound flat-topped clusters.
Flowering time: summer–mid-autumn.
Harvesting time: summer.
Use: as well as being ornamental, tansy has pharmaceutical properties in its flowering heads and dried leaves. These are used to make infusions and a liquid extract as a home treatment for intestinal worms, fleas and lice and as an insecticide.
Propagation: by seed or division in spring.
Environment and light: full sun.
Type of soil: poor and quite sandy.
Remarks: the leaves and stems are poisonous, but when the flower heads are steeped in liquid, the flavoured fluid can be used for cheeses, cakes and puddings.

---

408 **DANDELION**

Taraxacum officinale:

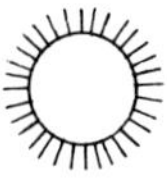

3

Family: Compositae. Dandelion, from French *dent de lion*, lion's tooth. *Taraxacum* from ancient Persian meaning bitter herb.
Place of origin: Europe; now almost worldwide in distribution; restricted garden use, where it is a noxious weed.
Description: perennial herb with long, stout root. Leaves smooth, deeply lobed, arranged in rosette. Flower heads about $1\frac{1}{2}$ in. (3–6 cm) across, bright yellow, borne on smooth, hollow stalks to 20 in. (50 cm) high.
Flowering time: spring–autumn.
Harvesting time: late spring–mid-summer.
Use: large-leaved varieties cultivated as vegetables for use in salads; dandelion wine; dried roots used medicinally and, roasted, with coffee instead of chicory. Fed to rabbits.
Properties: cholagogic, diuretic, moderately laxative, tonic.
Propagation: by seed.
Environment and light: full sun to half shade.
Type of soil: no special features or requirements.
Remarks: do not allow plants to seed.

409 WALL GERMANDER
Teucrium chamaedrys

Family: Labiatae. Ancient Greek name, probably for Teucer, King of Troy, who is reputed to have used the plant medicinally.
Place of origin: Europe; naturalised in Britain.
Description: low, tufted, shrubby and branching perennial of 4–12 in. (10–30 cm). Leaves broadly oval, round-toothed, narrowing to short stalk. Flowers sage-like, pinkish-purple, clustered in irregular whorls.
Flowering time: late spring–early autumn.
Harvesting time: summer.
Use: for decorating small banks, stony slopes and parts of rock gardens.
Properties: long medicinal use as febrifuge, for stomach complaints, dropsy and gout.
Propagation: by seed or division in spring.
Environment and light: sun or light shade (found on banks in dry places in nature).
Type of soil: light, a little sandy.

⑤

---

410 VALERIAN
Valeriana officinalis:

Family: Valerianaceae. Name possibly from Latin, to be healthy.
Place of origin: Europe (including Britain), Asia.
Description: robust, upright, perennial herb $1\frac{1}{2}$–6 ft. 0·5–2 m) high. Leaves pinnate, pointed, very variable. Flowers pinkish-white, in wide, showy, flat-topped, terminal clusters.
Flowering time: spring–early summer.
Harvesting time: spring to late summer.
Use: may be used in the garden to make small clumps.
Properties: Valerian has anti-neurotic and sedative properties, used as a condiment, perfume (in eastern countries mainly to scent tobacco), and in herbal remedies. Rhizome with roots in 2nd and 3rd years, with which tisanes, tinctures and liquid extracts are made.
Propagation: by division, by seed in spring.
Environment and light: shady, wooded, slightly damp places.
Type of soil: ordinary fertile garden soil.
Remarks: cats adore this plant yet the roots have been used as a rat-bait.

⑤

411 ORANGE MULLEIN

Verbascum phlomoides:

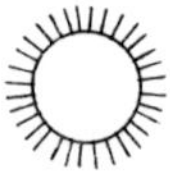

Family: Scrophulariaceae. *Verbascum*, old Latin name for this plant.
Place of origin: Southern Europe, Caucasus; introduced into Britain in 1739.
Description: upright biennial, 2–3 ft. (60–90 cm) high, with dense, woolly, white to yellowish hairs. Leaves large, ovate or oblong, entire, lower ones in a rosette. Flowers bright yellow or orange-yellow, about $1\frac{1}{2}$ in. (3–5 cm) across, in thick racemes.
Flowering time: summer–early autumn.
Use: a good ornamental species for backs of borders, wild gardens etc., formerly used in domestic medicine and (the ground capsules and seed) for stypefying fish.
Propagation: by seed in spring.
Environment and light: full sun.
Type of soil: no special requirements.

6

---

412 MISTLETOE

Viscum album:

Family: Loranthaceae. *Viscum*, old Latin name for the plant; *mistletoe*, from Anglo-Saxon.
Place of origin: Europe, Northern Asia.
Description: evergreen, semi-parasitic plant growing on the trunks and branches of many deciduous and some coniferous trees; branches greenish-yellow, mostly pendulous, dichotomously-branched, forming roundish growth 16–36 in. (40–90 cm) across. Leaves greenish-yellow, flattened, leathery, oblong, rounded at tip. Flowers unisexual, yellowish, inconspicuous, stalkless, in axils of the leaves; followed by round, white berries.
Flowering time: spring.
Use: the berries have poisonous properties but have been used as a home remedy for epilepsy and for making bird-lime; widely used at Christmastime.
Propagation: by seed inserted beneath the young bark of the host plant.
Remarks: this example is the European mistletoe which does not thrive in the US. The American mistletoe (*Phoradendron flavescens*) does well in zone 7 and further south.

7

LATE BLOOMING PLANTS

413 ABELIA

Abelia chinensis (A. rupestris):

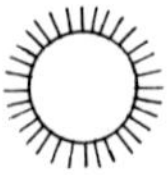

Family: Caprifoliaceae. Named after Dr Clarke Abel (1780–1826), botanist in China.
Place of origin: Central and Eastern China; introduced into Europe in 1844.
Description: a small shrub with opposite, short-stemmed, oval-lanceolate leaves and masses of small, tubular, white, rose-tinted, fragrant flowers.

Flowering time: late summer.
Use: in cool climates, as a wall shrub. In warm areas with only light frosts, as isolated specimens in shrubberies or to form loose hedges.
Propagation: by half-ripe summer cuttings, taken in mid-summer and rooted with bottom heat.
Environment and light: sunny position, protected from cold winds.
Type of soil: ordinary garden soil.
Remarks: prune out old shoots occasionally.

(5)

---

414 LOVE-LIES-BLEEDING

Amaranthus caudatus:

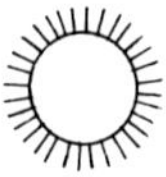

Family: Amaranthaceae. Name from Greek *amarantos*, everlasting; some species can be dried.
Place of origin: Tropics; introduced into Britain in 1596.
Description: a striking annual which under good conditions reaches 3–4 ft. (90–120 cm). Leaves ovate, simple, alternate, light green. Flowers in long pendent racemes 18 in. (45 cm) or so in length, crimson. The variety "Viridis" has pale green flowers.

Flowering time: mid-summer–mid-autumn.
Use: for cutting purposes or annual borders or containers.
Propagation: in cool climates, by seed in early spring in seedboxes. In frost-free areas, by seed outdoors.
Environment and light: sunny, even if not in direct sun, but not too exposed.
Type of soil: ordinary garden soil.
Soil moisture: the soil should always be fairly moist.

415 MICHAELMAS DAISY
Aster novi-beglii "Marie Ballard":

Family: Compositae. Name from Latin *aster*, a star; the plants are often called Starflowers.
Place of origin: North America; introduced into Europe in 1710.
Description: an important group of late-flowering herbaceous perennials, all derived from a rather weedy lilac-pink species. Cultivars come in various heights from 1–6 ft. (30–180 cm) and colours (white, cream, pink, red, crimson, mauve and purple); semi-doubles and doubles. Leaves alternate, lanceolate, smooth; stems branching; flowers many, daisy-like. The variety "Marie Ballard", 3 ft. (90 cm) in height, has fine double, light blue flowers.
Flowering time: early to mid-autumn.
Use: for various positions in herbaceous borders; as cut flowers. The smaller types are good for edging.
Propagation: by division.
Environment and light: sunny, open position.
Type of soil: fertile, but well-drained.
Soil moisture: water generously if soil becomes dry.
Remarks: taller kinds need staking with twiggy supports, Cut stems to ground level in early autumn and divide occasionally—otherwise the clumps will deteriorate.

---

416 ORNAMENTAL KALE; BORECOLE
Brassica oleracea var. *acephala*:

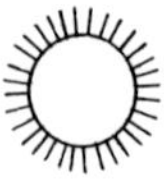

Family: Cruciferae. Old Latin name for cabbage.
Place of origin: garden form.
Description: a variety of kale used for decorative purposes, which comes to its best after the first winter frost. Foliage frilled, in shades of pink, purple and purplish-green.
Flowering time: autumn.
Use: for winter decoration and flower arrangements.
Propagation: by seed in early summer and planted out late summer.
Environment and light: sunny and well exposed.
Type of soil: rich, well worked to quite a depth; appreciates a little lime.

417 **CHINA ASTER**
Callistephus chinensis:

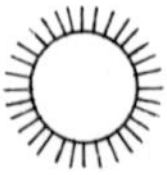

(5)

Family: Compositae. Name from Greek, *kalli*, beautiful and *stephanos*, fit for a wreath, referring to the flowers.
Place of origin: China, Japan; introduced into Europe in the eighteenth century.
Description: an annual of a monotypic genus which has produced countless cultivars. Height 18 in. (45 cm) (but varieties 9–30 in. (22–75 cm)), flowers solitary, dark purple, set off by a ring of green sepals. Leaves ovate, coarsely toothed. Varieties occur having pink, red, white, mauve, violet etc; long or short petalled; single, semi-double or double flowers; also dwarfs of 9 in. (22 cm).
Flowering time: late summer–autumn.
Use: to form colourful clumps in self or mixed borders; for edging and cut flowers.
Propagation: by seed; seedlings are planted out in early summer. They are not frost tolerant.
Environment and light: full sun to filtered sun (particularly in hot places).
Type of soil: any good, fertile garden soil.
Soil moisture: water regularly, more in summer—they suffer in drought.

---

418 **BLUE SPIRAEA; COMMON BLUEBEARD**
Caryopteris incana (C. mastacanthus):

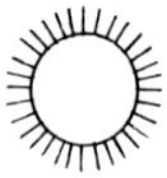

(7)

Family: Verbenaceae. Name from Greek *karyon*, nut and *pteron*, wing, referring to the winged fruits.
Place of origin: China, Japan; introduced into Europe in 1844.
Description: a deciduous shrub of 3–5 ft. (90–150 cm), delicate-looking and often killed to ground-level in cold climates. Leaves opposite, coarsely toothed, entire. Flowers pale blue in clusters in terminal and axillary cymes. A much better garden plant is the violet-blue, 3 ft. (90 cm) *C. xclandonensis* or any of the named varieties.
Flowering time: late summer–mid-autumn.
Use: valued for its late flowering; grow amongst herbaceous perennials, or at front of shrub borders.
Propagation: by cuttings (seed also for species).
Environment and light: well-drained, sunny position, sheltered from cold winds.
Type of soil: sandy loam.
Soil moisture: water if necessary.
Remarks: prune hard back in spring, especially any frosted growths.

419 COCK'S COMB

Celosia argentea "Cristata" *(C. cristata):*

Family: Amaranthaceae. Name from Greek *keleos*, burning, referring to the colour of the flower.
Place of origin: tropical Asia and Africa; introduced to Europe in 1570.
Description: annual with showy flower-heads, the latter congested into flat, crested heads and brilliantly coloured. Height $1\frac{1}{2}$–2 ft. (45–60 cm). Leaves ovate, pointed.
Flowering time: autumn.
Use: in cool climates, for cool greenhouses or conservatories; sometimes bedded out in early summer. In the tropics, for flowerbeds.
Propagation: by seed raised under glass in most climates.
Environment and light: sunny, sheltered positions outdoors; in a light place in the greenhouse but not too hot.
Type of soil: deep, rich, well-drained. Feed pot plants in summer.
Soil moisture: water pot plants regularly as required.

---

420 CELOSIA

Celosia argentea "Plumrosa"*:*

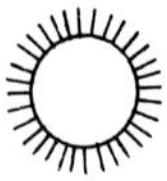

Family: Amaranthaceae.
Place of origin: tropical regions.
Description: another garden form of the annual *C. argentea* and similar to it except that the flowers occur in feathery plumes instead of crested masses. Height around 18 in. (45 cm).
Flowering time: late summer.
Use: as pot plants and table decoration; for cool greenhouses, sun lounges etc. or outdoors in warm sheltered situations.
Propagation: by seed.
Environment and light: sunny, sheltered positions outdoors; in a light place in the greenhouse but not too hot.
Type of soil: deep, rich, well-drained. Feed pot plants in summer.
Soil moisture: water pot plants regularly as required.

421 BLUE CERATOSTIGMA; FALSE PLUMBAGO

Ceratostigma plumbaginoides (Plumbago larpentae):

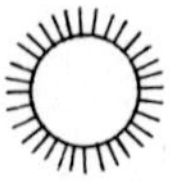

Family: Plumbaginaceae. Name from Greek *keras*, horn and *stigma*, stigma, referring to the horn-like excrescence on the stigma.
Place of origin: China; introduced into Europe in 1846.
Description: a shrubby perennial with herbaceous stems which are killed to the ground in winter. Leaves small, alternate, obovate, ciliate. Flowers in terminal and axillary clusters, rich purplish blue which, with the autumnal red tints of the leaves, make a beautiful picture. Height 1–1½ ft. (30–45 cm).
Flowering time: early–mid-autumn.
Use: for fronts of shrubberies, rock garden pockets.
Propagation: by cuttings or division.
Environment and light: sunny.
Type of soil: sandy loam.
Remarks: this species is not suitable for places with cold winters.

7

---

422 CHRYSANTHEMUM

Chrysanthemum × hortorum:

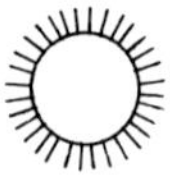

Family: Compositae. Name from Greek *chrysos*, gold and *anthos*, flower.
Place of origin: China and Japan. Cultivated varieties reached Europe in 1789, having been grown in China since 500 B.C.
Description: well-known, woody-stemmed perennials, much grown for the cut flower trade and for autumn bedding. Leaves obovate, lobed on stems of various height, aromatic when bruised. Flowers single or double, in a wide range of colours, round, daisy-like. See classification on next page. Illustration shows a large-flowered single.
Flowering time: early–mid-autumn; winter (under glass), but, by special techniques, will bloom all the year round.
Use: the small types are good for edging or flower beds and the taller for the backs of borders; as pot plants grown under glass for winter bloom and as cut flowers.
Propagation: *see* Nos 423/4.
Environment and light: sun.
Type of soil: *see* Nos 423/4.
Soil moisture: *see* Nos 423/4.
Remarks: *see* Nos 423/4.

423 & 424 *Chrysanthemum × hortorum:*

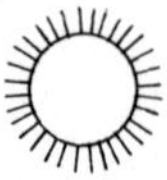

Family: Compositae.

Description: florists' chrysanthemums are mainly derived from two species of Chinese origin—*Chrysanthemum vestitum (C. morifolium)* and *C. indicum*, the first hybrids of which were probably all yellow.

Today's varieties are broken up into seven main groups, classified according to the way the petals turn and the flower shapes. These are:

—Incurved, florets curved inwards to make a round ball of close, tight petals. (No 424 shows "Mavis Shoesmith", a large incurved pink with broad florets making a globular flower);

—Reflexed, petals falling outwards, drooping and overlapping like the feathers on a bird;

—Intermediate, flowers coming between these two, that is semi-reflexed or partially incurved;

—Singles (No 422);

—Anemone-flowered, the central disk having raised, tubular florets;

—Pompons, small quite round flowers, like globes;

—Other types, that is Spoon or Rayonnante Chrysanthemums. (No 423 shows Rayonnante "White Spider"); spray types and cascades.

Flowering time: *see* No 422.

Propagation: by soft cuttings from base of mother plant, which is brought under glass in warmth to encourage sprouting. Also division and seed (latter giving unreliable results).

Environment and light: sun.

Type of soil: fertile, preferably containing lime; manured for a previous crop. Feed during summer.

Soil moisture: water plentifully in growing season.

Remarks: for good flowers, disbudding and staking are vital.

425 CUP AND SAUCER PLANT

Cobaea scandens:

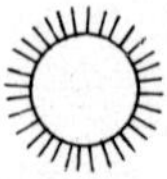

(9)

Family: Polemoniaceae. Named after a Jesuit missionary and naturalist, Bernardo Cobo (1572–1659).
Place of origin: Mexico; introduced into Europe in 1787.
Description: a vigorous climbing perennial, usually treated as annual in cool climates, where it readily succumbs to frost and becomes too large for small glasshouses. Leaves alternate, dark green, with 3-pairs leaflets and terminating in a branched tendril. Flowers large (3 in. (7 cm) or more), on long slender stems, campanulate, green at first developing to deep purple; calyx green, prominent, saucer-like. Height around 20 ft. (6 m). There is a white form.
Flowering time: late summer–early autumn.
Use: trained up conservatory pillars or trellis under glass. Outdoors, for screening, covering walls, growing on fences, arbours, etc.
Propagation: by seed.
Environment and light: sheltered, full sun.
Type of soil: light, sandy. Feed pot plants weekly in summer.
Soil moisture: needs plenty of water in the growing season and, under glass, frequent syringing.

---

426 NAKED BOYS; SHOWY AUTUMN CROCUS

Colchicum speciosum:

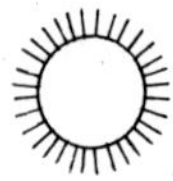

(4)

Family: Liliaceae. Name given because it was once abundant in Colchis (Caucasus).
Place of origin: Asia Minor, Caucasus.
Description: often erroneously called autumn crocus, but distinct from the genus *Crocus* in flower, leaves and tuber. Height up to 1 ft. (30 cm) flowers large, tulip-like, pale rosy-lilac to deep reddish-purple with a pale throat, in clusters from a large tuber. Leaves not appearing till spring, large, broadly ovate on tall stems carrying large seed pods.
Flowering time: early–mid-autumn.
Use: among grass round a tree-trunk, in clumps in open shrubberies, between dying stems of herbaceous plants, or in large rock gardens.
Propagation: by division of the tubers in late autumn 20–30 days after flowering or by seed.
Environment and light: sun or semi-shade.
Type of soil: well-drained.
Remarks: guard against slugs at flowering time.

427 & 428 DAHLIA

Dahlia: sp.

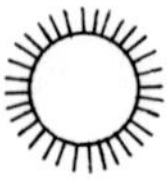

4

Family: Compositae. Named after the Swedish botanist, Dr Anders Dahl (1751–1789).
Place of origin: Mexico; introduced into Europe in 1789.
Description: there are some 20 species of these tuberous-rooted perennials, but almost without exception the plants cultivated today are of garden origin. Because of interbreeding, these are extremely varied so that the National Dahlia Society of Britain has divided them into 10 classes and some sub-divisions.
The main types are Singles; Anemone-flowered; Collerettes; Paeony-flowered; Decorative (full doubles, but subdivided according to size of flower (*see* No 428); Cactus, with quill-petalled flowers (No 427); Double Show and Fancy (double but more globular than preceding); Pompon, small, round doubles; various Dwarf Bedding Dahlias (*see* No 200).
General characteristics include tuberous rootstocks, pinnate leaves with ovate leaflets, rich green except for a few bronze-foliaged forms, and large, showy flowers, singles or doubles, many "petalled", fleshy; shades from white, cream and yellows to pink, red, purple and bronze.
Flowering time: late summer–autumn.
Use: for flowerbeds, containers, borders, small isolated clumps and cut flowers. Plant out when risk of frost is past.
Propagation: by division of tubers, by soft, basal cuttings in spring, rooted with bottom heat. Bedding dahlias, by seed.
Environment and light: open, sunny position.
Type of soil: heavy soil, well fertilized weeks in advance with rotted manure.
Soil moisture: water generously in dry weather.
Remarks: remove dead flowers regularly to prolong the season. When flowering is over, when the plant is pruned and the foliage has yellowed, dig up the tubers, clean them, and put them in cool dark frost-free place on peat until spring.

429 JAPANESE PLUM; LOQUAT
Eriobotrya japonica (Mespilus japonica):

Family: Rosaceae. Name from Greek *erion*, wool and *botrys*, cluster, referring to the woolly flower clusters.
Place of origin: China, Japan; introduced into Europe in 1787.
Description: an evergreen tree with handsome foliage; the latter large, 6–12 in. (15–30 cm) long and 3–6 in. (7–15 cm) broad, dark glossy green, under-surface brown, deeply ribbed. Flowers yellowish, fragrant, in woolly clusters followed by edible, pear-shaped fruits.
Flowering time: late-autumn–winter.
Harvesting time: fruit, plum-sized, orange-yellow, pulpy, edible; they ripen in early spring.
Use: as an isolated specimen for its decorative foliage, or as a fruit tree in warm countries, but in most parts of Britain it needs the shelter of a wall.
Propagation: by seed or layering.
Environment and light: sunny to half-shade.
Type of soil: ordinary dry garden soil.
Soil moisture: water regularly. The plant dislikes moisture via the roots but thrives in a humid atmosphere, especially in winter.

---

430 SNEEZEWEED; SNEEZE WORT
Helenium autumnale:

Family: Compositae. Name from Greek *helenion*, used for a plant named after Helen of Troy.
Place of origin: North America; introduced into Europe in 1729.
Description: coarse, herbaceous perennial, 4–6 ft. (1–1·8 m) in height, smooth, stout, leafy and winged stems, branched near the tops. Leaves alternate, entire, lanceolate. Flowers plentiful, rayed, yellow with darker disk-florets. Many hybrids with copper-orange, clear yellow and red-crimson flowers.
Flowering time: late summer–mid-autumn.
Use: for flowerbeds, borders, small clumps and as cut flowers.
Propagation: by division in spring or by seed.
Environment and light: sunny.
Type of soil: any good but light soil.

431 JERUSALEM ARTICHOKE

Helianthus tuberosus:

4

Family: Compositae.
Place of origin: North America; introduced into Europe in 1617.
Description: herbaceous perennial, 7–10 ft. (2–3 m) high with leaves well-stemmed, almost all opposite, oval and with large teeth, 4–8 in. (10–20 cm) long, the lower rounded, or heart-shaped, at the base; $1\frac{1}{2}$–3 in. (4–8 cm) capitula with yellow peripheral ligules in a row, and similarly yellow disk.
Flowering time: early–mid-autumn.
Use: for borders, flowerbeds, small clumps, slopes and banks, if well exposed etc., for cut flowers.
Planting: tubers planted out in spring.
Properties: despite the handsome flowers this plant is grown primarily for its edible root.
Propagation: by division of tubers in spring.
Environment and light: full sun.
Type of soil: ordinary garden soil, very fertile with manure or organic fertilizer.
Soil moisture: water generously almost daily.
Remarks: if this plant is to be used decoratively prune the plant back after flowering. Only rarely cultivated for its bloom, in its native area it is a rampant weed.

---

432 SPIDER LILY

Lycoris radiata:

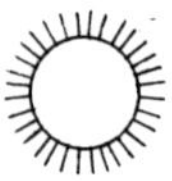

7

Family: Amaryllidaceae. Named after a mistress of the Roman general, Mark Antony.
Place of origin: China.
Description: bulbous plants somewhat like *Nerine*, the flowers in rounded umbels before the leaves. These are funnel-shaped, bright red or deep pink with wavy-edged, reflexed perianth segments and long, protruding stamens. Leaves linear, strap-shaped, glaucous. Height to 18 in. (45 cm).
Flowering time: late summer–early autumn.
Use: not hardy except in very warm, sheltered situations and fares best in pots in cool greenhouses. In warmer regions, in borders or as cut flowers.
Propagation: by division of the bulbs or by seed sown as soon as it is ripe; seedlings will flower after about four years.
Environment and light: full sun or at least quite sunny. Need shallow planting with necks of bulbs exposed.
Type of soil: ordinary garden soil with some sand.
Soil moisture: water when in active growth, then rest the bulbs.

433 CAPE COLONY NERINE
Nerine bowdenii:

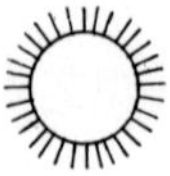

9

Family: Amaryllidaceae. Named after the sea-nymph, Nerine, in Greek mythology.
Place of origin: South Africa; introduced into Europe in 1889.
Description: handsome, bulbous plants of which this species is the hardiest. Stem stout, smooth, fleshy, to 2 ft. (60 cm) terminating in large, round umbels of tubular flowers, each up to 3 in. (7 cm) long; pale pink with a darker line down each sepal. Varieties with deep pink, light red and cherry-rose flowers exist. Leaves long, narrow and strap-like, long-lasting.
Flowering time: early to mid-autumn.
Use: for warm, sunny corners, frames, pots, cool greenhouses and for cutting.
Propagation: by division of bulbs.
Environment and light: plant bulbs 6 in. (15 cm) deep in a warm, sheltered place in full sun.
Type of soil: acid with plenty of humus; a good mixture is made up of compost, sand and peaty soil.
Soil moisture: water pot plants when in growth but keep dryish when plants are resting.

---

434 TUBEROSE
Polianthes tuberosa:

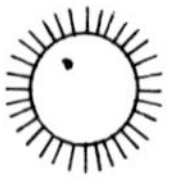

9

Family: Agavaceae.
Place of origin: Mexico; introduced in 1629.
Description: a monotypic genus, the species one of the most fragrant plants in the world. Flowers white, waxy, funnel-shaped, in terminal spikes. Leaves linear, glaucous, deeply chanelled. Height around 2 ft. (60 cm). Illustration shows the double form, "The Pearl".
Flowering time: late summer but by forcing can be induced to bloom throughout the year.
Use: for cut flowers, buttonholes etc. In pots for cool house cultivation. In warm climates, in borders.
Propagation: by division of tubers in autumn (but these do not usually ripen well) or imported annually.
Environment and light: full sun. Not hardy in temperate areas so are discarded after flowering.
Type of soil: loam, leaf-mould, rotted manure and sand.
Soil moisture: water plentifully whilst growing only.
Remarks: after flowering the tubers should be taken up and the large ones discarded as they will produce no more flowers. The small tubers should be stored in a cool, dry place until the following spring. If properly ripened they will flower in the third year and should then be discarded.

435 STAR IPOMOEA; SCARLET MORNING-GLORY

Quamoclit coccinea:

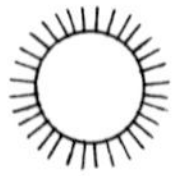

Family: Convolvulaceae. Origin of generic name obscure.

Place of origin: Mexico, Arizona; introduced into Europe in 1769.

Description: a climbing annual, to 8 ft. (2·4 m). Leaves entire, sagittate, slender, pointed. Flowers axillary, flaring tube opening to an umbrella shape with yellow throat, 1 in. (2·5 cm), scarlet. Plants with toothed or lobed leaves (as in illustration) have now been separated as *Q. hederifolia.*

Flowering time: late summer–mid-autumn.

Use: as a climbing plant in greenhouses in cool climates and good for covering walls, arbours, pillars and the base of statues, balustrades etc.; sometimes also grown in pots. Outdoors, in tropics and sub-tropics.

Propagation: by seed in spring.

Environment and light: full sun.

Type of soil: quite fertile, made up of peaty soil, loam and a little sand.

Soil moisture: water regularly, but generously, 2–3 times a week.

Remarks: the illustration shows the plant climbing through a shrub.

---

436 CANADA GOLDENROD

Solidago canadensis:

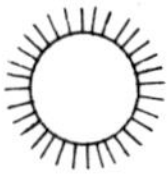

Family: Compositae. Name from Latin *solido*, to make entire, referring to the medicinal properties of some species.

Place of origin: Eastern N. America; naturalised in parts of Britain and originally introduced in 1648.

Description: a common late summer perennial with stiff, leafy stems, rough to touch, 3–5 ft. (1–1·5 m) tall and terminating in broad panicles of many, small, yellow flowers. Leaves narrowly oblong, rough above. Parent of many hybrids, which are to be preferred for garden use.

Flowering time: summer–mid-autumn.

Use: for borders, open woodland, shrub borders, slopes and banks.

Propagation: by division in spring or autumn.

Environment and light: full sun.

Type of soil: ordinary garden soil, but it should be fed from time to time as the plants tend to exhaust it.

Soil moisture: water in dry weather only.

3

Remarks: these plants contrast well with Michaelmas daisies (*Aster* sp.).

437 LILY OF THE FIELD; WINTER DAFFODIL

Sternbergia lutea:

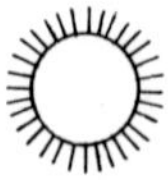

⑦

Family: Amaryllidaceae. Named after the Austrian botanist Count Kaspar von Sternberg (1761–1838).
Place of origin: Mediterranean region; introduced into Britain in 1596.
Description: a crocus-like plant with rich golden, solitary flowers with a satiny sheen, about 2 in. (5 cm) long, on 10 in. (25 cm) stems. Bulb like that of a small *Narcissus*, dark brown. Leaves deep green, strap-shaped, after flowering.
Flowering time: late summer–late autumn.
Use: for small borders, slopes, rockeries, banks; also for cut flowers.
Propagation: by division in summer, also by seed; flowers three years after seed is sown.
Environment and light: full sun in cool climates, otherwise half-shade. Need a good summer ripening or they fail to flower.
Type of soil: good drainage essential; likes lime. Add a little sand to ordinary garden soil.
Soil moisture: water only in very dry weather; dislikes too much wet.
Remarks: considered by some authorities to be the "lilies of the field" of the Bible.

---

438 AUTUMN ZEPHYR LILY; FLOWER OF THE WESTERN WIND

Zephyranthes candida:

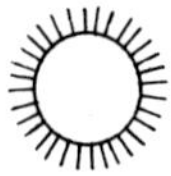

⑧

Family: Amaryllidaceae. Name from Greek *zephyros*, west wind and *anthos*, flower, referring to their New World (i.e. western) habitat.
Place of origin: South America; introduced in 1822.
Description: little bulbous plant with pure white flowers about 2 in. (5 cm) long, on 8 in. (20 cm) stems. Flowers crocus-like, with 6 perianth segments, green at base. Leaves rush-like, narrow, longer than flower stem.
Flowering time: autumn.
Use: as an edging plant (the foliage persists most of the year), in pots, borders and rock pockets.
Propagation: by offsets from bulbs.
Environment and light: hardy in sheltered areas particularly in drier zones; aim to keep bulbs dry in winter, with little frost (cover with glass or similar). Full sun. Found along river banks but not advisable in gardens.
Type of soil: any good potting compost for containers. Outside, well-drained, fertile, sandy loam.
Soil moisture: water regularly and generously.
Remarks: in winter, in cold climates, the bulbs should be stored in a cool dry place.

ROCK GARDEN
PLANTS

439 SWEET ALYSSUM

Alyssum maritimum (now more correctly *Lobularia maritima*):

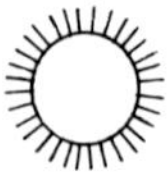

Family: Cruciferae. Name from Latin *lobulus*, small pod.
Place of origin: Europe, W. Asia.
Description: spreading, mat-forming, woody-stemmed perennial, rarely more than 9 in. (22 cm) high. Leaves narrow, entire, sessile, whitish-haired. Flowers white or pinkish, small, honey-scented, in dense terminal clusters.
Flowering time: summer–mid-autumn.
Use: as a summer bedding plant and for edging borders and sowing in crevices in crazy paving and dry walls; as a temporary filling in the rock garden.
Propagation: by seed in spring. The plant is invariably treated as annual in cultivation.
Environment and light: full sun or, if necessary, partial shade.
Type of soil: any light, well-drained soil.

(4)

---

440 GOLD DUST; GOLDEN-TUFT; ROCK ALYSSUM

Alyssum saxatile (more properly *aurinia saxatilis*):

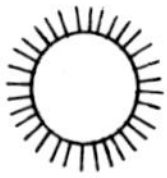

Family: Cruciferae. Name from Greek *a*, against and *lyssa*, madness; the plants were regarded as an antidote to madness.
Place of origin: central and S.E. Europe; intoduced into Britain in 1710.
Description: shrubby-based perennial growing to 9–10 in. (22–25 cm) high. Leaves oblong-ovate, grey-green and velvety. Flowers golden-yellow, numerous, in close flat-topped corymbs. There are cultivars with lemon, pale gold and double flowers.
Flowering time: spring–early summer.
Use: for rock gardens, dry walls, crazy paving, banks and fronts of borders.
Propagation: by cuttings rooted in summer in a cold frame.
Environment and light: full sun.
Type of soil: no special requirements, but must have good drainage.
Remarks: protect the plants in very cold climates. (Not necessary in Britain.)

(3)

441 **ALPINE ASTER**
Aster alpinus:

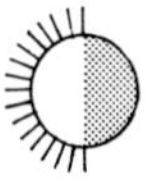

Family: Compositae. Name from Latin *aster*, star, referring to the shape of the flower heads.
Place of origin: mountains of central and E. Europe; introduced into Britain in 1658.
Description: low, spreading, hairy perennial, 6 in. (15 cm) high. Leaves entire, the basal ones obovate, more or less in rosette, stem-leaves lanceolate. Flowers violet-blue with central disk florets yellow, in large, usually solitary heads, 1–2 in. (2·5–5 cm) across. Cultivated forms include white and red flowered varieties.

Flowering time: late spring–mid-summer.
Use: for rock gardens, rocky slopes and banks; fronts of borders.
Propagation: by division.
Environment and light: half-shade.
Type of soil: any good garden soil with sharp drainage; likes lime.
Soil moisture: water if necessary.

---

442 **PURPLE ROCK CRESS**
Aubrieta deltoide (often misspelt *Aubrietia*)*:*

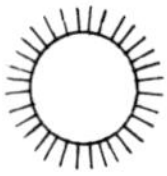

Family: Cruciferae. Named after Claude Aubriet (1668–1743), French botanical artist.
Place of origin: mountains of Sicily, southern Greece and Asia Minor.
Description: a very variable, mat-forming of trailing evergreen perennial up to 1 ft. (30 cm) high. Leaves simple, oblong, greyish-hairy. Flowers conspicuous in broad sheets, lilac-mauve, deep purple or red-purple (occasionally white). Many forms of garden origin, differing principally in flower colour; also one with variegated foliage.

Flowering time: spring–early summer.
Use: for borders, rock gardens, cracks in walls or rocks, in crazy paving; for trailing over dry walls.
Propagation: named sorts, by cuttings in summer; for mixed seedlings, by seed in spring.

Environment and light: sunny.
Type of soil: well-drained garden soil, with lime.
Soil moisture: water regularly but never over-water.
Remarks: after flowering cut old growths back to encourage new shoots. Dry wall trailers; shorten by half. Does best in a mild Mediterranean type climate.

(4)

443 BELLFLOWER; DWARF CAMPANULA

Campanula garganica:

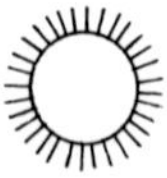

(5)

Family: Campanulaceae. Name from Latin *campana*, bell, referring to the shape of some of the flowers.
Place of origin: Greece, Italy.
Description: tufted perennial, 5–6 in. (12–15 cm) high. Leaves kidney-shaped, somewhat toothed and more or less downy, basal ones long-petioled and rising in a rosette. Flowers very profuse, hiding the foliage when in full bloom, light blue with white centre, star-shaped, in axillary clusters. "W. H. Paine" is a form with deep blue flowers.
Flowering time: late spring–early autumn.
Use: for rock gardens, crazy paving; in pots on balconies and terraces.
Propagation: by seed or spring cuttings rooted under glass.
Environment and light: open and sunny.
Type of soil: good garden soil, preferably with some lime.
Soil moisture: water container plants especially in summer.

---

444 CAPER-BUSH

Capparis spinosa:

(9)

Family: Capparidaceae. *Kapperis*, ancient Greek name for these plants.
Place of origin: Southern Europe.
Description: a spiny, deciduous shrub 3–5 ft. (1–1·5 m) high, of spreading habit. Leaves oval, somewhat fleshy, blunt or indented at the tip. Flowers large, white tinged reddish or lilac, 2–3 in. (5–7 cm) across with numerous projecting stamens, solitary. The flowers are fairly short lived.
Flowering time: late spring–late summer.
Use: for rock gardens and stony slopes in frost-free areas; as a pot-plant in cool climates. Raised commercially—flower buds are pickled as the capers used in cooking.
Propagation: in zone 8 by seeds in cracks in walls and rocks; elsewhere, by seed and by cuttings.
Environment and light: full sun.
Type of soil: in sub-tropical gardens, poor, made up of rock chippings, stones, with a little sand added; temperate zones, well-drained, sandy loam for pot plants.
Soil moisture: when the plant is young or has just been planted, sprinkle only in order to retain the small amount of soil it needs; thereafter, water regularly.

445 RED VALERIAN

Centranthius (Kentranthus) ruber:

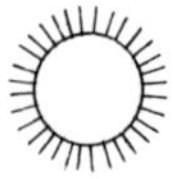

Family: Valerianaceae. Name from Greek *kentron*, spur and *anthos*, flower, referring to the spurred corolla.
Place of origin: Europe; naturalised in Britain.
Description: smooth, upright, rather glaucous perennial, 12–40 in. (30–100 cm) high. Leaves pointed, ovate, shallow-toothed which emit a cat-like smell when bruised. Flowers in rich clusters, pink or red (occasionally white), corolla tube slender with a backwardly projecting spur.
Flowering time: late spring–late summer.
Use: to make clumps of colour in very large rock gardens and borders, on banks etc.
Propagation: by seed sown in early summer where plants are to flower, or in pans.
Environment and light: sun.
Type of soil: the plants are happy in poor, well-drained soil, particularly on limestone.

4

---

446 SCALY SPLEENWORT; RUSTY-BACK FERN

Ceterach officinarum (Asplenium ceterach):

Family: Aspleniaceae. The name *Ceterach* is of Arabic origin.
Place of origin: Europe (including Britain), N. Africa, W. Asia to the Himalayas.
Description: a dwarf wall fern, evergreen, with sage-green fronds covered all over the undersides with silvery scales which become brown with age. Fronds up to 6 in. (15 cm).
Use: for dry stone walls, rock crevices in limestone, rock gardens and containers.
Propagation: by spores (sown in pans and kept in humid conditions) or by division.
Environment and light: shade to half-shade; roots must be shaded.

Type of soil: compost with added lime; otherwise any good soil.
Soil moisture: a sturdy plant which makes surprising recovery even after severe drying out.

3

447 YELLOW CORYDALIS
Corydalis lutea:

Family: Papaveraceae. Name from Greek *korydalis*, lark, referring to the spurs behind the flowers which resemble the long hind-claws of larks.
Place of origin: Europe, including Britain.
Description: branched, spreading, hairless perennial, 8–12 in. (20–30 cm) high, with slightly glaucous stems. Leaves soft, 2-pinnate with lobed, stalked leaflets. Flowers tubular and spurred, yellow, about $\frac{3}{4}$ in. (1–2 cm) long, in free-flowering racemes, somewhat nodding.
Flowering time: spring–late-autumn.
Use: for rock gardens, borders, old walls etc.
Propagation: usually propagates naturally from self-set seedlings; otherwise sow seed in situ.
Environment and light: sun or shade.
Type of soil: any fertile garden soil.
Remarks: can become a nuisance but readily checked by removing unwanted seedlings.

(5)

---

448 GARLAND FLOWER; ROSE DAPHNE
Daphne cneorum:

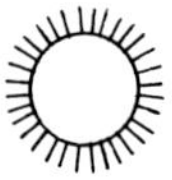

Family: Thymelaeaceae. *Daphne*, Greek-name for the bay-tree, transferred to this genus.
Place of origin: Central and Southern Europe; introduced in 1752.
Description: procumbent, evergreen shrub, which forms a dense mat covered with fragrant flowers in spring. Height 6 in. (15 cm) spread 2–3 ft. (60–90 cm). Leaves oblong, linear, slightly leathery, glaucous beneath, more numerous towards the end of downy branchlets. Flowers pink or rosy-red, richly fragrant, in rounded terminal clusters. White and pygmy varieties in cultivation.
Flowering time: spring–early summer.
Use: for rock gardens or alpine gardens.
Propagation: by heel cuttings in late summer rooted in a mixture of sand and peat mixture in a cool place.
Environment and light: sun or partial shade.
Type of soil: ordinary well-drained garden soil.
Soil moisture: water if necessary in the hot months. Ground must always be damp.
Remarks: when buying plants, ensure that these are on their own roots and not grafted. The crushed bark was used in Spain to stupefy fish.

(4)

49
43
39

1.31

1.19
74 2

193 2

449 ALPINE PINK
Dianthus alpinus:

Family: Caryophyllaceae.
Place of origin: Austrian Alps; introduced into Britain in 1759.
Description: a small species of about 4 in. (10 cm) in height, forming close mats of linear leaves. Flowers 1–1½ in. (2–4 cm) wide, pale pink to purple, dentate petal edges, white eyes and purple spots. Not fragrant.
Flowering time: late spring–late summer.
Use: for rock and alpine gardens, walls, sink gardens.
Propagation: variable results if raised from seed; good from cuttings. Increase regularly every two years as the plants are short-lived.
Environment and light: full sun.
Type of soil: tolerant of lime, salt spray and smoky atmospheres. Any good, well-drained soil that is not too acid.

④

---

450 ROYAL BROOM
Genista radiata (Cytisus radiatus):

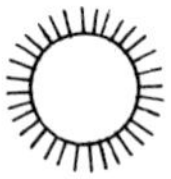

Family: Leguminosae. The Latin *planta*, plant and *genesta*, broom, hence the name of the Plantagenet kings of England whose badge bore a sprig of broom.
Place of origin: south-eastern France, central and eastern Europe; introduced into Britain in 1750.
Description: a densely branched shrub up to 1½ ft. (45 cm) high with apparently leafless, switch-like, green branches. Leaves tri-foliate, very small, soon falling. Flowers yellow, silky-haired outside, in dense terminal clusters.
Flowering time: late spring–mid-summer.
Use: for slopes, banks, rock gardens and alpine gardens.
Propagation: by seed or cuttings in late summer, in sandy soil.
Environment and light: full sun.
Type of soil: mainly calcareous, stony-rocky, and poor.

⑤

451

Gentiana sino-ornata:

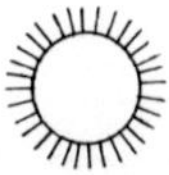

(5)

Family: Gentianacea. Named in honour of King Gentius of Illyrica, who is said to have discovered the medicinal virtues of the root.
Place of origin: West China and Tibet.
Description: a prostrate growing perennial, ascending at the tips. Leaves narrow, up to $1\frac{1}{2}$ in. (4 cm) long; flowers showy, solitary, terminal, deep blue but pale at the base.
Flowering time: late summer–early autumn.
Use: rock pockets, edging small beds.
Propagation: spring cuttings or division.
Environment and light: semi-shade, or in the sun provided the roots are kept cool.
Type of soil: will not tolerate lime; prefers a mixed sand and peat or leaf-mould soil.
Soil moisture: water in spring and early summer.
Remarks: this is a temperamental and unpredictable plant but once established is one of the loveliest of flowering plants. Very worth experimenting until success is achieved.

---

452 **GLOBE DAISY; HEARTLEAF GLOBULARIA**

Globularia cordifolia:

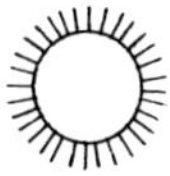

(9)

Family: Globulariaceae. Name from Latin, *globulus*, globe, referring to the shape of the inflorescence.
Place of origin: Europe, W. Asia; introduced into Britain in 1633.
Description: a mat-forming, dwarf perennial with woody stems and branches. Leaves in rosettes, shiny, dark green, somewhat fleshy, rounded-ovate. Flowers in rounded heads, terminal, blue, occasionally white or rose.
Flowering time: summer.
Use: for rock or alpine gardens.
Propagation: by seed or division.
Environment and light: sunny, dry spot.
Type of soil: mainly calcareous (for example, a mixture of clayey-calcareous soil, sand and leaf-mould).

453 SUNROSE; ROCKROSE

Helianthemum nummularium (H. chamaecistus):

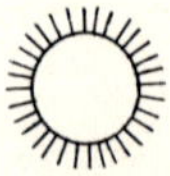

⑥

Family: Cistaceae. Name from Greek *helios*, sun and *anthemon*, flower.
Place of origin: Europe (including Britain).
Description: spreading, semi-shrubby evergreen, covering an area of 1–2 ft. (30–60 cm) and about 1 ft. (30 cm) high. Branching stems with elliptic, narrow, oblong leaves, grey and downy beneath, green above, Flowers free, yellow to rose, coppery red and crimson, also white. Many doubles have been raised, the "Ben" series particularly good. The plant illustrated is "Ben More", a rich orange-red.
Flowering time: early to mid-summer.
Use: for rock gardens, slopes and pockets in crazy paving.
Propagation: by soft cuttings rooted in gentle heat.
Environment and light: full sun. They dislike shade and damp.
Type of soil: free, open, light soil with lime (though this is not essential).

---

454 ALPENCRESS; HUTCHINSIA

Hutchinsia alpina:

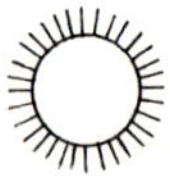

⑥

Family: Cruciferae. Named after Ellen Hutchins (1785–1815), an Irish botanist.
Place of origin: Pyrenees; introduced into Britain in 1775.
Description: tufted, herbaceous perennial, only 2 or 3 in. (5–7·5 cm) high, with basal rosettes of stemmed, pinnatifid leaves. Flowers white, very small, in short-stemmed clusters.
Flowering time: late spring–mid-summer.
Use: for rock gardens.
Propagation: by seed in spring or division.
Environment and light: open, sunny.
Type of soil: well-drained, sandy.

455 EDELWEISS

Leontopodium alpinum:

Family: Compositae. *Leontopodion*, Ancient Greek name meaning lion's foot.
Place of origin: European Alps; introduced into Britain in 1776.
Description: a tufted, woolly, herbaceous perennial of 6–8 in. (15–20 cm) spreading, with basal grey-green, lanceolate leaves on stalks; stem-leaves linear, sessile. Flowers in terminal, clustered heads, very tiny and insignificant but enveloped in showy, woolly bracts.
Flowering time: summer.
Use: for rock gardens.
Propagation: by division in spring or by seed.
Environment and light: sun to half-shade.
Type of soil: well-drained, sandy or calcareous soil.
Soil moisture: like most woolly-leaved plants, resents wet in winter.

---

456 BLUE LOBELIA; LOBELIA

Lobelia erinus:

Family: Lobeliaceae. Named after Matthias de l'Obel (1538–1616), botanist and physician to James I of England.
Place of origin: South Africa; introduced into Britain in 1782.
Description: a low-growing, about 6 in. (15 cm) high, perennial, treated as annual in frost-prone areas. Lower leaves, obovate, stalked, toothed along the margins; upper leaves, almost sessile, narrow, lanceolate. Flowers irregular in shape, pale blue with white or yellowish throat, in great profusion. Varieties occur with white, crimson, dark blue flowers; also doubles and trailing varieties.
Flowering time: summer–mid-autumn.
Use: for edgings, summer bedding, rock garden pockets, hanging baskets, window boxes, containers, dry walls, crazy paving crevices; also winter flowering in the greenhouse.
Propagation: by seed.
Environment and light: sun.
Type of soil: light, moist soil.
Soil moisture: soil should be kept moist.

457 **FLOWER OF JOVE**
Lychnis flos-jovis:

⑤

Family: Caryophyllaceae. Name from Greek *lychnos*, lamp; the leaves of some species were formerly used as lamp wicks.
Place of origin: European Alps; introduced into Britain in 1726.
Description: a woolly-leaved perennial of 1–2 ft. (30–60 cm). Leaves thick, acute, lanceolate, velvety grey. Flowers many, simple, regular, bright crimson-magenta to scarlet; occasionally white.
Flowering time: summer.
Use: for large rock gardens and borders.
Propagation: by division in spring; by seed planted out in spring.
Environment and light: full sun or light shade.
Type of soil: well-drained, fertile, slightly sandy.
Soil moisture: water in summer to keep the soil moist.

---

458 **GROUND PINK; MOSS PHLOX; MOSS PINK**
Phlox subulata:

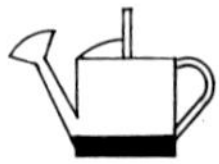

③

Family Polemoniaceae. *Phlox*, Greek word for flame.
Place of origin: Eastern United States; introduced into Europe in 1746.
Description: a low-growing, spreading perennial, sub-shrubby, forming mats of linear, mid-green, rigid leaves. Flowers profuse, in terminal panicles, each bloom having 5 petals; colours variable from pale pink to red, mauve, lavender and magenta in the named forms.
Flowering time: spring–early summer.
Use: for banks, rocky slopes or for making splashes of colour between paving stones, rock garden pockets, sink gardens, alpine houses.
Propagation: by basal shoots used as cuttings in mid-summer.
Environment and light: full sun. Survives a little shade but not happily.
Type of soil: any good garden soil.
Soil moisture: water if necessary in dry summers.

459 HART'S TONGUE FERN

Phyllitis scolopendrium:

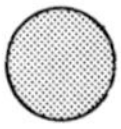

Family: Aspleniaceae. Name from Greek *phyllon*, leaf.
Place of origin: northern hemisphere.
Description: a beautiful evergreen fern with bright green, entire, strap-shaped fronds. Varieties occur with waved edges, crisped curly fronds like lettuce leaves, forked tips etc.
Use: fine indoor plant; also for recesses, old walls, cracks in rocks, rockeries, well heads etc.
Propagation: by spores and by division.
Environment and light: dimly lit places, but best if in total shade, with good humidity.
Type of soil: two parts ordinary garden soil to one of peat and one of sand.
Soil moisture: water often, but sparingly. The soil must always be damp.

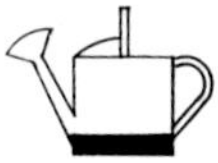

③

---

460 RAMPION

Phyteuma comosum:

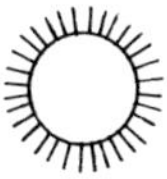

Family: Campanulaceae. Ancient Greek name.
Place of origin: mountains of Europe, in particular the Dolomites; introduced into Britain in 1752.
Description: a low-growing perennial of 2–4 in. (5–10 cm) of spreading habit and forming a tufted plant with smooth, ovate, pointed, coarsely toothed leaves. Flowers on very short stalks, flask-shaped, purple or blue, inflated at base and in clusters; each head about $1\frac{1}{2}$ in. (4 cm) across.
Flowering time: mid-summer.
Use: for alpine houses in pans; rock gardens, moraine or scree.
Propagation: seed or division.
Environment and light: full sun.
Type of soil: well-drained; found in nature in limestone crevices.
Soil moisture: water regularly, very frequently in hot months.
Remarks: protect against slugs.

⑦

461 BASTARD BOX; GROUND BOX

Polygala chamaebuxus:

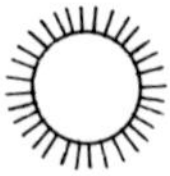

⑥

Family: Polygalaceae. Name from Greek *polygalon*, much milk; some species were supposed to increase lactation.
Place of origin: mountains of Europe; introduced into Britain in 1658.
Description: a dwarf evergreen shrub with numerous stems. Height 6 in. (15 cm), spread 8–12 in. (20–30 cm). Leafless at base, leafy above. Foliage leathery, elliptic-lanceolate, almost sessile. Flowers slightly fragrant, cream or yellow tipped with purple, in racemes of 1–6 blooms.
Flowering time: late spring–early summer.
Use: for small rock garden pockets; pans in alpine houses.
Propagation: by soft cuttings in late summer, or divided in spring.
Environment and light: full sun.
Type of soil: well-drained, enriched with leaf-mould or peat. Use a lime-free compost for pan culture.
Soil moisture: water if necessary; regularly, if under glass.

---

462 MINIATURE RHODODENDRON

Rhodothamnus chamaecistus:

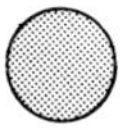

⑥

Family: Ericaceae. Name from Greek *rhodo*, red and *thamnos*, shrub, referring to the flower colour.
Place of origin: European Alps, Siberia; introduced into Britain in 1786.
Description: an evergreen shrub with slender prostrate stems, seldom more than 16 in. (40 cm) high. Branches glandular, hairy; leaves small, oval to obovate. Flowers in terminal clusters, 5-lobed, pinkish-violet with long, purple-tipped stamens.
Flowering time: spring.
Use: for rock garden pockets and alpine gardens, in lime-free soils.
Propagation: by seed, cuttings, layering, air layering in summer.
Environment and light: half-shade. Protect roots from strong sun or the plant will die.
Type of soil: light, lime-free with added humus.
Soil moisture: water in hottest and driest period.
Remarks: Blooms later in areas with heavy frost.

463 DWARF WILLOW; NEATLEAF WILLOW
Salix reticulata:

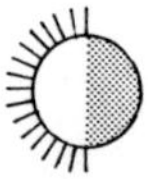

Family: Salicaceae. *Salix* Latin name for willow.
Place of origin: mountains of Europe (including Scottish Highlands); Labrador.
Description: a low or prostrate deciduous shrub, spreading to broad patches but only 5–6 in. (12–15 cm) high, rarely to 12 in. (30 cm). Young branches shiny brown. Leaves dark green above, glaucous white beneath, elliptival ovate, much wrinkled and prominently veined. Catkins $\frac{1}{2}$–1 in. (1–2·5 cm) long.
Flowering time: late spring.
Use: for rock or alpine gardens.
Propagation: by cuttings in spring or layering in summer.
Environment and light: sun or half-shade.
Type of coil: any good damp soil, including calcareous.
Soil moisture: water if necessary.
Remarks: this plant does best in very cold climates and does not do well south of zone 3.

①

---

464 GOLD MOSS; STONE CROP; WALLPEPPER
Sedum acre:

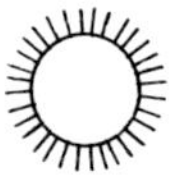

Family: Crassulaceae. From Latin *sedere*, to sit, referring to the manner in which some species grow on rocks.
Place of origin: Europe (including Britain), N. Africa, Western Asia.
Description: small, mat-forming plant, evergreen with mid-green to yellow, small, thick, conical, obtuse leaves which have a peppery taste. Flowers bright yellow, in terminal cymes, 5-petalled, almost star-shaped. Gold and variegated leaved forms exist.
Flowering time: early to mid-summer.
Use: for edging borders, dry walls, rock gardens, crevices in walls or stonework, pockets in crazy paving.
Propagation: by cuttings or division.
Environment and light: full sun.
Type of soil: poor and dry.

③

465 HOUSELEEK; ST PATRICK'S CABBAGE; HEN AND CHICKENS

Sempervivum tectorum:

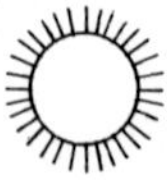

Family: Crassulaceae. Name from Latin *semper*, always and *vivus*, living.
Place of origin: Pyrenees, Alps; naturalised in Britain.
Description: this fleshy plant was formerly planted on roofs (where it survives for years) to ward off lightning. Rosette-forming with green, fleshy leaves which have red tips. Flowers in full, thick corymbs, dark or light purplish-red, up to 12 in. (30 cm) long.
Flowering time: early–mid-summer.
Use: for rock gardens, roofs, walls and cracks in rocks.
Propagation: by division of rosettes growing at base of mother plant.
Environment and light: full sun.
Type of soil: ordinary garden soil, light and porous.

⑤

---

466 YELLOW HOUSELEEK

Sempervivum wulfenii:

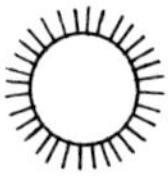

Family: Crassulaceae. *See* No 465.
Place of origin: Austrian and Swiss Alps.
Description very similar to No 465 but with fewer leaves and without the purplish tips. Bases rosy-purple and flowers greenish-yellow on 8 in. (20 cm) stems.
Flowering time: mid-summer.
Use: for cracks in rocks and walls, rock gardens.
Propagation: by division of rosettes growing from mother plant.
Environment and light: full sun.
Type of soil: ordinary garden soil, but light and porous.

⑤

467 DROOPING CATCHFLY
Silene pendula:

Family: Caryophyllaceae. *Silene*, a Greek name originally applied to *viscaria*.
Place of origin: southern Europe; introduced into Britain in 1731.
Description: a showy annual with erect 6–9 in. (15–22 cm) stems with oblong or lance-shaped, hairy leaves and drooping sprays of $\frac{1}{2}$ in. (about 1 cm) pale pink, 5-petalled flowers. White, purple and deep rose forms occur, also doubles.
Flowering time: late spring–early autumn, depending on when seed is sown.
Use: for rockeries, sinks and other containers, alpine gardens, walls and borders.
Propagation: by seed.
Environment and light: full sun.
Type of soil: any good but well-drained soil.

⑤

---

468 LONG-SPURRED PANSY
Viola calcarata:

Family: Violaceae. Old Latin name used by Pliny.
Place of origin: mountains of Central Europe.
Description: a plant of alpine and subalpine meadows; perennial, growing some 3–4 in. (7–10 cm) high. Leaves oval-oblong, mostly forming a rosette, sometimes deeply lobed, entire or toothed. Flowers violet or yellow; sometimes white, sky blue or parti-coloured.
Flowering time: early–mid-summer.
Use: for rock gardens, rockeries, slopes and banks, but the plant is not long-lived under cultivation.
Propagation: by seed.
Environment and light: full sun to half-shade.
Type of soil: mainly calcareous and well fertilized.
Soil moisture: water regularly, more often in hottest period.

⑥

MEDITERRANEAN PLANTS

469 CENTURY PLANT

Agave americana:

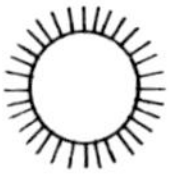

⑥

Family: Agavaceae. From Greek *agavos*, admirable, said to refer to the spectacle of the plants in flower.
Place of origin: Mexico; introduced into Mediterranean region 1640.
Description: succulent, virtually stemless plants growing in rosettes, often several feet across. Leaves spine-tipped, sword-shaped, grey-green, leathery, up to 3 ft. (90 cm) long. Flowers yellowish-green, crowded together at the ends of lateral branches on giant flowering spikes up to 25 ft. (7·5 m) tall; inflorescence appears after a long period, thirty or forty years (once believed to be a century), after which the rosette dies.
Flowering time: late summer.
Use: for rock slopes, sunny banks, or in large pots for entrance halls etc.; as a summer bedding plant.
Propagation: by offsets near the parent plant. Allow to dry for several days before potting up in good compost.
Environment and light: sunny. Winter under cover in areas subjected to frost.
Type of soil: good potting compost.
Soil moisture: water freely during the growing period.
Remarks: species of *Agave* are important economic plants, used for liqueur and other alcoholic drinks. Also the source of sisal.

---

470 ANEMONE

Anemone hortensis var. *stellata:*

Family: Ranunculaceae. Name possibly from Greek *anemos*, wind.
Place of origin: Mediterranean region from France to Greece, often in cultivated fields.
Description: perennial, 4–8 in. (10·20 cm) high. Radical leaves palmately divided, the lobes toothed; stem leaves narrow and more lance-shaped. Flowers star-shaped, purple, varying in shade; rarely white with lance-shaped petals.
Flowering time: late winter–late spring.
Use: for borders, rock gardens, cut flowers.
Propagation: by seed or division.
Environment and light: full sun; it is as well to protect the plants with leaves or the like in places with cold winters.
Type of soil: any good, well-drained soil that will hold moisture.

⑤

471 SNAPDRAGON

Antirrhinum majus:

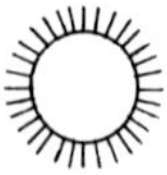

7

Family: Scrophulariaceae. Name from Greek *anti*, counterfeiting and *rhis*, nose, referring to the shape of the flower—like a dragon's mouth.
Place of origin: Mediterranean region; naturalised in Britain.
Description: erect, woody-based perennial, 10–32 in. (25–80 cm) high. Leaves entire, narrow, lance-shaped. Flowers about $1\frac{1}{2}$ in. (3·5–4 cm) long, reddish-purple with yellow throat (in wild form), in dense terminal racemes. Cultivars occur in wide range of colours and combinations: whites and yellows, through to mauve, scarlet and crimson. Cultivated forms usually grown as annuals.
Flowering time: spring–autumn.
Use: for bedding and grouped in borders to provide clumps of colour; as cut flowers. Container work. Found in nature on old walls.
Propagation: by seed.
Environment and light: full sun.
Type of soil: any good, well-cultivated soil, preferably light and well-manured.
Soil moisture: water in very dry seasons.
Remarks: north of zone 7 to be treated as an annual.

---

472 PINK MASTERWORT

Astrantia major:

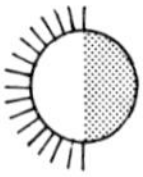

6

Family: Umbelliferae. Medieval plant-name possibly referring to the star-shaped flower-heads.
Place of origin: Alpine meadows, Europe.
Description: erect, little-branched perennial, 2 ft. (60 cm) high. Leaves ovate-lanceolate, dark shining green, lighter beneath; basal leaves, stalked and deeply divided into coarsely-toothed lobes; stem leaves, sessile. Flowers pinkish- or greenish-white, surrounded by large pointed bracts, on slender-stalked, rounded umbels, up to 2 in. (5 cm) across. They have a sickly smell.
Flowering time: early to mid-summer.
Use: for flowerbeds, rock gardens.
Propagation: by seed or by division.
Environment and light: half-shade, but sun if soil is moist in summer.
Soil moisture: water regularly so that soil is always moist.
Remarks: plants sometimes need staking.

473 FAIRY'S THIMBLE
Campanula cochleariifolia:

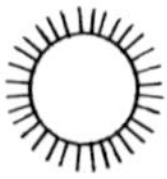

Family: Campanulaceae. Name from Latin *campana*, bell.
Place of origin: mountains of Europe; introduced into Britain in 1813.
Description: cushion-forming, herbaceous perennial, 4–6 in. (10–15 cm) high, with underground runners. Leaves shining, small; basal ones, rounded, long-stalked, in rosette; stem leaves, narrow. Flowers hanging, bell-shaped, about ¾ in. (1–2 cm) across, blue. White and deep blue forms in cultivation.
Flowering time: summer.
Use: fronts of borders, large rock gardens, containers, sink gardens etc. In alpine house, in pans for early flowering.
Propagation: by division in autumn or spring; by seed in autumn.
Environment and light: full sun or partial shade.
Type of soil: ordinary well-drained garden soil.
Soil moisture: the ground should always be fairly moist.

6

---

474 DANESBLOOD; CLUSTERED BELLFLOWER
Campanula glomerata:

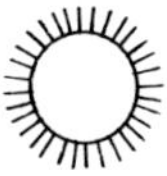

Family: Campanulaceae.
Place of origin: Europe (including Britain), temperate Asia.
Description: erect, unbranched, hairy perennial, 4–36 in. (10–90 cm) high. Lower leaves long-stemmed, oval or oblong to lanceolate; upper leaves, narrower, sessile, partly clasping stem. Flowers sessile, funnel-shaped, about 1 in. (1·5–3 cm) erect in terminal heads, deep blue to purple. There is a white form, "Alba".
Flowering time: summer.
Use: for herbaceous borders, bedding between shrubs; as cut flowers.
Propagation: by seed or division.
Environment and light: sun or light shade.
Type of soil: good garden soil with good calcium percentage.
Soil moisture: soil should be moist and fertile; often found on chalk or limestone.

3

475 SMOOTH CARLINE; STEMLESS CARLINE THISTLE

Carlina acaulis:

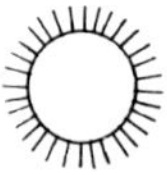

6

Family: Compositae. Medieval name for Carolus (Charles) and referring to Charlemagne, who is reputed to have used the roots to cure plague in his army.
Place of origin: mountains of Europe; introduced into Britain in 1640.
Description: low perennial, some 8 in. (20 cm) high. Leaves in large rosette, spiny, thistle-like, shiny. Flowers usually solitary,, 2–5 in. (5–13 cm) across, disk-florets white or reddish-white on very short stalk surrounded by spreading silvery-white, spiny, lance-shaped bracts.
Flowering time: early to mid-summer.
Use: for rock gardens, rockeries and slopes.
Planting: seedlings are planted out in late spring.
Propagation: by seed in early spring.
Environment and light: full sun.
Type of soil: rocky stony, not very calcareous.
Remarks: used as a weather guide, the flowers (bracts) closing under humid conditions; root used in herbal remedies.

---

476 MOUNTAIN BLUET; MOUNTAIN KNAPWEED

Centaurea montana:

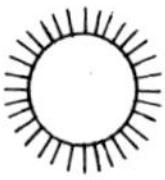

3

Family: Compositae. *See* No 357.
Place of origin: mountains of Central Europe; introduced into Britain in 1596.
Description: perennial, to $1\frac{1}{2}$ ft. (45 cm) high, with underground creeping stems. Leaves entire, downy, oblong, lanceolate. Flowers about 3 in. (6–8 cm) across, blue to violet, florets deeply cut. Cultivars range from white and pale yellow to deep reddish-purple.
Flowering time: spring–mid-summer.
Use: for borders and flowerbeds, and for cutting.
Propagation: by division, or seed.
Environment and light: full sun.
Type of soil: any fertile, well-drained soil.
Soil moisture: water if necessary.

477 **PINK ROCKROSE**

Cistus incanus (C. villosus):

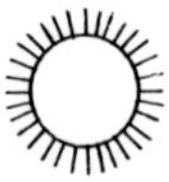

Family: Cistaceae. *Kistos*, Greek name for the plant.
Place of origin: Europe, Mediterranean region; introduced into Britain in 1650.
Description: densely-branched, evergreen shrub, 1–5 ft. (30–150 cm) high. Leaves opposite, entire, rounded, downy, greenish-grey, paler beneath. Flowers pink to rosy-purple with numerous bright yellow stamens about 2 in. (4–6 cm) across, prolific, in terminal clusters. White and wavy-petalled forms in cultivation.

Flowering time: spring–early summer.
Use: for small hedges, flowerbeds, clumps of colour.
Propagation: by seed in boxes and by cuttings after flowering.

Environment and light: full sun. Rockroses are difficult to grow in northern areas unless especially well exposed places are chosen which are also sheltered from cold winds.
Type of soil: dry and light, drained, best if mainly siliceous.

7

Soil moisture: water regularly, more often in summer.
Remarks: source of Labdanum, a bitter gum used in perfumery and medicine.

---

478 **SAGE-LEAVED CISTUS; SAGE-LEAVED ROCK-ROSE**

Cistus salvifolius:

Family: Cistaceae. *See* No 477.
Place of origin: Southern Europe; introduced into Britain in 1548, into the U.S.A. in 1550.
Description: spreading or erect, branched, evergreen shrub, 2–3 ft. (60–90 cm) high. Leaves stalked, rough, oblong to oval, grey-green, sage-like. Flowers: petals white with yellow bases, about 1–1½ in. (2–4 cm) across, in lateral clusters.

Flowering time: spring–early summer.
Use: for large rock gardens, slopes and well-drained flowerbeds.
Propagation: by seed or cuttings after flowering.

Environment and light: sunny, sheltered place, warm with well-drained soil. Renew frequently from cuttings as older plants are often killed in hard winters.
Type of soil: dry and light, well-drained.
Soil moisture: water if necessary.
Remarks: roots used medicinally in Arabic countries.

7

479 EUROPEAN CYCLAMEN; SOWBREAD
Cyclamen europaeum:

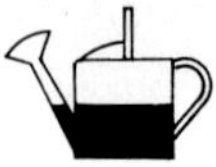

7

Family: Primulaceae. Name from Greek *kyklos*, circle, referring to the spiral twisting of the peduncle after flowering in some species.
Place of origin: Central and Southern Europe to Transcaucasus; introduced into Britain in 1613.
Description: low perennial with large globular or flattened corm. Leaves long-stalked, heart-shaped, silvery-zoned above, often purplish below. Flowers sweetly scented, rich carmine, occasionally white or pink, with reflexed petals; flowering stems 4–12 in. (10–30 cm) long, appearing with the leaves.
Flowering time: late summer–early autumn.
Use: for growing in small patches in rock gardens and in pans in alpine houses; also in pots on balconies and terraces.
Propagation: by seed.
Environment and light: shelter from hot sun and wind.
Type of soil: leaf-mould with loam and sand for good drainage.
Soil moisture: water if necessary; flowering plants like damp soil.
Remarks: the corms of *Cyclamen* are regarded as a favourite food for swine in parts of Southern Europe (hence the name, sowbread). Used in domestic medicine as a purgative and pain-killer.

---

480 FEBRUARY DAPHNE; MEZEREON
Daphne mezereum:

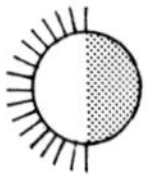

5

Family: Thymelaeaceae. *Daphne*, Greek name for the bay-tree, transferred to this genus.
Place of origin: Europe, Western Asia; introduced into Britain in 1561.
Description: erect, deciduous shrub, up to about 5 ft. (1·5 m) high. Leaves oblong, lanceolate, short-stemmed, greyish-green beneath. Flowers deep pink, fragrant, in dense lateral clusters on previous year's stems; the flowers appear before the leaves and are followed by round, scarlet berries. White and purple flowered varieties in cultivation.
Flowering time: late winter–spring.
Use: grown for its sweet scent and early flowers in borders and rock garden pockets etc.
Propagation: by half-ripe summer cuttings rooted in peat and sand or by seed.
Environment and light: sun or partial shade.
Type of soil: ordinary garden soil, including chalk, but must be well-drained.
Soil moisture: water in hot months to keep soil damp.
Remarks: poisonous. A diuretic and stimulant is derived from the dried bark.

481 YELLOW FOXGLOVE

Digitalis grandiflora (D. ambigua):

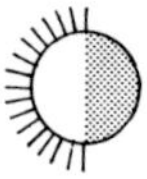

(3)

Family: Scrophulariaceae. *See* No 390.
Place of origin: mountainous regions in Europe; introduced into Britain in 1596.
Description: erect perennial of 2–3 ft. (60–90 cm), with hairy stems. Leaves oval, lance-shaped, toothed, downy on veins beneath. Flowers tubular, pale yellow, reticulated brown, 2 in. (5 cm) long, borne on slender spikes.
Flowering time: late spring–summer.
Use: for shady borders, amongst perennials in sunny borders, for cutting.
Propagation: by seed.
Environment and light: full sun to half-shade.
Type of soil: ordinary garden soil which does not dry out in summer.
Soil moisture: water if required in summer.
Remarks: poisonous.

---

482 FIREWEED; ROSEBAY WILLOW-HERB

Epilobium (Chamaenerion) angustifolium:

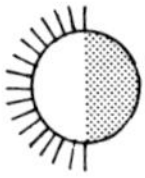

(3)

Family: Oenotheraceae. Name from Greek *epi*, upon and *lobos*, a pod, referring to the position of the petals.
Place of origin: Europe, including Britain.
Description: erect, little-branched perennial, up to about 5 ft. (150 cm) high. Leaves long, narrow, lance-shaped, marked venation on underside. Flowers rose-purple, about 1 in. (2–3 cm) across, 4-petalled, in long, leafless, terminal spikes. Seeds readily and can become a pest, so plant with caution. A white-flowered form, "Alba", is also cultivated; does not set seed.
Flowering time: summer–early autumn.
Use: for wild gardens, open woodlands etc.; white forms in herbaceous borders.
Propagation: by division or by seed.
Environment and light: sun or half-shade in cool places.
Type of soil: good but moist while well-drained.
Soil moisture: water if necessary.
Remarks: the leaves are used for making a tea in parts of Russia.

483 DOG'S TOOTH VIOLET; EUROPEAN FAWN-LILY; TROUT-LILY

Erythronium dens-canis:

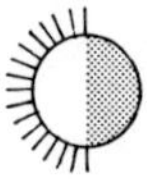

③

Family: Liliaceae. Name from Greek *erythros*, red, referring to the flowers of this species.
Place of origin: Europe, Asia; introduced into Britain in 1596.
Description: erect, bulbous perennial, with flowering stems usually about 6 in. (15 cm) high. Leaves variable, lanceolate, slender-pointed, usually marbled with grey or purple-brown. Flowers cyclamen-like, solitary, pink, nodding, perianth segments lanceolate and reflexed, $1\frac{1}{4}$ in. (3 cm) long. White and deep purple flowering forms exist in cultivation.
Flowering time: early spring.
Use: for rock gardens, light shady spots, edging borders or alpine pans.
Propagation: by seed or, occasionally, offsets.
Environment and light: half-shade.
Type of soil: moist but not waterlogged, with plenty of humus.
Soil moisture: water regularly; the ground should always be moist.
Remarks: the roots are a source of starch, which is utilized in Japan. In Mongolia and Siberia the leaves and bulbs are collected for food.

---

484 STEMLESS GENTIAN; TRUMPET GENTIAN

Gentiana acaulis:

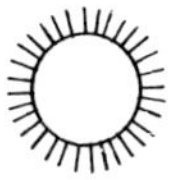

③

Family: Gentianaceae. Named after Gentius, King of the Illyrians, said to have discovered the medicinal value of the root.
Place of origin: mountains of Central and Southern Europe; introduced into Britain probably in 1888.
Description: this is a variable plant and embraces a number of species such as *G. kochiana, G. clusii* and *G. angustifolia*; modern authorities now refer them all to *G. excisa*. Low, mat-forming, herbaceous perennial of about 3 in. (7–8 cm). Leaves leathery, entire, ovate, in tight basal rosette. Flowers large, trumpet-shaped, about 2 in. (5–6 cm) long, solitary, bright blue, on short stalks. Blooming is erratic, some flower while others not at all. Various colour forms in cultivation.
Flowering time: late spring–early summer.
Use: for rock gardens or alpine houses.
Propagation: by division after flowering or seed grown in pans. Germination will hasten if the seeds are first frozen.
Environment and light: sunny position.
Type of soil: leafy soil, lime free potting compost.
Soil moisture: water regularly, more generously in summer, so that the soil is always moist.

485 WILLOW GENTIAN

Gentiana asclepiadea:

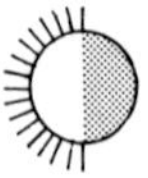

③

Family: Gentianaceae. *See* No 484.
Place of origin: woods and mountains of Europe; introduced into Britain in 1629.
Description: herbaceous perennial with leafy arching stems, 8 in.–2 ft. (20–60 cm) tall. Leaves willow-like, lanceolate, strongly-veined. Flowers trumpet-shaped, dark blue, striped paler and spotted with purple, $1\frac{1}{4}$–$2\frac{1}{4}$ in. (3·5–5·5 cm) long, in groups of 1–3 in axils of upper leaves. Dwarf and white-flowered varieties exist in cultivation.
Flowering time: late summer–early autumn.
Use: in light woodland, beneath trees, in grass; for mixed borders.
Propagation: by seed.
Environment and light: damp, partially shaded spot.
Type of soil: humus type soil but well-drained.
Soil moisture: keep ground moist during growing period.

---

486 SPOTTED GENTIAN

Gentiana punctata:

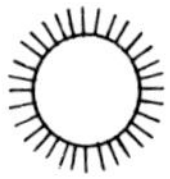

③

Family: Gentianaceae. *See* No 484.
Place of origin: mountains of central Europe, Alps and Balkans.
Description: a vigorous, stiff, erect, unbranched perennial, 1–2 ft. (30–60 cm) high, with a long tap-root. Leaves elliptic, strongly-veined, greyish-green. Flowers yellow, purple-spotted, bell-shaped, about $5\frac{1}{2}$ in. (3–4 cm) long, in dense terminal and axillary clusters.
Flowering time: summer.
Use: for large rock or alpine gardens.
Propagation: by seed.
Environment and light: full sun, where it will not be disturbed.
Type of soil: deep and fertile; tolerant of lime.
Soil moisture: water so that the ground is always damp to the touch.

487 YELLOW HORNED POPPY; SEA POPPY

Glaucium flavum:

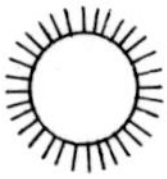

8

Family: Papaveraceae. Name from Greek *glaukos*, greyish-green.
Place of origin: coastline of Mediterranean and Western Europe (including Britain) usually on shingle; introduced to and naturalised in North America.
Description: erect biennial or short-lived perennial, 12–24 in. (30–60 cm) high. Leaves glaucous, rough, quite fleshy, deeply lobed and toothed, upper ones clasping the stem. Flowers 4-petalled, bright yellow, 3 in. (7–8 cm) across. The sap is yellow. Fruits narrow, 1 ft. (30 cm) long, splitting into 2 valves.
Flowering time: summer.
Use: for borders, clumps and flowerbeds.
Propagation: by seed in late spring sown where it is to flower; the seedlings do not transplant well.
Environment and light: full sun.
Type of soil: ordinary but well-drained soil.
Soil moisture: water regularly, more in summer, but do not let water stagnate.
Remarks: the root is poisonous. Oil pressed from the seeds has culinary uses; also manufactured into soap.

---

488 SNAKE'S HEAD IRIS

Hermodactylus tuberosus (Iris tuberosa):

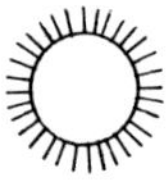

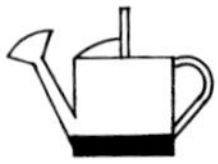

7

Family: Iridaceae. Name from Greek *Hermes*, Mercury and *daktylos*, finger, referring to the form of the tubers.
Place of origin: rocky and stony places of Central and Eastern Europe; introduced into Britain in medieval times.
Description: iris-like perennial, with slender, hollow stem 8–16 in. (20–40 cm) high and swollen, tuberous roots. Leaves rush-like, lanceolate, erect. Flowers striking, greenish-yellow with reflexed segments blackish- or brownish-purple, overarched by long green spathe; solitary.
Flowering time: late winter–spring.
Use: for rock garden pockets, flowerbeds, and for cutting.
Propagation: by division of tubers in early autumn.
Environment and light: warm, sunny position in cool temperate climates. Resents cold, wet winters.
Type of soil: good loamy soil, quite fertile and well-drained.
Soil moisture: water if necessary whilst growing.

489 SOLOMON'S SEAL
Polygonatum multiflorum:

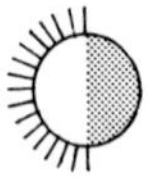

Family: Liliaceae. Name from Greek *poly*, many and *gony*, knee-joint, referring to the jointed rhizomes.
Place of origin: Europe (including Britain), Northern Asia.
Description: herbaceous perennial with leafy, arched stems 2–4 ft. (60–120 cm) long and white, creeping rhizomes. Leaves oblong, clasping the stem. Flowers white with green tips, tubular with slightly constricted waist, about 1 in. (2–3 cm) long, hanging in clusters of 2–5 on slender stalks rising from the axils of the leaves.
Flowering time: spring–early summer.
Use: for shady borders and open woodland in parks and gardens.
Propagation: by division of rhizomes.
Environment and light: half-shade.
Type of soil: ordinary garden soil.
Remarks: this plant does not thrive south of zone 8. The Solomon's Seal of gardens is considered to be a hybrid between *P. multiflorum* and *P. odoratum*. The rhizomes have been used in herbal remedies.

(5)

---

490 BISTORT; SNAKEROOT; SNAKEWEED
Polygonum bistorta:

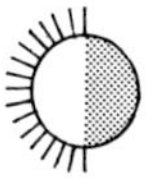

Family: Polygonaceae. Name probably from same derivation as No 489 and refers to the many-jointed rhizome.
Place of origin: Europe; including Britain (in damp meadows), Northern and Western Asia.
Description: erect, vigorously-growing, unbranched perennial, 1–2 ft. (30–60 cm) high. Leaves light green, ovate, the lower ones with broadly winged stalks; upper leaves sessile, clasping stem. Flowers pink (more rarely white), in dense cylindrical, terminal spikes.
Flowering time: late spring–mid-summer.
Use: for grassy banks and damp meadows, moist slopes and rockeries.
Propagation: by division.
Environment and light: half-shade.
Type of soil: moist but well-drained garden soil.
Soil moisture: water if essential; keep ground moist.
Remarks: the dried rhizomes are used as a tonic and astringent. The leaves are eaten in the English Lake District under the name Easterledges.

(6)

491 ENGLISH PRIMROSE; PRIMROSE

Primula acaulis (more correctly *P. vulgaris*):

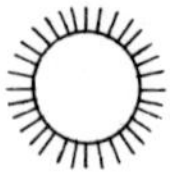

Family: Primulaceae. Name from Latin *primus*, first (early flowering).
Place of origin: Southern and Western Europe, including Britain.
Description: a favourite spring perennial. Leaves oblong, rounded at tip, rough textured, downy and lighter green beneath, narrowed to winged stalk. Flowers freely-produced, pale yellow, about 1 in. (2–3 cm) across, on slender, erect, downy, leafless stalks, 4–6 in. (10–15 cm) high. Many forms in cultivation, simple- or double-flowered and ranging in colour from white to pink, purple and blue.
Flowering time: spring.
Use: borders, flowerbeds, rock gardens, wild and woodland gardens.
Propagation: by seed or division in autumn.
Environment and light: sun or half-shade, according to climate.
Type of soil: good loam-clay soil that is moisture retentive.
Soil moisture: water if necessary to keep soil moist.
Remarks: does best where the climate is mildly humid.

(5)

---

492 AURICULA; AURICULA PRIMROSE; BEAR'S EAR

Primula auricula:

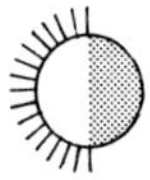

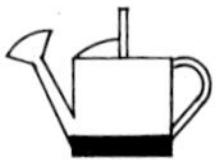

Family: Primulaceae.
Place of origin: mountains of Central Europe; introduced into Britain in 1596.
Description: a variable perennial which is the parent of countless cultivars in various colours and combinations of shades. Leaves in lax rosettes, obovate, more or less entire, slightly fleshy and usually powdery. Flowers sweet-scented, bright yellow (in the species), sometimes purple, about 1 in. (1·5–3 cm) across, 3–20 together in umbels on upright 5–25 cm stalks.
Flowering time: spring.
Use: for rock gardens, shady borders, or can be grown in pots.
Propagation: by division or by seed.
Environment and light: half-shade.
Type of soil: well-drained, gritty, with plenty of humus.
Soil moisture: water regularly to keep soil moist.

(3)

493 SHOWY PRIMROSE

Primula spectabilis:

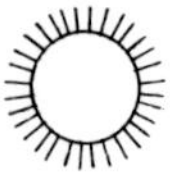

Family: Primulaceae.
Place of origin: Eastern Alps; introduced into Britain in 1879.
Description: one of the finest European primulas but unfortunately very shy flowering. Forms flat, rosettes of shiny green, entire, ovate, acute, fleshy leaves, pitted above. Flowers clear rose-pink, often with a white eye, about 1 in. (2–3 cm) across, borne in umbels of 2–7 flowers.
Flowering time: late spring–mid-summer.
Use: for rock gardens.
Propagation: by division or by seed.
Environment and light: full sun, in a pocket high up in a rock-garden; half-shade in warm areas.
Type of soil: stony mixture to afford a good root run. Mulch occasionally with leaf-mould.
Soil moisture: water regularly in hot weather to keep soil damp.

(5)

---

494 ALPENROSE; ROCK RHODODENDRON

Rhododendron ferrugineum:

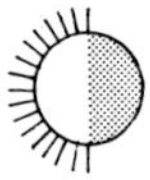

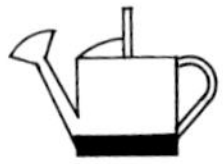

Family: Ericaceae. Name from Greek *rhodon*, rose and *dendron*, tree.
Place of origin: mountains of Central Europe; introduced into Britain in 1752.
Description: evergreen shrub, 3–4 ft. (90–120 cm) high, with twisted branches. Leaves leathery, elliptic, shiny and dark green above, honey-coloured beneath. Flowers plentiful, funnel-shaped, about 1 in. (2–3 cm) long, pinkish-red, in umbel-like clusters of 6–12 flowers. White and scarlet varieties in cultivation.
Flowering time: early to mid-summer.
Use: for isolated clumps in open woodland, large rock gardens.
Propagation: by cuttings, air layers and stem layers.
Environment and light: half-shade.
Type of soil: rich and acid; compost made up of leaf-mould, loam and peat.
Soil moisture: water if necessary to keep the soil damp.

(4)

495 BUTCHER'S BROOM
Ruscus aculeatus more properly *Aculeatus:*

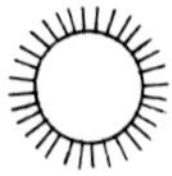

Family: Liliaceae. *Ruscus*, an old Latin name for this plant.
Place of origin: Northern Asia, Southern and Eastern Europe (including Britain).
Description: dense, evergreen shrub, 3 ft. (1 m) high, with grooved stem bearing stiff, dark green, flattened, spiny-pointed branchlets (cladodes) resembling leaves. True leaves scale-like. Flowers tiny about one tenth of an inch (3 mm) across, greenish, 1–2 together in centre of cladode. The plants are monoecious and their real interest lies in the large, round, scarlet berries which appear in the autumn.
Flowering time: early spring.
Use: for small hedges, borders, wild gardens; a good plant for edging.
Propagation: by seed or division.
Environment and light: sun or dense shade.
Type of soil: ordinary dry garden soil, also clays and chalk soil.
Remarks: plant in groups containing one male plant in order to have berries. The branches of this plant are sometimes used to make brooms, and were once employed to sweep butchers' counters and chopping-blocks.

(7)

---

496 COMMON GLOBE FLOWER
Trollius europaeus:

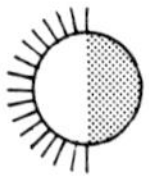

Family: Ranunculaceae. From the German *trollblume*, globe flower.
Place of origin: Europe, including Britain.
Description: erect, little-branched perennial, some 1–2 ft. (30–60 cm) high. Leaves buttercup-like, dark green, stalked, lobed and deeply divided; upper leaves sessile. Flowers globular, lemon yellow, 1–2 in. (3–5 cm) across, solitary. Many garden hybrids with flowers up to $2\frac{1}{2}$ in. (6·5 cm) across, pale lemon to gold and orange.
Flowering time: late spring–mid-summer.
Use: for borders or small clumps by streams, wells, ponds, in damp places.
Properties: poisonous.
Propagation: by division in spring or autumn.
Environment and light: half-shade to complete shade; quite sunny in cooler climates.
Type of soil: fertile, but moist.
Soil moisture: if the soil is not damp enough naturally, water daily; adjust amount of water to climatic conditions.

(4)

WATER AND POOL PLANTS

497 MARSH MARIGOLD; KINGCUP

Caltha palustris:

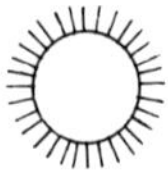

Family: Ranunculaceae. Name refers to yellow petals (possibly derived from *calendula).*
Place of origin: northern temperate (including Britain) and Arctic regions.
Description: smooth perennial growing 9–15 in. (22–37 cm) high with hollow stems, entire round to kidney-shaped crenate leaves and golden yellow, buttercup-like flowers on branching stems. Double and white-flowered forms exist.
Flowering time: spring.
Use: an early bloomer for bog gardens, river banks, wet meadows; also in shallow water at pond margins.
Propagation: by division in spring.
Environment and light: full sun.
Type of soil: any marshy soil, or heavy loam.
Remarks: the buds have been used as a substitute for capers; leaves eaten as "spring greens". Flowers once used for dyeing yarn.

(3)

---

498 ELEPHANT'S EAR

Colocasia esculenta var. *antiquorum (C. antiquorum):*

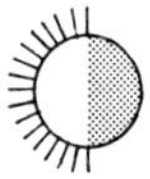

Family: Araceae. Name from Greek *kolokasia*, used originally for another water plant.
Place of origin: tropical Asia.
Description: an ornamental aroid with large edible tubers and huge, 2 ft. (60 cm), ovate, cordate leaves shaped like the ears of an elephant and on stout stems. Flowers pale yellow, 15 in. (20 cm) spathes; spadix with a very long sterile appendage.
Flowering time: summer, but flowers rarely.
Use: cool climates; for indoor pools or as a pot plant plunged in outside pools for summer and then wintered indoors. In tropics, grow outside all the time—moist soil or shallow water.
Properties: Colocasias have edible rhizomes when, when boiled, loose their poisonous properties.
Propagation: by division of tubers in spring.
Environment and light: sunny to half-shade, in shallow water or bog garden.
Type of soil: ordinary fertile garden soil, without stones, pebbles etc.

(10)

499 **UMBRELLA FLATSEDGE; UMBRELLA GRASS**
Cyperus alternifolius:

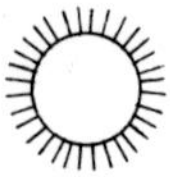

Family: Cyperaceae. Name from the Greek for sedge.
Place of origin: Madagascar; introduced into Europe around 1780.
Description: a sedge 1–3 ft. (30–90 cm) high with flat-topped, umbrella-like inflorescences set off by narrow grassy leaves. Stems triangular. Of the several forms the one with variegated leaves is the most interesting.
Flowering time: late summer.
Use: as a pot plant stood in very shallow water; for bog gardens in subtropical countries, fountain basins and the like.
Propagation: by division.
Environment and light: sun or light shade. Too tender to winter outdoors except in frost-free environment.
Type of soil: loam and sand with a little peat.
Soil moisture: needs constant watering.

(10)

---

500 **EGYPTIAN PAPER-PLANT; PAPYRUS**
Cyperus papyrus:

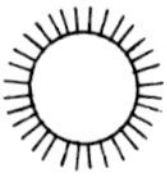

Family: Cyperaceae.
Place of origin: Syria, tropical Africa; introduced into Europe in 1803.
Description: a noble reed with large, round "mop-heads" of greenish-brown inflorescences on stout, triangular, bare stems. Leaves reduced to sheaths. Height 6–8 ft. (1·8–2·4 m), or up to 16 ft. (4·6 m) in its native habitat.
Flowering time: summer.
Use: for large containers, indoor pools. In warm climates, as an aquatic for the margins of ponds and lakes.
Propagation: by division or by pegging down the flower-heads in wet mud, where the seedlings germinate.
Environment and light: full sun.
Type of soil: heavy loam, lump charcoal and a little bonemeal.
Soil moisture: needs shallow water or wet soil all the time.
Remarks: the pith of this plant supplied the paper (papyrus) of the ancient Egyptians; and these were the "bullrushes" that sheltered the infant Moses.

(9)

501 WATER HYACINTH

Eichhornia crassipes (E. speciosa):

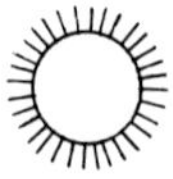

Family: Pontederiaceae. Named after J. A. Fr. Eichhorn (1779–1856), a Prussian Minister of Education.
Place of origin: South America; introduced into Europe in 1879.
Description: a showy, floating aquatic with rosettes of shiny, pale green, smooth, cordate leaves which have huge, sausage-like, swollen petioles filled with spongy tissue (aerenchyma). This makes them buoyant and the long black roots trail down into the water. Flowers pretty, borne in spikes, pale violet blue with conspicuous blue and gold peacock markings on the upper petals.
Flowering time: summer.
Use: for indoor pools, aquaria, or outdoor pools in summer in temperate climates. Should not be introduced to water features in tropics as it can spread rapidly and choke the pool.
Propagation: by detaching the runners from parent plants.
Environment and light: full sun.
Type of soil: none necessary.
Remarks: plant is killed by frost. To retain stock, pot several plants tightly together in a bowl of plain loam and keep damp (not in water) in a light, warm situation.

---

502 GINGER LILY

Hedychium gardnerianum:

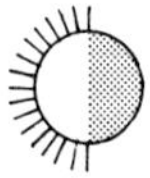

Family: Zingiberaceae. Name from Greek *hedys*, sweet and *chion*, snow; one species has white fragrant flowers.
Place of origin: Northern India; introduced in 1819.
Description: an erect, rhizomatous perennial with large, stiff stems. Leaves large, sessile (or stalked at tops of stems), lanceolate, up to 15 in. (37 cm) long. Flowers in bold spikes, pale yellow with red filaments to stamens.
Flowering time: summer.
Use: sub-tropical bedding; indoor pools for tropical plants, standing pots in shallow water; conservatory borders or large pots in cool climates; permanent beds or pools in tropics.
Propagation: by division of rhizomes in mid-spring or by seed.
Environment and light: half-shade to full sun; warm, moist.
Type of soil: rich loam with well-decayed manure and sand to ensure drainage. Feed in summer.
Soil moisture: stand in pools or water several times daily in summer.
Remarks: this is one of the hardiest species, but should be overwintered under cover when necessary—like cannas or dahlias.

503 YELLOW FLAG IRIS
Iris pseudacorus:

Family: Iridaceae. Named after Iris, Greek goddess of the rainbow.
Place of origin: Europe (including Britain), Asia Minor.
Description: a clump-forming, rhizomatous perennial of 2–3 ft. (60–90 cm). Leaves broadly sword-shaped. Flowers bright yellow with a deeper spot at throat and reddish veins. The variegated-leaved form is the most garden-worthy.
Flowering time: early summer.
Use: for shallow water in ponds and lakes; by fountains and streams.
Propagation: by division of rhizomes.
Environment and light: full sun.
Type of soil: heavy clay loam.
Soil moisture: shallow water of 2–3 in. (5–8 cm) all the time.
Remarks: the species is the original Fleur-de-lis or Flower-de-luce of French heraldry. The root was used at one time as a remedy for coughs, toothache and dyspepsia, and the roasted seeds as a coffee substitute.

(5)

---

504 EAST INDIAN LOTUS; HINDOO LOTUS
Nelumbo nucifera (Nelumbium speciosum):

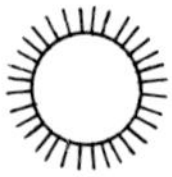

Family: Nelumbonaceae. Sinhalese name for the plant.
Place of origin: Asia; introduced into Europe in 1787.
Description: a spectacular aquatic with banana-like rhizomes. Leaves large, round, glaucous, with metallic sheen and centrally poised on 3–6 ft. (90–120 cm) stems. Flowers fragrant, large, showy, up to 12 in. (15 cm) across, vivid rose which pales with age. White, deep red, purplish and pink varieties exist, also many doubles.
Flowering time: summer.
Use: temperate climates: for indoor pools, tubs or sometimes planted in outside tanks for summer, then either wintered indoors or pools are drained and plants protected with leaves, glass etc. Tropics: for lakes and large pools.
Propagation: in spring by division of rhizomes.
Environment and light: full sun.
Type of soil: well fertilized soil with peat.
Remarks: in late autumn empty the pond and cover the plants with fertilized peat until the following spring. Buddha is supposed to have been born in the "heart of a lotus", so the plant has been held sacred in India and China from very early times.

(6)

505 BRANDY BOTTLE; EUROPEAN COW-LILY; YELLOW WATER-LILY; NENUPHAR

Nuphar Lutea:

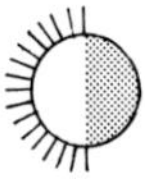

Family: Nymphaeaceae. Arabic name.
Place of origin: Europe (including Britain), temperate Asia, N. America.
Description: a coarse aquatic perennial with huge fleshy rhizomes, sometimes greenish but generally white with brown markings. Leaves floating, orbicular, large, lobed at base. Flowers unpleasant smelling, leathery, globular, cup-shaped, yellow, just above the water.
Flowering time: summer–autumn.
Use: for running water, shady situations and deep pools where the true water-lilies (*Nymphaea*) will not thrive. Can take over a small pool however, so plant with care.
Propagation: by division.
Environment and light: half-shade to deep shade; only flowers well, however, in sun.
Type of soil: clay, loam.
Remarks: water should be 1–3 ft. (30–90 cm) deep, or more.

③

---

506 PYGMY WATER-LILY

Nymphaea tetragona (pygmaea) "Helvola"*:*

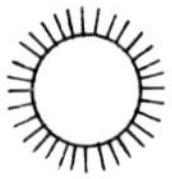

Family: Nymphaeaceae. Name from Greek *nymphe*, water nymph.
Place of origin: garden origin.
Description: a small perennial water-lily, free flowering, with crenulate, soft yellow, many-petalled flowers and fleshy, chocolate blotched leaves from a short, thick rhizome.
Flowering time: summer.
Use: for rock garden pools, containers, both indoors and out of doors (summer only) in frost-prone climates.
Propagation: by division in spring, after at least 3 years.
Environment and light: full sun.
Type of soil: peat, garden soil, leaf-mould, coarse sand; all well fertilized.
Remarks: a charming little plant that has to be protected in winter and only requires 3–4 in. (7–10 cm) of water.

④

507 FRAGRANT WATER-LILY; ALLIGATOR BONNET

Nymphaea odorata:

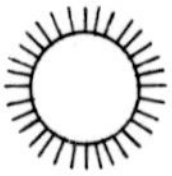

Family: Nymphaeaceae.
Place of origin: Eastern U.S.A.; introduced into Britain in 1786.
Description: a very sweet-scented hardy water-lily. Leaves orbicular, purplish beneath. Flowers usually floating, 3–6 in. (7–15 cm) across, sepals 4, petals 23–32, smaller than sepals, pure white. Rhizome stout.
Flowering time: summer–mid-autumn.
Use: for shallow water pools or tubs (12–18 in. (15–20 cm)).
Propagation: in spring by division.
Environment and light: full sun.
Type of soil: fibre-free loam, with bonemeal.

③

---

508 RED WATER-LILY

Nymphaea rubra:

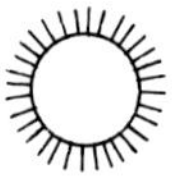

Family: Nymphaeaceae.
Place of origin: India; introduced into Britain in 1803.
Description: a tropical water-lily, with fairly small, rounded tubers, only hardy outside in warmer climates. Leaves large, bronzed, becoming green with age, margins waved. Flowers large, 6–10 in. (15–25 cm) across, stellate, deep purplish-red, nocturnal flowering (opening evening, closing mid-morning), petals narrowly oval, stamens cinnabar-red.
Flowering time: summer.
Use: for large conservatories or sun-lounge tanks; appreciated for its fragrant blooms at night.
Propagation: by seed.
Environment and light: full sun.
Type of soil: loam, charcoal and bonemeal.
Remarks: water should be 4–12 in. (10–30 cm) deep. When plants die down in autumn, drain tank and dry off tubers; store in moist sand and start again in spring.

⑤

509 WATER LETTUCE
Pistia stratiotes:

Family: Araceae. Name from Greek *pistos*, water.
Place of origin: New World tropics; introduced into Britain in 1843.
Description: a tropical, floating aquatic which forms rosettes of light green, wedge-shaped, slightly concave, heavily-ribbed leaves, 2–5 in. (5–12 cm) long. These are softly downy due to a covering of fine hairs. Flowers greenish, insignificant.
Use: for tropical tanks or aquaria, where the trailing roots form nurseries for fish. Will also grow under bog conditions in suitable climates.
Propagation: by stolons. Increase naturally and rapidly.
Environment and light: sun or half-shade, airy, or in well-lit places if in aquaria or under glass. Summer temperature of water must always be at least 70°F (21°C).
Type of soil: good loamy soil.
Soil moisture: if the plant is not directly in water the soil must always be very damp.

8

---

510 PICKEREL WEED; WAMPEE
Pontederia cordata:

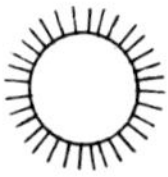

Family: Pontederiaceae. Named after Giulio Pontedera (1688–1757), botanist at Padua.
Place of origin: North America; introduced into Europe in 1597.
Description: a robust, herbaceous perennial of $1\frac{1}{2}$–3 ft. (45–90 cm). Leaves smooth, ovate-cordate, dark green, on erect stems. Flowers in terminal spikes, sky-blue with a white mealy background.
Flowering time: summer–early autumn.
Use: for margins of ponds, lakes etc.
Propagation: by division at any season.
Environment and light: full sun; hardy in temperate areas.
Type of soil: heavy loam.
Remarks: plant in 6–12 in. (15–30 cm) of water.

3

511 ARROWHEAD; OLD-WORLD ARROWHEAD

Sagittaria sagittifolia:

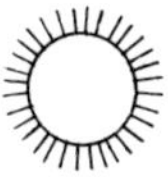

Family: Alismataceae. Name from Latin *sagitta*, arrow, referring to the shape of the leaves.
Place of origin: Europe, including Britain.
Description: herbaceous plant with an almost round, tuberous rootstock. Leaves, when immersed, slender and grasslike; floating, rounded and emergent leaves arrow-shaped. Flowers white, 3-petalled, in whorls around 12–18 in. (30–45 cm) stems. The double form, which looks like a white stock, is the best for garden pools and unlike the species does not become a rampant nuisance.
Flowering time: early summer.
Use: for pool margins.
Propagation: double form, by divisions; otherwise by division or seed.
Environment and light: sun.
Type of soil: loam.
Remarks: tubers eaten, particularly by the Chinese; the green parts are fed to pigs.
The type can spread rapidly, so plant with caution.

⑤

---

512 POWDERY THALIA; WATER CANNA

Thalia dealbata:

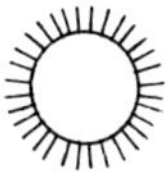

Family: Marantaceae. Named after Johann Thal (1542–1583), German naturalist.
Place of origin: South Eastern U.S.A.; introduced into Europe in 1791.
Description: a fine-foliaged aquatic up to 7 ft. (2 m) tall, with broad basal leaves, covered with white bloom. Flowers on leafless, waxy stems, above the foliage, purplish, 6-petalled.
Flowering time: late summer–early autumn.
Use: frost-free climates: marginal aquatic for ponds and lakes. Temperate zones: grow in large pots plunged in outside pools for summer or all the time in warm indoor pools.
Propagation: by division in spring.
Environment and light: full sun or sunny and warm.
Type of soil: good loamy soil.

⑦

513 ROYAL WATER-LILY; ROYAL WATER PLATTER

Victoria amazonica (V. regia):

Family: Nymphaeaceae. Named after Queen Victoria.
Place of origin: tropical South America.
Description: huge, densely prickly aquatics with short, thick rhizomes. Mature leaves up to $6\frac{1}{2}$ ft. (2 m) peltate to orbicular, floating, lower surface spined, margins turned up to form a continuous rim; juvenile leaves linear to orbicular. Flowers just above the surface, up to 40 cm across, numerous petals, red, pink or white; seeds pulpy.
Flowering time: summer.
Use: for large, indoor warm tanks (as in botanic gardens) in temperate climates. Tropics, large ponds or lakes.
Propagation: treated as an annual in temperate zones, seed being sown in spring under glass in pots with good loamy soil, immersed in water at 83°F (28°C) which should cover it to a height of about 2 in. (5–6 cm). After a series of transplantings plant is taken to flowering site.
Environment and light: full sun.
Type of soil: good rich soil, with rotted cow manure.
Remarks: in frost-prone areas treated as an annual for outdoor garden pools.
Seeds rich in starch and used for flour in S. America. Rhizomes used in dyeing and tanning.

⑧

---

514 CALLA LILY; ARUM LILY

Zantedeschia aethiopica (Calla aethiopica):

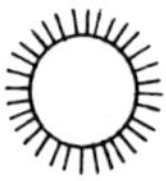

Family: Araceae. Named after Giovanni Zantedeschi (1773–1846), an Italian botanist.
Place of origin: South Africa; introduced in 1731.
Description: herbaceous, moisture-loving perennial of $2–2\frac{1}{2}$ ft. (60–75 cm). Leaves smooth, fleshy, arrow-shaped, rich green on long stems. Flowers pure white, 3–8 in. (7–20 cm) long, on stout, leafless stems. Variety "Crowborough" hardy in south of England.
Flowering time: under glass, in spring; outdoors in summer.
Use: pot plant, cut flowers, edges of pools in warm climates; or may survive in winter in $2–2\frac{1}{2}$ ft. (60–75 cm) of water in temperate climates like the south of England. Often raised under glass in northern Europe for the Easter market.
Propagation: by division in spring.
Environment and light: full sun. A semi-aquatic plant; thus may be grown in pots if partly immersed in water.
Type of soil: good garden soil with sand, and some organic fertilizer.
Soil moisture: reduced in winter so that the rhizomes can lie dormant, unless totally submerged.

⑦

ORCHIDS

515 **BLETILLA STRIATA**
Bletia hyacinthina:

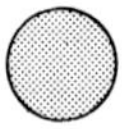

(10)

Family: Orchidaceae. Named after Luis Blet, who owned a botanic garden in Algeciras, Spain, in the eighteenth century.
Place of origin: China; introduced into Europe in 1802.
Description: a terrestrial orchid, very variable and the only member of the genus cultivated. Species is hardy in favoured localities in mild temperate climates. Height 1 ft. (30 cm). Leaves grassy- to sword-shaped, basal, pleated. Flowers on erect stems carrying 6–10 rich purple flowers—occasionally white, pink or striped.
Flowering time: spring–early summer.
Use: moist, shady spots in sheltered woodland gardens. In pots or pans in cold areas.
Propagation: by division of pseudobulbs at the base of the plant, after flowering.
Environment and light: in areas subject to frost, grow in small pots of peaty soil and plunge into ground outside to flower; shade.
Type of soil: equal parts of peat and loam with a little sand and leaf mould.
Soil moisture: water plentifully whilst growing but in winter only enough to keep compost from drying out.

516

Cattleya labiata: hybr.

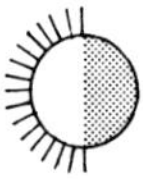

(10)

Family: Orchidaceae. Named after William Cattley of Barnet, England (d. 1832), patron of botany.
Place of origin: South and Central America and West Indies; introduced into Britain from Brazil in 1818.
Description: there are about 60 species of *Cattleya*, all epiphytic. This species has numerous forms and is very popular with florists on account of the large, flamboyant flowers. *C. labiata* has pseudobulbs, each carrying a single, leathery, oval leaf. Flowers sometimes 8–10 in. (20–25 cm) across in the cultivars, deep velvety crimson, but lighter and darker shades abound.
Flowering time: most forms in late autumn.
Use: for cut flowers, corsage work, growing in warm greenhouses in hanging pots. In tropics, on trees.
Propagation: by division when repotting.
Environment and light: light important, especially in winter. Temperatures:
summer: day, 70°–80°F (21°–27°C), night, 60°F (15·6°C);
winter: day, 65°F (18°C), night, 55°F (13°C).
Type of soil: osmunda fibre and sphagnum moss.
Soil moisture: water regularly when substratum is almost dry; stop when dormant.

517

Cymbidium: sp.

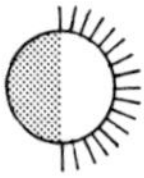

(10)

Family: Orchidaceae. Name from Greek *kymbe*, boat, referring to the hollow recess in the lip of the flowers.
Place of origin: Asia, Australia; in Europe since about 1838.
Description: most popular group of orchids for temperate climate and one of the easiest to grow under glass. Numerous cultivars, in every shade except blue, exquisitely marked, with 15–25 blooms per stem on a well-grown plant—and up to 20 sprays. Leaves strap-shaped, from large pseudobulbs.
Flowering time: winter to early summer, according to variety and species.
Use: for home decoration. Flowers last up to 3 months on the plant; cut blooms up to 8–9 weeks. Used for corsage sprays and the like.
Propagation: by division when repotting (about every third year).
Environment and light: cool, frost-free house. Plants survive in temperatures down to 45°F (7°C), but advisable to aim at 50°–55°F (10°–13°C).
Type of soil: fibrous loam with sphagnum moss mixed with broken crocks and some osmunda fibre.
Soil moisture: water generously in summer; sprinkle daily in winter.

---

518 **LADY'S SLIPPER**

Cypripedium calceolus:

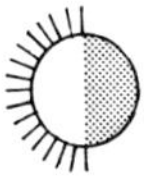

(3)

Family: Orchidaceae. Name from Aphrodite's association with Cyprus and the Greek *pedilon*, slipper (latinized by Linnaeus to *pedium*).
Place of origin: Europe (including Britain), N. Asia and North America.
Description: a terrestrial orchid with a thick, short-jointed, creeping rhizome carrying numerous roots. Leaves stem-clasping, ribbed, about 1 ft. (30 cm). Flowers solitary, bright yellow pouches and brownish-purple sepals and petals, about 3 in. (8 cm) across, with a fruity smell.
Flowering time: summer.
Use: cool, damp places, e.g., near water.
Propagation: by division after flowering.
Environment and light: half-shade.
Type of soil: well-drained, damp and leafy.
Soil moisture: water regularly but stop virtually altogether when dormant.
Remarks: a protected plant in most countries, native of alpine woods and unlikely to survive in hot summers in dry lowland areas.

519 *Dendrobium:* hybr.

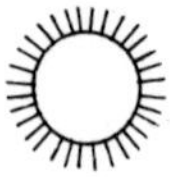

Family: Orchidaceae. Name from Greek *dendron*, tree and *bios*, life, referring to its epiphytic habit.
Place of origin: India to China and Japan, Australia and islands in south Pacific.
Description: handsome, epiphytic orchids possessing pseudobulbs. Leaves leathery; evergreen and deciduous species. Flowers variable in size, colour and markings; in long sprays, occasionally solitary. *D. nobile* (introduced in 1836) and its hybrids are among the easiest, best known and cheapest to buy.
Flowering time: winter–spring; varies between the different species.
Use: in temperate climates in hot houses, pots, hanging baskets etc. In tropics, grow on trees.
Propagation: by division when repotting.
Environment and light: hot house (or warm glasshouse) with high degree of humidity, well-lit and airy.
Type of soil: fern roots (polypody or osmundas) and one part sphagnum with organic fertilizer.
Soil moisture: water in summer, seldom when dormant.
Remarks: when *D. nobile* has stopped flowering, remove to a cool house and barely water it. The leaves will then drop, for it must have a ripening period. When growth restarts in spring needs plenty of water and high temperatures.

---

520 SLIPPER ORCHID
Paphiopedilum: var.

Family: Orchidaceae. Name from Greek *paphia*, Paphos on the island of Cyprus, known to Aphrodite, and *pedilon*, sandal.
Place of origin: tropical Asia.
Description: terrestrial orchids of which there are about 50 species, some with plain, strap-shaped, leathery leaves, others mottled. Flowers large and striking with variously coloured pouches and petals and sepals.
Flowering time: variable, according to species.
Use: ornamental in glasshouses, and for cut flowers. It is advisable to repot only when the roots have taken up nearly all the room in the pot.

Propagation: by division after flowering.
Environment and light: some need more warmth than others. Temperature demands vary according to species, but usually those with plain leaves need winter temperatures around 55°F (13°C) mottled-leaved kinds 65°F (18°C).

Type of soil: three parts fibrous loam to one each of osmunda fibre, sphagnum moss and plenty of finely broken crocks.
Soil moisture: water generously, less in mid-winter.

521 MOTH ORCHID

Phalaenopsis: sp.

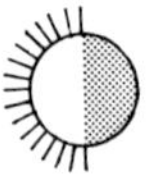

Family: Orchidaceae. Name from Greek *phalaina*, moth and *opsis*, like.
Place of origin: widely distributed throughout the East—Philippines, Burma, Eastern India, Borneo, New Guinea.
Description: epiphytic orchids with showy flowers, usually in clusters, varying in colour from white to pink to violet-red. Leaves few in number, leathery, broad, thick, 2-ranked, notched at the top.
Flowering time: variable, according to species.
Use: for cut flowers; also for adorning warm conservatories, suspended from rafters in pans with holes round the sides, openwork teak boxes, hanging baskets or fastened to tree trunks.
Propagation: by division, but it is not an easy job. *See* Remarks.
Environment and light: hot house, with high humidity and lots of light. Never in direct sun.
Type of soil: osmunda fibre, decayed oak leaves and sphagnum moss.

Soil moisture: water often and generously, also sprinkle. When the leaves are fully developed, let the plant lie dormant for a couple of months, and water less.
Remarks: all species resent root disturbance, so renew compost with caution, piece by piece.

522

Stanhopea oculata:

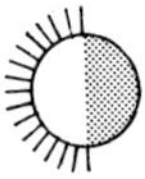

Family: Orchidaceae.
Place of origin: Mexico; introduced into Europe in 1829.
Description: epiphytic orchid with thick pseudobulbs. Leaves large, plicate and narrowing to a stem. Flowers short-lived but fragrant, lemon or yellow with crimson sepal markings. A very free flowering species.

Flowering time: summer.
Use: ornamentally in warm glasshouses in pots or hanging baskets. Less good for cut flowers, because they do not last long.
Propagation: by division.

Environment and light: warm glasshouse, quite humid, not over lit.
Type of soil: peaty soil with sphagnum moss, osmunda fibre and charcoal chippings or broken crocks.
Soil moisture: water often and generously from spring to autumn, less or not at all at other times when the plant is dormant.

GLOSSARY

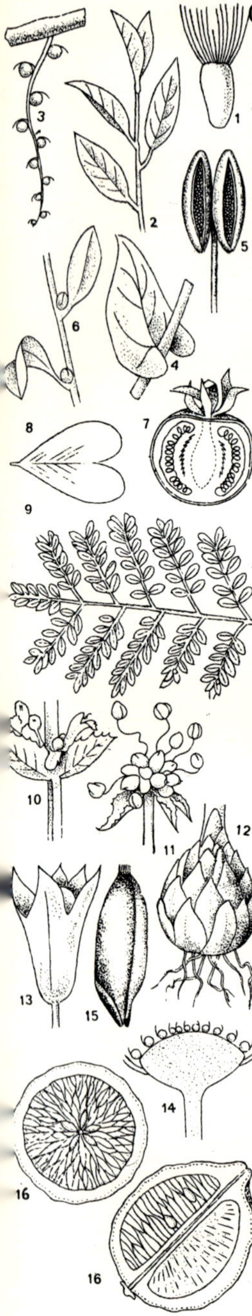

achene dry, one-seeded, indehiscent fruit (1).
adventitious of organs that arise spontaneously.
alternate of leaves appearing singly (not in pairs) at the nodes (2).
amentum spike of unisexual flowers; a catkin (3).
amplexicaul clasping or embracing the stem (4).
annual plant that lives for one year or season.
anther lobed, upper part of stamen where pollen is produced (5).
antispasmodic with properties to alleviate spasms or fits.
antitussive cough-relief.
aperitif serving to excite the appetite.
apex terminal part of leaf, stem, root etc.
areole organ peculiar to cacti, bearing spines and produced in leaf axils.
aril accessory seed covering.
aromatic fragrant.
astringent substance that checks secretion; (i.e. binds as opposed to laxative) a styptic.
axillary of bud etc. arising in the angle between main axis and a branch or leaf (6).
balsam resinous product used as a soothing agency.
berry fleshy, indehiscent fruit usually containing more than one seed (7).
biennial plant making growth in one year and flowering and fruiting in the next.
bifid divided by a cleft into two parts (8).
bipinnate of leaves divided and re-divided into regular segments (9).
bottle garden a garden made inside a large bottle, carboy, etc.
bottom heat warmth below the ground, normally applied to propagating frames or benches.
bract small leaf or scale below calyx (10).
bulbil small, usually aerial, axillary bulb, e.g. in lilies (11).
bulb swollen stem, usually underground, with persistent fleshy leaf-bases (12).
caducous quickly falling (of leaves).
calyx outer whorl of a flower constituting the sepals (13).
campanulate bell-shaped.
capitulum inflorescence of numerous, sessile flowers (14).
capsule dry seed-case, opening when ripe by parting of valves.
carnose fleshy.
carminative assisting to expel wind.
carpel ovule-bearing part of flower.
caryopsis dry, indehiscent, one-seeded fruit, characteristic of grasses; a grain (15).
cespitose low-growing; cushion-like in habit. Growing in tufts.

chlorophyll green constituent of the cells of leaves, essential for the synthesis of carbohydrates.
cholagogic discharging bile.
ciliate fringed.
citrus pertaining to the genus including citron, grapefruit, lemon, lime, orange and other fruit (16).
cladode flattened, leaf-like stem (17).
clone vegetatively produced progeny of a single individual—as by cuttings, grafts etc.
compound of leaf divided into segments.
cordate heart-shaped (18).
corm a swollen, underground root-stock.
corolla inner whorl of a flower; the petals (20).
corymb flat-topped raceme formed by proportionally longer lower flower-stalks.
crenolate leaf-margins which are shallow-toothed (21).
cross (X) See hybrid.
culm the straw or hollow stem of grasses.
cultivar a cultivated variety.
cutting part taken from parent plant for propagation.
cuttings:
- **heel** young side shoot pulled from adult plant with a sliver of the old wood attached.
- **leaf** leaf separated from parent and induced to form its own roots.
- **soft** young leafy shoots rooted in a moist atmosphere, e.g. frame (to prevent wilting).

cyme inflorescence where primary axis ends in a flower, further growth being continued by lateral branches which may again end in a flower (22).
deciduous leaves etc. that are shed annually by the plant.
decoction liquor or essence concentrated by boiling.
dehiscent of fruits or anthers which open at maturity to discharge contents (23).
dentate toothed (24).
dichotomous dividing equally.
digitate leaves with deep, finger-like lobes; palmate (25).
dioecious unisexual plants; stamens and carpels borne on different plants.
disk florets central part of flower-head of members of the compositae (26).
distichous two ranked, i.e. fruit, leaves etc. arranged in two lines on opposite sides of stem.
diuretic exciting, or substance inducing, discharge of urine.
division separation of bulb, roots etc. for propagation purposes (27).
drainage of soil: well-drained, due to the presence of coarse particles which permit ready passage of surplus water (28).
drupe fruit with outer skin, inner fleshy layer and central woody stone or pip; a "stone-fruit" (29).
embrocate bathe etc. to mitigate disease.
emmenagogic promoting menstrual discharge.
emmolient softening or relaxing application.
endemic specific to (a country or region).

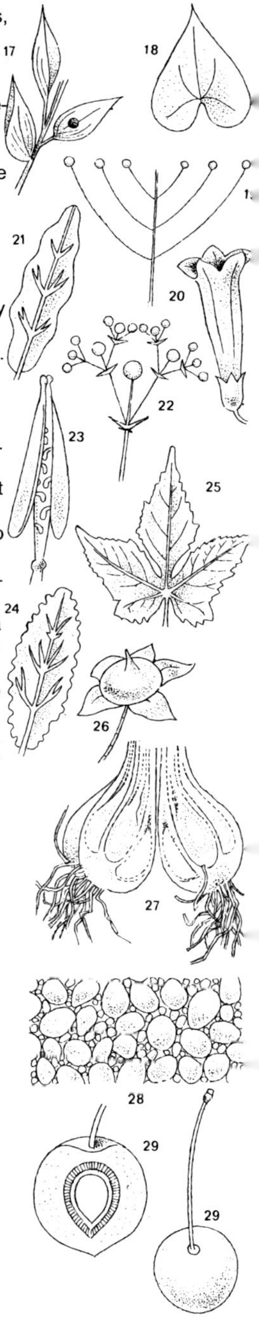

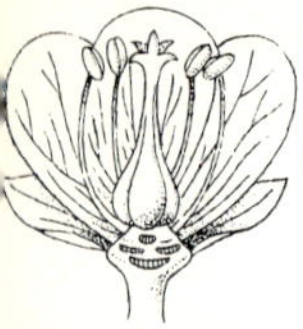
30

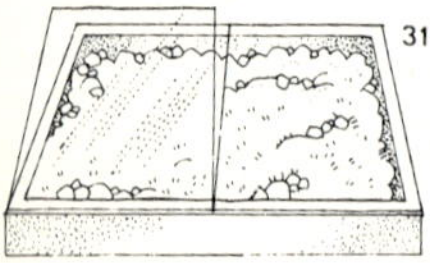
31

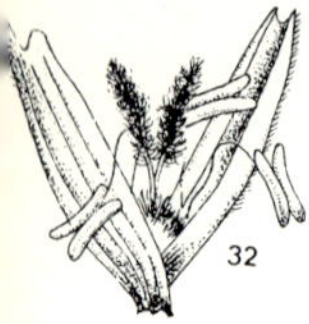
32

33

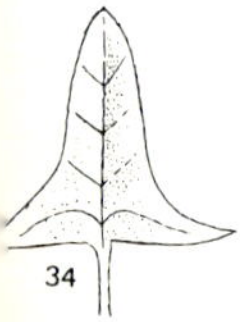
34

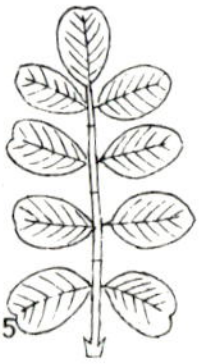
35

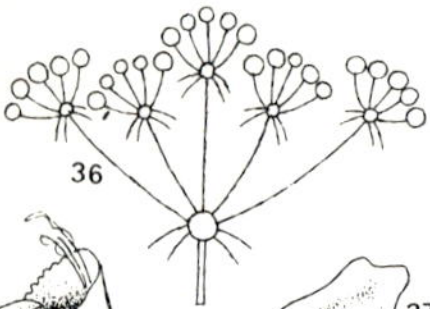
36

37

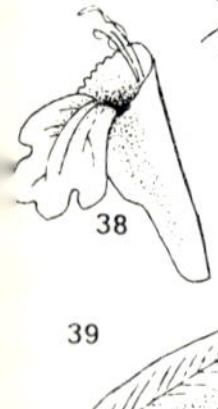
38

39

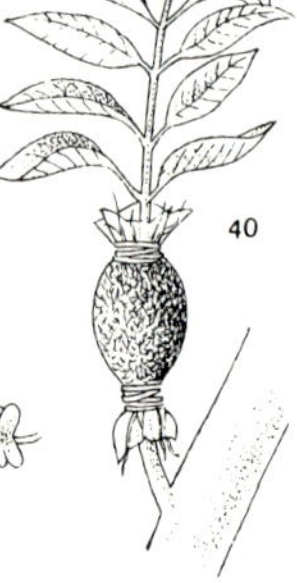
40

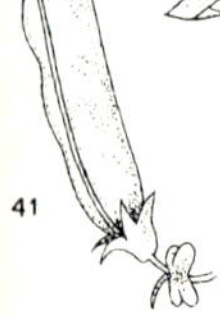
41

ensiform sword-shaped.
entire leaf-margins without divisions.
epiphyte plant growing on another, but physiologically independent.
espalier framework upon which fruit-trees or shrubs are trained.
evergreen of leaves that are persistent.
excitent drug etc. that stimulates activity.
exotic of plants which are not native; alien.
expectorant that which promotes ejection of phlegm etc. from chest or lungs.
falls hanging perianth segments of iris flower.
false fruit type of fruit of which the fleshy part is not derived from the ovary.
family group of genera with common characteristics.
febrifuge medicine to reduce fever.
filament stalk of the stamen.
fimbriate edged or bordered.
flower reproductive shoot of plant formed of perianth segments, the sepals and petals (where present), stamens and/or carpels (30).
follicle single-carpelled fruit dehiscing by ventral suture.
forcing to induce growth and/or flowering prematurely.
frame glazed, box-like structure used to protect plants from excessive cold (31).
frond leaf-like organ in ferns, differing from leaves in bearing spores.
frutescent woody-stemmed; shrublike.
genus group of species with common characteristics.
germ embryo.
gland cell or cells secreting various substances such as oils.
glaucous with smooth, blue-green bloom.
glume chaff-like bract at base of the inflorescence of grasses (32).
glumella inner glume or palea (33).
habit general form of a plant.
habitat environment in which a plant lives.
hair unicellular or multicellular outgrowth of epidermis.
hastate spear-shaped (34).
herbaceous usually refers to perennial plants which are not woody and die to the ground annually.
hothouse artificially heated structure, usually glazed, for the growth of plants belonging naturally to warmer climates.
humus decomposed organic matter in soil.
hybrid offspring derived from two species, often combining characteristics of each.
hydroculture (hydroponics) system of culture in liquid nutrients.
imparipinnate unequally pinnate leaves (35).
indehiscent of fruits and other structures which do not open.
inflorescnce flower-bearing stem axis (36).
infusion liquid containing soluble constituents extracted from herb.

labellum lip-like lower petal or perals of some orchids (37).
labiate of flowers where the petals protrude to suggest lips, especially of the families Labiatae and Scrophulariaceae (38).
lacinate fringed or divided into irregular segments.
lamina leaf blade.
lanceolate lance-like (39).
latex milky secretion produced by some plants.

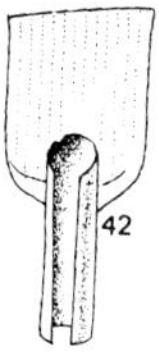
42

43

layering method of propagation. Illustration shows air layering of woody plant by removing part of outer bark of young stem, wrapping around it with damp moss, covered with polythene bag to form roots (40).
leaf-mould rich fibrous, usually woodland soil, composed of rotted leaves, pieces of wood, seeds, etc.
legume dehiscent fruit splitting at maturity into two valves; a pod (41).
ligule membranous outgrowth, as from the base of leaves in grasses (42).

44

lobate lobed.
mildew small parasitic fungi forming a loose growth of filaments on the host plant.
mist propagation irrigation of cuttings by automatic overhead watering to prevent wilting.
monoecious with stamens and ovary on same plant.
monotypic having one type or representative, e.g. a genus with one species.
mucronate terminally in a hard sharp point (43).
mulch layer of organic material spread over soil to conserve moisture.

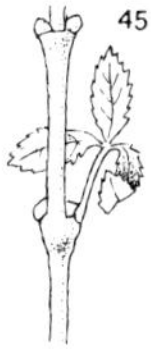
45

46

narcotic inducing insensibility or drowsiness.
nervate leaves with prominent ribs or veins (44).
node joint at which leaves are borne on stem (45).
nut dry, one-seeded, indehiscent fruit with woody pericarp.
oblanceolate lanceolate with the wider part towards the apex.
oblong of leaves rounded at tip, longer than broad (46).
obovate inversely ovate, with broader end uppermost (47).

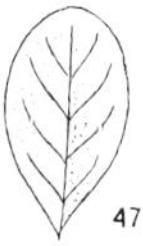
47

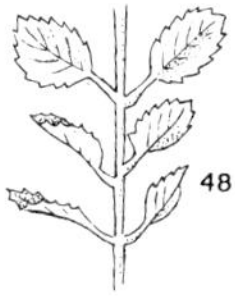
48

obtuse blunt.
offset short runner with clusters of leaves at tip.
offshoot side growth or shoot—as in bulbs.
opposite leaves inserted opposite each other in pairs (48).
orbicular disk-shaped (49).
organ part of a plant with a particular structure and function.

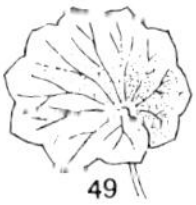
49

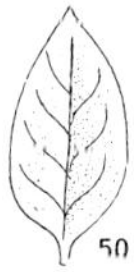
50

ovate of leaves oval in shape and broadest at their base (50).
palmate see digitate.
panicle a compound raceme, loosely branched (51).
papillose covered with little protuberances, or vesicles.
parallel-nerved of leaves with unbranched veins (52).
parasite organism living on and drawing nourishment from another.

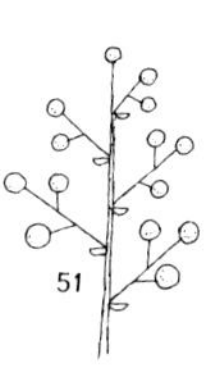
51

52

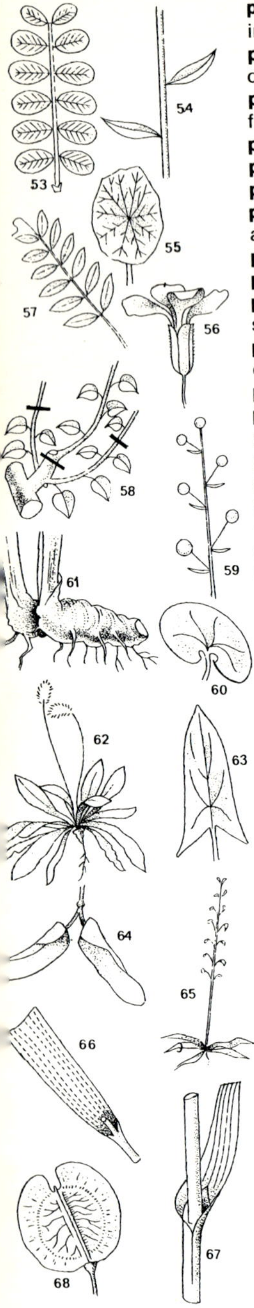

parenchyma undifferentiated tissue of cells present in various parts of plant.
paripinnate compound leaves with an even number of leaflets (53).
parthenogenesis development of a new organism from an unfertilized egg.
patens spreading (54).
pectin carbohydrate, present in cell-wall of plants.
peduncle main stalk of flower or inflorescence.
peltate shield-shaped; of leaves where the stalk arises from the geometric centre of lamina (55).
pendent hanging.
perennial plant living for several years.
perfoliate leaves with basal lobes uniting round the stem.
perianth outer floral leaves (the calyx and corolla) of flower (56).
pericarp fruit coat formed from ovary wall.
permeable of soil not impeding the diffusion of water.
petal unit of the corolla of a flower.
petiole leaf stalk.
phylloclade flattened stem resembling a leaf.
pinnate leaves composed of a series of leaflets on either side of a common petiole (57).
pinnule leaflets of a pinnately-compound leaf.
pith central tissue of stem or root.
pollinate to transfer pollen from the anther to the stigma.
procumbent lying flat or trailing.
prune to cut or lop superfluous branches etc. in order to induce regular growth (58).
Pseudobulb swelling of the lowest node of a stem, applied to orchids.
ptisan a nourishing decoction.
pubescent covered with downy hairs.
purgative aperient.
raceme flower-cluster with separate flowers at equal distances along central stem, the youngest at the top (59).
radical arising from the root stock at ground level.
ray florets outer petaloid extensions of flower-head of some members of the compositae.
reniform kidney-shaped (60).
rhizome swollen, elongated, usually horizontal, underground stem (61).
rock garden environment created in garden suitable for growing alpines and similar plants.
root part of plant normally below ground, serving as mechanical support and to convey nutrients from the soil.
rosette arrangement of leaves in a radial cluster (62).
runner creeping stem arising from main stem and taking root at the nodes, thus producing new plants vegetatively; a procumbent stolon.
rust small parasitic fungi.
sagittate arrow-shaped (63).
samara dry, indehiscent fruit with flattened winglike pericarp (64).

scape peduncle of inflorescence arising directly from root, as in primrose (65).
sedative substance with soothing properties.
seed a ripened ovule capable of development into another plant.
sepal part of the outer whorl or calyx of a flower.
serrate of leaves with toothed, saw-like margins.
serrulate finely serrated.
sessile without a stalk (66).
setaceous bristly.
sheath part of a plant, wrapped round a stem or other body (67).
shrub woody plant branching near ground.
silicula a short, broadened form of siliqua (68).
siliqua two valved fruit, divided internally by a replum, which dehisces from the base upwards (69).
sinuate wavy-edged.
soils acidic (clay types)
calcareous (chalky)
fibrous
peaty (acid)
sandy (light)
spadix spike of flowers closely arranged on fleshy axil, enclosed in a spather (70).
spathe a large, sheathlike bract surrounding an inflorescence (71).
spatulate broad and rounded.
species group of organisms gentically similar and normally producing fertile offspring.
spike a raceme of sessile flowers (72).
spine pointed structure usually derived from a leaf.
spore cell capable of germination.
spur slender, hollow projection of petal or sepal.
stamen male, pollen-producing organ of flowering plant (73).
staminode sterile stamen.
standard upper perianth segments of iris flower.
stellate star-shaped.
stem main stalk of a plant, usually above ground and supporting leaves and flowers.
stem cutting method of propagation using a cut shoot which is placed in well-moistened soil to induce root formation (74).
sterile incapable of reproduction.
stigma upper part of style or ovary-surface that receives pollen (75).
stimulant that which excites or produces a transient increase of energy.
stipe stalk of ferns or palms.
stipule outgrowth at base of leaf stem (76).
stock established root-base of host plant into which scion or grafting slip is inserted in propagation (77).
stolon an elongated shoot tending to produce roots and to form a new plant (78).
stratified exposing seeds to elements to hasten germination.
style part of flower connecting ovary and stigma (79).
subulate awl-shaped.

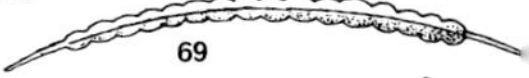
69
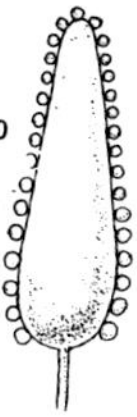
70
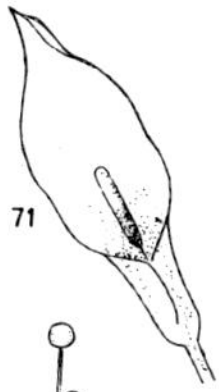
71

72
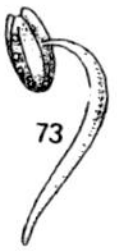
73
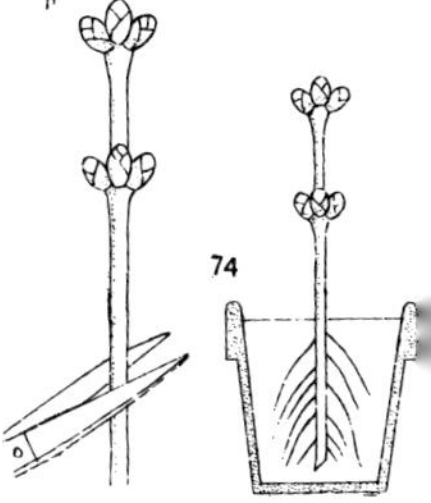
74

75
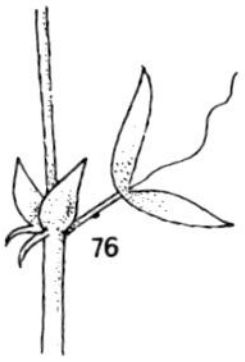
76
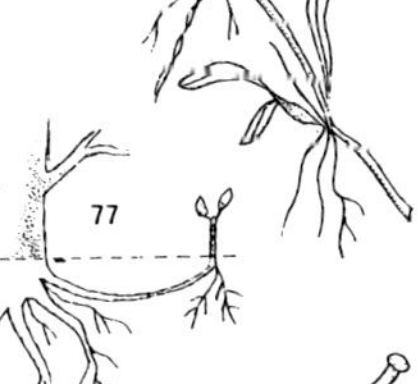
78
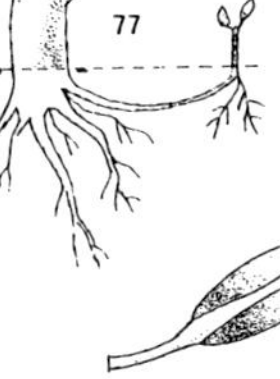
77

79

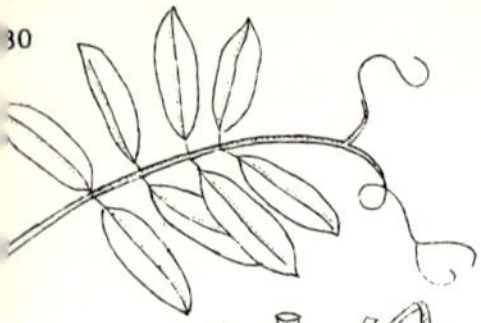
80

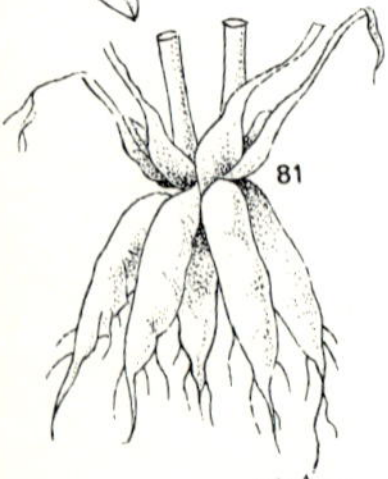
81

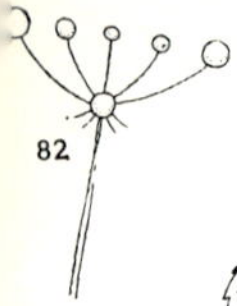
82

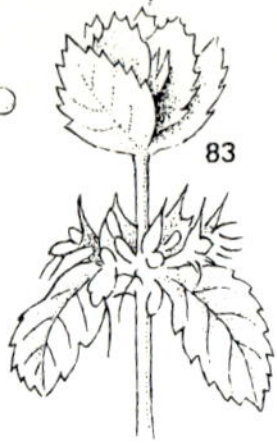
83

succulent a juicy, fleshy plant.
sucker a shoot arising just below ground.
sudorific inducing sweat-production.
tanniferous of tannic acid, and astringent.
tap root strongly developed primary root.
tendril sensitive, coiling plant organ that assists in climbing (80).
ternate formed or arranged in threes.
tincture alcoholic solution of vegetable essence used medicinally.
tomentose woolly.
trifoliate three parted (of leaves).
trigonal three-sided.
tubercle nodule, hard swellings, e.g. on roots of leguminous plants harbouring nitrogen-fixing Bacillus.
tuber swollen tip of underground stem.
type species individual embodying the distinctive characters of the species.
umbel flat-topped raceme with flowering stalks arising from a single point (82).
variety modification within a species.
vasodilatory of drug causing dilation of blood-vessels.
venation arrangement of veins on leaf.
vermifuge drug that expels intestinal worms.
verticil, verticillate whorl, set of parts radiating from axis, as in flowers of the Labiatae (83).

INDEX

Almost all the illustrations of the plants were taken by Azzurra Carrara Pantano of Verona, and all of the part illustrations are by courtesy of Foto Pictor, Milan, with the exception of that of Spring and Summer Plants which is by Giuseppe Mazza. The following illustrations are courtesy the Harry Smith Collection, Chelmsford, Essex: 53, 56, 115, 166, 226, 248, 253, 257, 259, 263, 265, 267, 270, 271, 323, 329, 331, 338, 423, 439, 457, 465, 474. The publishers also wish to thank Frances Perry for the following photographs: 190, 375, 399, 444, and 451.